POLITICAL (DIS)ENGAGEMENT

The changing nature of the 'political'

Nathan Manning

First published in Great Britain in 2017 by

Policy Press
University of Bristol
1-9 Old Park Hill
Bristol
BS2 8BB
UK
t: +44 (0)117 954 5940
pp-info@bristol.ac.uk
www.policypress.co.uk

North America office:
Policy Press
c/o The University of Chicago Press
1427 East 60th Street
Chicago, IL 60637, USA
t: +1 773 702 7700
f: +1 773-702-9756
sales@press.uchicago.edu
www.press.uchicago.edu

British Library Cataloguing in Publication Data
A catalogue record for this book is available from the British Library

Library of Congress Cataloging-in-Publication Data
A catalog record for this book has been requested

ISBN 978 1 44731 701 2 hardcover
ISBN 978-1-4473-1702-9 paperback
ISBN 978-1-4473-2134-7 ePub
ISBN 978-1-4473-2135-4 Mobi
ISBN 978-1-4473-1704-3 ePdf

Cover design by Qube Design Associates, Bristol
Printed and bound in Great Britain by CPI Group (UK) Ltd,
Croydon, CR0 4YY
Policy Press uses environmentally responsible print partners

Contemporary Issues in Social Policy

Series editor: Charles Husband

This exciting new series brings together academics, professionals and activists to link cutting-edge social theory and research to contentious issues in social policy, challenge consensus and invite debate. Each text provides a critical appraisal of key aspects of contemporary theory and research to offer fresh perspectives.

Research and policy in ethnic relations: Compromised dynamics in a neoliberal era
Charles Husband (editor)

New philanthropy and social justice and social policy: Debating the conceptual and policy discourse
Behrooz Morvaridi (editor)

Political disengagement: The changing nature of the 'political'
Nathan Manning (editor)

See more at http://bit.ly/1AWjClV

Contents

List of figures and tables

Figures

Tables

Notes on contributors

Parveen Akhtar is Lecturer in Sociology at the University of Bradford, UK. Prior to this she was a British Academy Research Fellow at the University of Bristol. She has held academic positions at a number of universities and research institutes, including: Sciences Po, Paris; the Institut für die Wissenschaften vom Menschen (Institute for Human Sciences), Vienna; Institute for Migration and Ethnic Studies, Amsterdam; School for Postgraduate Interdisciplinary Research on Interculturalism and Transnationalism, Aalborg and Lahore University of Management Sciences, Lahore. She has published widely on political participation, Islam, migration and social change. Her monograph, *British Muslim Politics*, was published by Palgrave in 2013.

Andre Banks has spent most of the last decade harnessing the power of storytelling and technology to build powerful social movements in the US and around the world. He is the co-founder and executive director of All Out (www.allout.org), a new organisation mobilising in every region to create a world where no person will have to sacrifice their family or freedom, safety or dignity because of who they are or whom they love. In its first three years, All Out grew from a few thousand friends and followers to more than two million people standing up for equality in every country in the world.

Francine Fernandes has worked to promote social justice and tackle inequality for over 15 years. Managing several award-winning programmes, she has worked with government ministers, senior parliamentarians, political parties and local authorities to realise the benefits of positive BME engagement. In 2009, she was appointed as a Special Adviser & Strategic Partner on the UK Government's Black, Asian and Minority Ethnic Women Councillors Taskforce.

Her programmes have enjoyed considerable success, producing over 100 magistrates, 30 councillors, numerous public appointments, and made political history with the election in 2010 of the Conservative's first African Caribbean woman MP.

Marie Gillespie is Professor of Sociology at The Open University, and Co-Director of the Centre for Research on Socio-cultural Change. Her research and publications focus on issues of diaspora and transnationalism in relation to questions of social and cultural change.

For a list of publications see www.open.ac.uk/socialsciences/main/staff/people-profile.php?name=Marie_Gillespie

Yashpal Jogdand completed his PhD 'On the experience and consequences of humiliation' in the School of Psychology at University of St Andrews, UK. He is currently working as a research fellow in the School on a project about replication and reinterpretation of Stanley Milgram's famous obedience studies.

Mina Lami is a media analyst who specialises in Arabic and jihadist media. She works at BBC Monitoring. Prior to that she was a senior visiting fellow at the London School of Economics and Political Science, where she did research on online radicalisation and jihadism. She has worked on a number of academic projects at Royal Holloway, University of London and at The Open University that looked at diverse aspects of Arabic and jihadist media.

Nathan Manning is Lecturer in Sociology at the University of York, UK. His PhD research explored the ways in which young adults understand and practise politics. This work resulted in publications for the *Journal of Youth Studies*, *Journal of Sociology* and Sociological Research Online. Recently his interests have turned to adult political dissatisfaction and the role emotions may play in political (dis)engagement with work featuring in *The Sociological Review*, *Citizenship Studies* and *Sociology*. He is currently working on a project funded by the British Academy to use the Mass Observation Archive to explore political (dis)engagement and feelings of dissatisfaction longitudinally.

Michele Micheletti holds the Lars Hierta Chair of Political Science at Stockholm University, Sweden. Her current research focuses on sustainable citizenship and angry citizens (*Wutbürger*) mobilised in urban renewal projects. Her most recent publications are the co-authored *Political consumerism: Global responsibility in action* (Cambridge University Press, 2013) and 'Consumer strategies in social movements' (in *The Oxford handbook of social movements*, 2014).

Therese O'Toole is Senior Lecturer in the School of Sociology, Politics and International Studies and the Centre for the Study of Ethnicity and Citizenship at the University of Bristol, UK. Her research focuses on political participation and debates on ethnic and religious identities and the impact of forms of participatory governance on the governance of ethnic and religious diversity. These interests were explored in her most recent book, with Richard Gale, *Political engagement amongst ethnic minority young people: Making a difference* (2013), a large AHRC/ESRC-funded project, with Tariq Modood, on Muslim participation in contemporary governance, and her current ESRC project on Muslim participation in local governance in Bristol. She is co-editor of, and contributor to, Public Spirit: an online forum on religion and public policy for researchers, policymakers, politicians and practitioners from the voluntary and community sectors (www. publicspirit.org.uk).

Stephen Reicher is Professor of Psychology at the University of St Andrews, UK. He works on processes of social identity and collective action. He has studied such topics as crowd behaviour, nationalism, political rhetoric and leadership, intergroup antagonism and, latterly, the psychology of obedience and tyranny.

Caoimhe Ryan completed her Masters in Social Psychology at the London School of Economics and Political Science. She is currently completing a PhD in the School of Psychology at the University of St Andrews, UK, looking at processes of mobilisation in anti-deportation campaigns.

Nesrine Abdel Sattar is a communication strategist and a media and internet policy researcher. She has worked on a wide range of academic, policy and practitioner-related research projects at The Open University and Oxford University, UK. She received her DPhil degree from the Oxford Internet Institute, University of Oxford in 2013.

Tim Street is an activist with UK Uncut and a director of UK Uncut Legal Action. He has also worked as a campaigner and researcher with several peace and disarmament groups. He is currently completing his PhD on nuclear disarmament at Warwick University.

Acknowledgements

This book is the product of many people's hard work and commitment. I would like to give special thanks to Charlie Husband; without his support and encouragement this book would not have been possible. Charlie had a key role in this project from the beginning and I hope the book reflects some of his integrity, passion for inquiry and dedication to progressive change.

This volume began life as a symposium funded by the University of Bradford's Centre for Applied Social Research and I am very grateful for the opportunity to have brought together many of the contributors to this event for the chance to engage with each other's work. I'm also very thankful to each of the contributors who have shared their excellent work in a genuinely collegiate spirit. As the book's editor I am very grateful to Laura Vickers and the Policy Press team for their support and professionalism in helping to make this book a reality. Thanks also goes to Mary Holmes who (as always) provided insightful and constructive feedback.

Special thanks also goes to Fiona Whelan, for just about everything.

ONE

Introduction

Nathan Manning

"That's what I mean about politics, it's just everywhere, you know. Um, it's a political choice as to what I would order for lunch, you know." (Patrick,[1] 19 years)

The above quote is taken from research I conducted in Australia (see Manning, 2014). When I met Patrick he was not involved with electoral politics or activism, nor did he regularly volunteer his time for a cause or organisation. Based upon orthodox ways of measuring political participation he would likely be deemed part of that group often invoked in discussions of contemporary political involvement, the disengaged youth. However, Patrick was interested in political issues and, significantly, he understood politics to be a part of everyday life and how we live. He was a committed vegetarian and had concerns about the industrial production of meat. He understood his daily life to be enmeshed with politics, particularly through his consumption choices. He boycotted companies like McDonald's and Nike because he "disagrees with the philosophies behind [them]". He was a keen recycler and tried to minimise his energy consumption, for example, by using public transport. He avoided processed food and shopped for organic produce and locally produced goods from small local businesses. These personalised, individualised ways of practising politics gave Patrick a sense of political agency. He believed we have "an obligation to not do nothing", to not "be a part of the problem, basically by agreeing with it, saying, 'oh, it's just the way it goes'". While Patrick did want to get involved in more collective forms of political participation, he had already developed a sense of himself as a political being, a person whose everyday life and decisions held broader socio-political meaning and implications.

Patrick's ability to understand himself as acting politically through individualised, everyday activities reflects profound socio-political and cultural changes that have taken place over the last several decades. Firstly, the example of Patrick points to the way politics is now often understood as having a life beyond the institutions and practices of electoral politics. While political consumerism has a long history (for example, see Micheletti, 2003, chapter 2; Kroen, 2004) politics is increasingly understood as occurring through our consumption in mundane places like supermarkets (Stolle and Micheletti, 2013). Further, Patrick's political consumerism highlights the importance of corporate targets, rather than a focus on the state. Related to this first change is the way Patrick understands his political involvement to be part of his everyday life and activities. Being political is conceived as something he is engaged in constantly as he makes his way in the world. This way of practising politics undermines traditional divisions between public and private, between political and non-political. Since the 1960s, social movements have pushed back the boundaries of politics and worked to politicise dimensions of everyday life – as discussed below, these movements echoed the questioning of the meaning and practice of politics by social movements of the early nineteenth century (Calhoun, 1993). The second-wave feminist mantra 'the personal is political' epitomises this idea. More recently, the campaigns for same-sex marriage equality occurring in many countries provide a contemporary example of politicising some of the most intimate, personal and 'private' aspects of life – the people we love and want to share our lives with. Another key feature found in Patrick's approach to politics is the absence of class. He is concerned about inequality, but this is not articulated in terms of class. Aside from a very recent renewed interest (for example, Jones, 2011), the language of class rarely features in public debate and it has been expunged from mainstream party-political discourse in many democracies. Also significant is how individualised Patrick's practice of politics is; when I met him he was a young man and he may well have gone on to be more involved with collective political activities. However, what is noteworthy in his account is that he doesn't need to be involved in any organised collective way with others to exercise his political beliefs and interests. From his perspective, he is already enveloped in vast global networks of trade and commerce that demand on-going action, to not "be a part of the problem, basically by agreeing with it". The challenges and opportunities posed by new personalised, individualised avenues for political participation are complex and will be discussed in more detail throughout this book, but processes of individualisation are pervasive and have seriously undermined the collective basis of politics. Patrick may not be a typical citizen, but his way of being political highlights some of the key dimensions of politics in our age.

The changing landscape of politics

The contributions to this book are contextualised by the fallout from the significant social change and disruption experienced across social and political life since the 1960s. Some of these changes have been hinted at above in the example of Patrick – changing political targets and repertoires; the challenges to established public/private divisions and the very meaning of politics; the disappearance of class from the mainstream political landscape; and the way individualisation has undercut the collective base of politics in many areas. This is the political world we live with and know, but to better understand our present situation it is useful to quickly sketch where we have come from.

The eighteenth and nineteenth centuries witnessed profound social change and upheaval. This was the time of the Enlightenment and the Industrial Revolution. New inventions like the steam engine and the modern factory were radically changing social life. Philosophers and social thinkers were advancing new ideas about relations between the state and its people in market societies with greater social diversity and mixing. Urban centres swelled in consequence of the incessant call for workers and individuals experienced a profound rupture or disembedding of social relations. A lifestyle centred on agriculture, the home, cottage industry and family and village life shifted to one encompassing a wider range of interactions and greater social distance. Local community life came to be replaced with an urban life-style revolving around the demands of wage labour and the market. In Karl Polanyi's words:

> To separate labor from all other activities of life and to subject it to the laws of the market was to annihilate all organic forms of existence and to replace them by a different type of organization, an atomistic and individualistic one. Such a scheme of destruction was best served by the application of the principle of freedom of contract. In practice this meant that the noncontractual organizations of kinship, neighborhood, profession, and creed were to be liquidated ... (Polanyi, 1957, p 163)

Social change and challenges to existing power relations continued as the pressures of economic growth and an organised labour movement eventually delivered universal suffrage (see Rueschemeyer et al, 1992). The struggle for suffrage was long and bitter and typically took a good deal longer for women and indigenous peoples than for men. While the erosion of aristocratic dominance in politics may have occurred at a glacial pace (Guttsman, 1967), the extension of voting rights injects modernity with a modicum of egalitarianism. However imperfect, mass democracy was a radical challenge to traditional power bases and it opened up political decision making for the majority to have some say. With the right to vote, the right to stand for office inevitably followed and age-old prejudices about working-class people's unsuitability to exercise leadership were gradually undermined.

In contrast to the tumultuous times described above, the period from the late nineteenth century until the early 1970s has been described as 'organised modernity' (Wagner, 1994). It is a period characterised by a reconfiguration of society designed to minimise uncertainty; wresting society under control after a period of great social, political and technological change. And this reconfiguration of society did result in relative political stability, with voting behaviour firmly aligned with social class position around the middle of the twentieth century (for example, see Butler and Stokes, 1969). Examples of the conventionalisation and homogenisation of practices that drove this restructuring include the emergence of mass political parties that marshalled modes of political participation; the Taylorist and Fordist modes of production that also extended and normalised consumption; and the introduction of social security (and later the welfare state), which helped to ensure material security but also opened up family life to surveillance and the disciplining and homogenising effects of the state and science (for example, see Rose, 1989). Organised modernity was characterised by an optimism about the future and society's ability to harness the power of science, technology and rationality to ensure the continuation of the prosperity enjoyed during the final decades of the era (Maier, 1970; Harvey, 1990; Rabinbach, 1992; Scott, 1998).

This period of relative control was not to last long. On a number of fronts the ability of science, technology and rationality to deliver progress, prosperity and peace was fundamentally contested. The combination of high inflation and high unemployment in the early 1970s brought an end to the post-war economic boom. These conditions produced a broader economic crisis because they could not be explained by the prevailing Keynesian economic theory. New social movements like second-wave feminism began to articulate a range of different and powerful challenges to patriarchal dominance. The anti-nuclear movement garnered large-scale public support in its opposition to the use of nuclear science as an instrument of war; a concern already made salient by the credible anxieties of nuclear annihilation unleashed by the Cuban missile crisis. In addition, various nuclear accidents (for example, Three Mile Island in 1979, Chernobyl in 1986) bolstered concerns about the dangers of nuclear power and worked to undermine confidence in new technology, science and notions of progress.

Sociological accounts argue that since the 1960s class and nation have gradually been displaced as *the* means of organising politics (Wagner, 1994). In his writing on these changes, the sociologist Ulrich Beck (1992) sees the unintended consequences and risks produced by industrial societies themselves (for example, environmental or nuclear catastrophe) as creating a realm of sub-politics that operates beyond the bounds of the institutionalised electoral politics of nation-states. For Beck, previously non-political spheres like scientific work on genetics or everyday consumption can be drawn into political struggles because they directly affect people's living conditions. Technological advances like *in vitro* fertilisation or genetically modified foods become publicly contested not only because social movements and individuals are more sceptical about the promised benefits, but also because such technologies have great influence on society and our everyday lives. Similarly, 'private' acts of consumption have been politicised by social movements in attempts to call corporations to account for how they produce goods and services; for example, demanding that they trade fairly or take responsibility for the environmental impact of their activities. Political consumerism is also about expanding people's sphere of concern by claiming a direct link between consumers and producers, despite the vast geographical, cultural and social distance that frequently exists between these groups (see Micheletti, 2003).

In a similar way, Giddens (1991) has argued that 'emancipatory' politics, exemplified by the Labour movement, is increasingly outstripped by 'life politics': a mode of political expression that is more individualised, tends to blur public and private making politics more about choice, self-expression and self-actualisation. If emancipatory politics aims to either 'release underprivileged groups from their unhappy condition, or to eliminate the relative differences between them', life politics, in contrast, is a politics of choice and personal decisions (Giddens, 1991, p 211). So, while responses to global warming require concerted collective action, they also involve widespread changes in life-style, which we can see in individual concern over food miles, energy conservation or recycling.

Political scientists have made similar claims about a culture shift among citizens. Some have described the rise of *Critical Citizens* (Norris, 1999), while others argue for a shift away from traditional voting along lines of social cleavage (for example, along divisions of social class) and towards a 'value cleavage', reflecting the move from a politics based on material needs to a new politics characterised by post-materialism (Inglehart, 1997). The dramatic economic growth of the post-war period, coupled with the development of the welfare state, has meant the struggle for mere survival and basic material needs has receded for many, providing space for values of autonomy and self-expression to be emphasised. The argument is that these values have fostered a post-materialist politics that is more concerned with matters of quality of life and individual freedoms than with a material agenda of economic security.

These accounts of socio-political change open up large questions about the continuity of the past with the present. Such questions of continuity and change will be explored throughout the book in a variety of contexts. Nonetheless, here we can note that recent research has challenged the polarisation of 'emancipatory' and 'life politics' (Sörbom and Wennerhag, 2013), finding that those engaged in 'life politics' are combining this with participation in the established institutions of electoral politics like political parties (see also Rheingans and Hollands, 2013). The Occupy movement (see Gitlin, 2012), which took root in many countries during 2011,[2] showed that in contrast to an emphasis on post-materialist politics, young people can still be mobilised around an agenda of material needs and inequality. The emergence of organisations like UK Uncut (see Street, Chapter Six in this volume) that campaign against the UK government's dramatic cuts in public spending, and the extensive anti-austerity protests taking place across much of Europe in recent years, also point to the continuing relevance of materialist agendas and issues of economic justice.

While material inequality remains an issue that people can be mobilised around, there can be no doubt that the social movements of the second half of the twentieth century have had a profound impact on the nature and practice of politics in contemporary society, particularly in their emphasis on issues of identity. The 1960s and 1970s witnessed the rise of various social movements across many industrialised countries (for a general discussion of social movements see Della Porta and Diani, 1999; Tilly, 2004; Tarrow, 2011). These movements included the student movements, women's liberation, peace movements, gay and lesbian liberation and environmental movements. As suggested above, in contrast to labour movements, these social movements placed an emphasis upon culture, identity and life-style. The gay and lesbian liberation movement is a good example of this, for while some activity took aim at discrimination – and recently we have seen strong campaigns in numerous countries for marriage-equality laws (see Banks, Chapter Three in this volume) – much of the movement has been about claiming positive non-heterosexual identities and pursuing social and cultural acceptance. Social movements, particularly the women's movement, challenged the very meaning of politics by arguing that politics should be understood in broad terms as being about power and power relations. As such, politics is everywhere, not just in 'public', in the offices and institutions of electoral politics. Politics was found to be lurking in many areas of life previously deemed to be private and non-political. Gays and lesbians politicised their sexuality, while feminists politicised gender and 'private' spaces like the home through campaigns on access to abortion and contraception, and domestic violence.

These social movements, emerging in the 1960s and 1970s, have been called 'new social movements' and sharply contrasted with the 'old' labour movements (see, for example, Touraine, 1971; Habermas, 1984; Offe, 1985; Melucci, 1989). It is variously claimed that these movements were different from the 'old' labour movements because, for example, they had a new focus on identity, autonomy and self-realisation, or were more middle class in make-up or because they politicised everyday life or allowed for partial and overlapping commitment. In contrast, Calhoun (1993) has shown that there is a great deal of continuity between mid-20th-century social movements and those of the late 18th and early 19th centuries. He argues that the aesthetic and cultural dimensions of earlier movements tended to be overlooked by classical theorists pursuing primarily instrumental lines of inquiry into social movements. While it may not be historically correct to describe these mid-20th-century movements as 'new', they certainly reopened questions about the boundaries of the public and private and reinvigorated the meaning and practice of politics.

In part, these challenges to the meaning and practice of politics were about the assertion of new identities, for example, out and proud non-heterosexuals; empowered, independent women, calling for self-determination and demanding full socio-political participation. These new identities challenge the assumed centrality of the working class as the key political actor for progressive politics. At the same time, since the 1970s, most industrialised countries have experienced deindustrialisation and a shrinking in the number of people involved in traditionally working-class jobs. As will be discussed below, not only has the central position of the working class been displaced in radical politics, but since the 1980s it has become less and less a feature of electoral politics too.

People involved with mid-20th- (and early 19th-)century social movements typically wanted to do politics differently. Many formed organisations that aimed to be more participatory and democratic and less hierarchical than the traditional institutions of electoral politics and trade unions. Their questioning of politics brought new political repertoires and targets for political action. As suggested above, the object or aim of political action was not necessarily the state, but could target everyday life, social attitudes and behaviours or corporations. And when actions did target the state they often centred on issues that concerned both the public and private spheres of life – women's-movement issues like equal pay, education and job opportunities; free contraception and abortion on demand; campaigns around gay pride; decriminalising homosexual sex or equalising the age of consent for homosexuals.

In recent years it has been the use of new media that has provided the dynamism for political participation. The internet has been a useful means of sharing alternative information and has provided activists with a powerful tool for organising and mobilisation. Various organisations have used the internet to conduct campaigns and draw attention to a range of neglected issues. Organisations like AVAAZ, Human Rights Watch, Change.org, GetUp!, MoveOn and 38 Degrees have become important political actors targeting electoral politics as well as working outside it. The role of social media has also been important in recent political unrest, from Istanbul and Egypt to Europe and North America (see, for example, Howard et al, 2011; Vicari, 2013; Bennett et al, 2014). Bennett and Segerberg (2012) argue that the way in which digital media is being used by some groups engaged in contentious politics has produced a new 'logic of connective action' that contrasts with the more familiar logic of collective action. While collective action is 'associated with high levels of organizational resources and the formation of collective identities' (Bennett and Segerberg, 2012, p 739), 'the starting point of connective action is the self-motivated (though not necessarily self-centred) sharing of already internalized or personalized ideas, plans, images, and resources with [mediated] networks of others' (Bennett and Segerberg, 2012, p 753). Examples of this kind of connective action are explored in Chapters Two, Four, Six and Nine.

New information technologies have made it possible for citizens to produce their own content and participate in the production of professional media content (see Chapter Four in this volume). Hartley highlights the shift from DIY (Do-It-Yourself) culture to Do-It-With-Others (DIWO) and the sharing, contributory and communitarian ethic facilitated by new technologies. Media consumers now co-create media content and interpret media products in various unintended and public/political ways. Examples of this kind of 'consumer productivity' and 'silly citizenship' can be seen in the homemade spoofs and parodies of election materials found on internet sites like YouTube that have been extremely popular and have featured in recent elections in a number of countries (for example, Hartley 2010, p 241). Of course, electoral politics is developing a greater presence on the internet and social media as a strategy to engage young people, Barack Obama's 2008 presidential campaign being a high-profile example (Katz et al, 2013).

These examples suggest the increasing importance of new information technology as a means of engaging in politics and activism and performing local and global citizenship that may or may not engage with local or national politics (Loader, 2007). Van Zoonen et al's (2010) work on the YouTube response to the anti-Islam film *Fitna* – made by a Dutch member of parliament – shows the multiple forms of citizenship that the film provoked. The film associated Islam with violence and terrorism and used images and statistics to suggest the Islamification of the Netherlands and Europe. There was an energetic and creative critique of the film via the internet. Young people engaged in collective and individual media production that articulated their dissent from the film as well as their religious and political identities, performing an 'unlocated citizenship' that helped to constitute and address a 'placeless public' about issues of transnational relevance.

New communication technology is also used in conjunction with older and 'offline' techniques for mobilisation and organising. In 2010 thousands of students across the UK were involved in protests against proposed government cuts to higher education and a dramatic increase in tuition fees, which involved over 35 universities. Theocharis (2012) has shown how the student occupations that took place in universities used a variety of online tools to organise and mobilise young people. Moreover, he found that older technologies were used in conjunction with newer, interactive forms; and in at least one instance new technology was created to aid effective mobilisation and protest. Significantly, e-tactics were used alongside extensive offline political activity (also see Chapters Three and Six in this volume). Occupy and other recent protest activity has also *combined* online and highly visible offline activities (Nielsen, 2013).

While social movements and new media have breathed fresh life into politics (to some extent within and) beyond the bounds of established institutions and practices, electoral politics has experienced a steady decline in participation across many democracies, along with increased feelings of cynicism and dissatisfaction.

Contemporary political (dis)engagements

For almost two decades now, young people's apparent disengagement from politics has been a feature of public debate and has prompted policy interventions like citizenship education (for example, Keating et al, 2010). During this time research has explored young people's relationship with politics, with some arguing that many young people lack interest in and knowledge of politics and participate at low levels (see, for example, Putnam, 2000; Torney-Purta et al, 2001; Park, 2004; Print et al, 2004; Fieldhouse et al, 2007; Wattenberg, 2011), while others have paid closer attention to young people's criticisms of the political system and the barriers to their participation (for example, Bhavnani, 1991; Marsh et al, 2007; Furlong and Cartmel, 2012; Henn and Foard, 2012; Manning and Edwards, 2014). However, it is clear that electoral turnout is particularly low among the young. For example, in the UK general elections of 2001 and 2005 more than half those aged 18–24 did not vote. 2010 saw an increase with just over half of 18–24 year olds voting, compared to 65% for all age groups (Dar, 2013). A lower youth turnout was recorded for the US presidential elections of November 2012, where 41.2% of 18- to 24-year-olds voted, while overall turnout was 61.8% (US Census Bureau, no date).

It may be that concern over young people's alleged failure to take up politics has masked a broader problem of general adult disengagement from and dissatisfaction with electoral politics. The evidence suggests that since the 1960s there has been a steady decline in the electoral participation of adults in many established democracies (see Dalton, 2004; Hay, 2007, pp 11–27). We can also note declining turnout among some Central and Eastern European countries since the transition to democracy (Mesežnikov, Gyárfášová and Smilov, 2008). Recent results from the UK show disaffection and withdrawal from electoral politics to be particularly acute (Curtice, 2012). Levels of knowledge and interest in politics, along with willingness to vote, continue to fall; most people are dissatisfied with the system of government and feel their involvement is unlikely to create change (Fox, 2012).

Given this long-term context of disengagement and dissatisfaction with electoral politics, it is perhaps not surprising that the global economic crisis post-2008 has compounded political disaffection. Recent comparative work covering 19 European countries found that levels of political trust and satisfaction with democracy have declined significantly across most countries. This was particularly the case for those countries worst hit by the economic crisis (Spain, Ireland and Greece), but also significant in the UK, Belgium, Denmark, Finland, France and Slovenia (Polavieja, 2013).

Decline in electoral participation is not just reflected in low voter turnout at elections. Over recent decades most major political parties have suffered a considerable decline in membership (Whiteley, 2011; Van Biezen, Mair and Poguntke, 2012). The drop in party membership also means a decline in partisanship among citizens (Dalton and Wattenberg, 2000; Clarke et al, 2004; Berglund et al, 2005; Curtice, 2012), which in turn increases electoral volatility. Social class may continue to shape life chances and have cultural meaning and relevance for some people's lives, but it no longer delivers the relative political stability driven by alignment between social class, party identification and voting that it did during organised modernity (for example, see Andersen, Yang and Heath, 2006). The hollowing-out of political parties also means that they no longer have a vibrant grassroots base providing a vital link to communities and everyday life, and this underscores the oft-remarked gulf between politicians and citizens.

One of the questions that arise from the general disaffection with electoral politics is: does this mean that people are rejecting politics overall, or are they simply doing politics differently and engaging less with electoral politics? In the US, Dalton (2009) has shown that while young people are less likely to participate in electoral politics they are more likely than older groups to engage in non-electoral forms of participation (such as signing a petition, protesting or boycotting). Martin (2012) has recently found these results to hold when applied to Australian data. These findings suggest that young people's preference for non-electoral engagement reflects generational change rather than life-cycle effects and that young people may be the vanguard of a new way of relating to electoral politics (see also Power Inquiry, 2006).

While extra-electoral politics may be a vibrant and dynamic political scene and globalisation has undermined the power and control of nation-states, a great deal of power still resides within the institutions and offices of electoral politics. However, the range of voices drawn upon to shape policy and party manifestos has narrowed with the collapse of the grassroots basis of party politics. Once in office, governments are pragmatically reactive to the pressures generated by extra-electoral politics and power-monitoring and power-controlling devices. Keane (2010) describes this situation as 'monitory democracy', wherein a whole raft of bodies, both within electoral politics and without, have come to play a role in scrutinising power, seeking transparency and accountability. While such checks on power may be welcomed, this dynamic further highlights the disjuncture between citizens and their elected representatives.

While it is important to analyse politics at a macro level, politics is experienced differently by different social groups, as suggested above in terms of young people. This insight underscores the importance of exploring particular social identities when thinking about contemporary politics. The complex relationships people from minority ethnic backgrounds have with politics are typically under-researched, and hence this volume attempts to address this imbalance with three chapters that explore different aspects of minority-ethnic political (dis)engagement in Britain. The example of the Bradford West by-election is discussed below, as it illustrates some key aspects of minority-ethnic participation: that electoral participation can be shaped by broader cultural practices, leading to patronage and bloc voting, and that this might currently be undergoing change (see Akhtar, Chapter Seven in this volume); and in contrast to some of the crisis narratives about the political disconnection of particular ethnic minorities (see O'Toole, Chapter Eight in this volume), ethnic minority citizens, like other groups, can be persuaded to vote when they feel a genuine alternative is available.

The politics of identity and marginalisation

In March 2012 a dramatic and unexpected by-election result occurred in the northern English city of Bradford. As noted above, England, like many other democracies, seems to be gripped by a growing dissatisfaction with, and disengagement from, electoral politics. Riots in London during the summer of 2011 that spread north to include Birmingham, Nottingham, Liverpool, Manchester, Leeds and Huddersfield reflected another dimension and expression of dissatisfaction (see Tyler, 2013, chapter 7 for a general discussion). Bradford did not riot in 2011, but saw considerable unrest in 2001, when, with nearby towns Burnley and Oldham, there were civil disturbances for some days and violent clashes between police and predominantly young people of South Asian background (Bagguley and Hussain, 2008). Following the 'riots', official reports highlighted the disengagement of such young people from the democratic process as a key factor (Cantle, 2001; see also DCLG, 2005 for comments about low Muslim youth participation following the London bombings of 2005). It was with this history, and amid a general context of unrest, that in March 2012 a by-election took place in which some 18,000 people turned out to elect George Galloway from the Respect Party as MP for Bradford West. While turnout was down to 50% from 65% in the general election of 2010, Galloway received almost 56% of the vote, overturning a 5,000-plus majority to win with a majority of 10,140 votes, and there were 20%-plus swings away from Labour and the Conservatives. Labour had held the seat since 1974 (except for a brief defection to the Social Democratic Party during the 1980s). Galloway referred to the result as the 'Bradford Spring', drawing a parallel with the Arab Spring of 2011.

Following the momentum generated in the by-election, the council elections held in May 2012 also proved successful for the Respect Party, with the election of five councillors and considerable support in several other wards. Respect was successful in wards with large populations of people from South Asian backgrounds. Prior to these elections, Respect did not hold any council seats in Bradford, had only ever run a few candidates and had garnered only a small proportion of the vote.

The party claims that many first-time voters, young and old, voted for Respect (Galloway, 2012). Media reports made similar comments and also highlighted the role of Muslim – especially Muslim women – voters (Goodhart, 2012; Pidd, 2012). Senior members of the Labour Party have noted their lack of connection with young people and Bradford's Asian community, particularly Muslim women (Cooper, 2012). Peace and Akhtar (2014) argue that the victory reflects the way young South Asian Muslim voters are beginning to break with a tradition of patronage and bloc voting. They also point to Respect's campaign strategy, which continued to take bloc votes when available while ostensibly positioning the party as anti-bloc vote, which held particular appeal for South Asian women and young people. However, the polling data remains in aggregate form and we have little direct evidence to draw upon in explaining this upsurge in electoral participation amid a UK-wide context of dissatisfaction and disengagement from electoral politics.

In addition to the explanations advanced by Peace and Akhtar (2014), we know also that George Galloway has been a vociferous opponent of the wars in Afghanistan and Iraq[3] (which were supported by both of Britain's major parties), is a strong supporter of the Palestinian cause and has close personal ties to Islam (Odone, 2012). The above factors also suggest that, unlike the common phrase 'politics is always local', Respect's success seems more likely to be the result of a complex interconnection of the kind of local issues identified by Peace and Akhtar within a national context of limited political choice due to party convergence and the ways in which social identity and faith can provide links to global issues and foreign policy (also see O'Toole, Chapter Eight in this volume).

The political representation of ethnic minorities in British electoral politics, especially at national level, is a relatively recent phenomenon, but has been gathering considerable pace in recent years. At the 2010 general election the number of MPs from a Black or minority ethnic (BME) backgrounds increased from 14 to 27. Organisations like Operation Black Vote (see Fernandes, Chapter Nine in this volume) have been working to further the education, participation and representation of BME people at all levels of politics and community life. The example of Bradford West also points to the way in which a growing number of electorates in numerous countries hold the potential for the BME vote to be decisive. Demographic trends suggest that the electoral power of British BME communities will continue to grow.

Shifting our focus from electoral politics towards the sub-political realm, we can see that despite the individualisation of political repertoires (think of signing e-petitions, recycling, energy conservation or political consumerism) there are a number of ways in which contemporary politics forges new solidarities. Within Islam the notion of the umma, a brotherhood or universal community of believers, is invoked by some as a means of political connection that binds Muslims together despite geographical, social and cultural distance (see Kamaludeen, 2013 for a discussion of Muslim hip-hop artists invoking the umma to articulate human rights concerns). Therese O'Toole's work (Chapter Eight in this volume, see also O'Toole and Gale, 2013) with young Muslim activists in the north of England brings this to the fore. Her work also highlights the importance of religious, rather than ethnic, identities for some activists. While Muslim faith provides this concept for believers, contemporary social conditions like the growth of transnational corporations, new communication technology, increasing international flows of goods and finance, the growth of diasporas and mass migration also facilitate and call for political activity that transcends national borders and connects people.

Globalisation undermines the autonomy of national governments, as finance and corporations increasingly operate globally – not to mention the role of transnational organisations like the International Monetary Fund or the World Trade Organization, which set agendas and have influence independent of national governments. The global financial crisis that began in the US housing market in 2007–08 and spread through the global financial system turned a problem of bad private debt into vast sovereign debt as governments bailed out various banks –

and in the case of Europe, bailed out a number of national economies – graphically highlights how enmeshed the international political economy has become. Given this situation, national governments are not always the best target for change, as they are poorly equipped to respond to many contemporary problems – tax evasion is a good current example, and the issue of climate change continues to remind us of the inability of governments to work together across national borders for international benefit. Various high-profile actions against the tax evasion of multinational companies have directly targeted these companies (see Street, Chapter Six in this volume), rather than taking direct aim at national governments and their tax legislation. As globalisation increasingly means the 'intensive entanglement of everyone with everyone else' (Connolly, 1991, p 188), various social movements have tried to exploit these points of connection to effect social and political change. The anti-sweat-shop and the fair-trade movements are good examples, as they call for a connection to be made between the conditions of production and producers of goods, and consumers, despite the typically vast geographical and social distances between these groups. In recent years concern has broadened from the production of food and clothing to also include the manufacture of electronic goods like smartphones (see Musgrove, 2006; Peralta, 2012; Chan, 2013). In Young's words:

> The discourse of the anti-sweatshop movement, as I hear it, draws attention to the complex structural processes that do connect persons and institutions in very different social and geographic positions. [...] We are all connected to them [sweatshop workers]; we wear clothes they make; we sell them in our stores. So the movement has done much to defetishize commodities, revealing market structures as complex human creations. (Young, 2003, p 40)

Political consumerism is broadly indicative of some of the ways in which political practices and understandings have shifted in recent years, namely in its transnational orientation, politicisation of everyday life and more individualised and personalised practices. These themes are reflected throughout the volume, but particularly in Chapters Three, Six and Eight. The social movements around political consumerism campaigns have creatively responded to the injustices of a globalised capitalism that exploits producers and workers in distant lands by arguing for an extension of the social and political imagination of 'wealthy' consumers and claiming that consumers themselves have a share of responsibility in the wages and conditions under which goods and services are produced/provided. Many of these campaigns go beyond a simple notion of consumer choice and power by trying to provide various assurances that goods have been produced and traded fairly and ethically. In part, this is about challenging the nature of capitalism by claiming that if a fair price is paid, then just and environmentally sustainable trade can occur (notably, this view ignores broader questions about global inequalities between 'producers' and 'consumers').

Recent scholarship has argued for the need to move beyond conceptions of fair trade as involving consumers individually invoking their ethical/political considerations, and instead to view it as operating within diverse social networks that frequently involve collective forms of activism as well as more individualised activity (Clarke et al, 2007). Nonetheless, political consumerism tends to be a more individualised activity, even if it is worked out and revised relationally with others or practised in conjunction with collective action. It is also one of those slippery activities that sit between the political and the non-political, the public and the private; it exists outside the bounds of institutionalised electoral politics. While political consumerism is exercised differently by different social groups (Adams and Raisborough, 2008; Beagan et al, 2010), it bears little relationship to collective class politics. In contrast, it is a form of political practice that is eminently suited to being reflexively used as part of one's everyday life-style and sense of identity.

Structure of the volume

Contemporary politics is a dynamic and contested field. It is increasingly global in scope, and yet national contexts and institutions remain powerful and continue to shape how many of us engage with politics. The meaning and practice of politics has reopened, generating effective and exciting actions by social movements and activists, but for many, electoral politics feels lifeless and disconnected from important issues. The range of social identities implicated in politics has broadened out to include, among others, gender, sexuality, disability, faith and ethnicity (and their intersections), but cross-cutting economic inequality has again become an increasingly salient issue. The internet and social media have become key tools for many activists and social movements, but have generally seen scant uptake across the institutions and practices of electoral politics. All forms of politics are experiencing profound change through processes of globalisation, individualisation and the impacts of communications technology. The contributions to this book attempt to grapple with these broad changes, both analytically and through the practices of activists and campaigners. The volume draws upon the insights of analysts and practitioners from different academic disciplines and forms of political engagement, using a variety of levels of analysis to help reveal the texture and dynamics of contemporary politics as well as the experience of politics in some of its variety.

The book is divided into three overlapping sections. Part One concerns the changing nature of politics, in particular new and blended forms of political participation. In the light of changing political practices, Michele Micheletti's Chapter Two asks bold questions about the democratic quality of various forms of participation and provides a broad overview of some of the ways in which citizenship may be changing. Andre Banks from the organisation All Out provides a first-hand account in Chapter Three of transnational activism that combines online and new media tactics with offline actions in the field of identity politics. Andre's work is an excellent example of the way contemporary politics can be transnationally oriented, combine online and offline action and politicise everyday life and social identities. Chapter Four, the final contribution to this section is from Marie Gillespie, Nesrine Abdel Sattar and Mina Lami and extends the focus on new media through a case study of BBC Arabic's attempts at participatory journalism. Citizen journalism is a key part of contemporary political repertoires, but mainstream media organisations have not been very successful in harnessing the interactive and participatory power of social media. Gillespie et al's chapter explores the challenges and potentials for media outlets to augment the public sphere through interactive technologies.

Part Two of the book provides several accounts of political life, all framed by a context of electoral disengagement. Nathan Manning's Chapter Five calls for us to take seriously the role that emotions play in our (dis)engagements with electoral politics. Significantly, this work draws upon research with working-class citizens who are typically overlooked in debates about new political practices, as they are frequently assumed to be disengaged and disaffected. In Chapter Six, Tim Street from the organisation UK Uncut discusses the way direct action and online organising have been used to oppose the UK government's austerity measures and highlight the tax avoidance of many high street companies. UK Uncut's work shows the on-going relevance of material issues for contemporary activism. Like All Out and other forms of contemporary activism, UK Uncut targets both the state and non-state actors like corporations, using the internet and social media to generate dynamic local and national campaigns both online and through direct action, like occupying shop-fronts. Chapter Seven, the final chapter in this section comes from Parveen Akhtar and draws upon ethnographic data to explore the impacts for young British Muslims of being both a minority within British politics and excluded from kin-based systems of patronage.

Part Three of the book deals with the politics of identity and marginalisation. In Chapter Eight, Therese O'Toole explores the varied forms of political engagement among young ethnic minority activists in the UK. Chapter Nine comes from Francine Fernandes, who works for the organisation Operation Black Vote. Her contribution provides some biographical insights into her work as an activist/campaigner and discusses the achievements and challenges of working for the political inclusion of BME citizens. These chapters on minority-ethnic (dis) engagement are significant, as such groups are frequently overlooked in work on political participation and citizenship. As these chapters show, BME citizens have complex relationships with the political. Akhtar's and Fernandes' chapters highlight the numerous ways in which ethnic minority groups are marginalised and disenfranchised from electoral politics, while O'Toole's work calls on us to expand definitions of politics and explore the ways in which young minority-ethnic citizens *do* participate. Chapter Ten comes from Stephen Reicher, Yashpal Jogdand and Caoimhe Ryan and highlights the importance of selfhood and social identity in political participation. This chapter emphasises the centrality of self and social identity that features in each of the preceding chapters and remains a mainstay of political (dis)engagement.

Notes

[1] 'Patrick' is a pseudonym.

[2] A database compiled by the *Guardian* newspaper listed 750 Occupy camps active in 2011; see http://www.theguardian.com/news/datablog/2011/oct/17/occupy-protests-world-list-map.

[3] See, for example, his 2005 appearance before the US Senate Homeland Security Subcommittee, http://www.youtube.com/watch?v=HrdFFCnYtbk.

References

Adams, M. and Raisborough, J. (2008) 'What Can Sociology Say About FairTrade? Class, Reflexivity and Ethical Consumption', *Sociology*, vol 42, no 6, pp 1165–82.

Andersen, R., Yang, M. and Heath, A.F. (2006) 'Class Politics and Political Context in Britain, 1964–1997: Have Voters Become More Individualized?', *European Sociological Review*, vol 22, no 2, pp 215–28.

Bagguley, P. and Hussain, Y. (2008) *Riotous Citizens: Ethnic Conflict in Multicultural Britain,* Ashgate: Aldershot.

Beagan, B.L., Ristovski-Slijepcevic, S. and Chapman, G.E. (2010) 'People Are Just Becoming More Conscious of How Everything's Connected? "Ethical" Food Consumption in Two Regions of Canada', *Sociology*, vol 44, no 4, pp 751–69.

Beck, U. (1992) *Risk society: Towards a new modernity*, London: Sage Publications.

Bennett, L.W. and Segerberg, A. (2012) 'The logic of connective action: digital media and the personalization of contentious politics', *Information, Communication and Society*, vol 15, no 5, pp 739–68.

Bennett, L., Segerberg, A. and Walker, S. (2014) 'Organization in the crowd: peer production in large-scale networked protests', *Information, Communication and Society*, vol 17, no 2, pp 232–60.

Berglund, F., Holmberg, S., Schmitt, H. and Thomassen, J. (2005) 'Party identification and party choice', in J. Thomassen (ed) *The European Voter*, Oxford: Oxford University Press, pp 106–24.

Bhavnani, K. (1991) *Talking Politics*, Cambridge: Cambridge University Press.

Butler, D. and Stokes, D. (1969) *Political change in Britain: forces shaping electoral choice*, London: Macmillan.

Calhoun, C. (1993) '"New Social Movements" of the Early Nineteenth Century', *Social Science History*, vol 17, no 3, pp 385–427.

Cantle, T. (2001) *Community Cohesion: A Report of the Independent Review Team,* London: The Home Office.

Chan, J. (2013) 'A suicide survivor: the life of a Chinese worker', *New Technology, Work and Employment*, vol 28, no 2, pp 84–99.

Clarke, H., Sanders, S., Stewart, M. and Whiteley, P. (2004) *Political Choice in Britain*, Oxford: Oxford University Press.

Clarke, N., Barnett, C., Cloke, P. and Malpass, A. (2007) 'The Political Rationalities of Fair-Trade Consumption in the United Kingdom', *Politics & Society*, vol 35, no 4, pp 583–607.

Connolly, W.E. (1991) *Identity/Difference*, Ithaca: Cornell University Press.

Cooper, Y. 2012 'Labour "failed to connect with Asians in Bradford"', BBC News [online], available at http://www.bbc.co.uk/news/uk-politics-17576752 (accessed 15 May2012).

Curtice, J. (2012) 'Political engagement: Bridging the gulf? Britain's democracy after the 2010 election', in A. Park, E. Clery, J. Curtice, M. Phillips and D. Utting (eds) *British Social Attitudes 28*, London: Sage, pp 1–20.

Dalton, R.J. (2004) *Democratic challenges, democratic choices: the erosion of political support in advanced industrial democracies*, Oxford: Oxford University Press.

Dalton, R.J. (2009) *The Good Citizen: How a Younger Generation is Reshaping American Politics* (revised edition), Washington: CQ Press.

Dalton, R.J. and Wattenberg, M.P. (2000) *Parties without partisans: political change in advanced industrial democracies*, Oxford: Oxford University Press.

Dar, A. (2013) *Elections: Turnout*, House of Commons Library Standard Note: SN/SG/1467, 16 April 2013 [online] available at: http://www.parliament.uk/business/publications/research/briefing-papers/SN01467/elections-turnout

DCLG (2005) *Preventing Extremism Together: Working Groups*, London: Department of Communities and Local Government.

Della Porta, D. and Diani, M. (1999) *Social Movements: An Introduction*, Malden, MA: Wiley-Blackwell.

Fieldhouse, E., Tranmer, M. and Russell, A. (2007) 'Something about young people or something about elections? Electoral participation of young people in Europe: Evidence from a multilevel analysis of the European Social Survey', *European Journal of Political Research*, vol 46, pp 797–822.

Fox, R. (2012) 'Disgruntled, Disillusioned and Disengaged: Public Attitudes to Politics in Britain Today', *Parliamentary Affairs*, vol 65, no 4, pp 877–87.

Furlong, A. and Cartmel, F. (2012) 'Social Change and Political Engagement Among Young People: Generation and the 2009/2010 British Election Survey', *Parliamentary Affairs*, vol 65, no 1, pp 13–28.

Galloway, G. (2012) 'This was Bradford's version of the riots', *Guardian*, 30 March [online], available at: http://www.guardian.co.uk/commentisfree/2012/mar/30/bradford-version-of-riots (accessed 4 May 2012).

Giddens, A. (1991) *Modernity and Self-Identity: Self and Society in Late Modern Age*, Cambridge: Polity Press.

Gitlin, T. (2012) *Occupy Nation: The Roots, The Spirit, and the Promise of Occupy Wall Street*, New York: Harper Collins.

Goodhart, D. (2012) 'Making sense of Bradford West', *Prospect Magazine* 4 April [online], available at: http://www.prospectmagazine.co.uk/2012/04/george-galloway-bradford-west-bloc-voting-labour-ethnic-minority/ (accessed 4 May 2012).

Guttsman, W.L. (1967) *The British Political Elite,* London: Macmillan.

Habermas, J. (1984) *The Theory of Communicative Action, Volume I: Reason and the Rationalization of Society*, Boston, MA: Beacon

Hartley, J. (2010) 'Silly citizenship', *Critical Discourse Studies*, vol 7, no 4, pp 233–48.

Harvey, D. (1990) *The Condition of Post-Modernity: An Enquiry into the Origins of Social Change,* Cambridge, MA: Blackwell.

Hay, C. (2007) *Why We Hate Politics*, Cambridge: Polity Press.

Henn, M. and Foard, N. (2012) 'Young People, Political Participation and Trust in Britain', *Parliamentary Affairs*, vol 65, no 1, pp 47–67.

Howard, P.N., Duffy, A., Freelon, D., Hussain, M., Mari, W. and Mari, M. (2011) *Opening Closed Regimes: What was the Role of Social Media During the Arab Spring* (working paper) [online] available at: http://pitpi.org/index.php/2011/09/11/opening-closed-regimes-what-was-the-role-of-social-media-during-the-arab-spring/ (accessed 31 July 2013).

Inglehart, R. (1997) *Modernization and Postmodernization: Cultural, Economic and Political Change in 43 Societies*, Princeton, NJ: Princeton University Press.

Jones, O. (2011) *Chavs: The demonization of the working class,* London: Verso.

Kamaludeen, M.N. (2013) 'The September 11 generation, hip-hop and human rights', *Journal of Sociology*, DOI: 10.1177/1440783313493029.

Katz, J.E., Barris, M. and Jain, A. (2013) *The Social Media President: Barack Obama and the politics of digital engagement*, New York: Palgrave Macmillan.

Keane, J. (2010) *The Life and Death of Democracy*, London: Pocket Books.

Keating, A., Kerr, D., Benton, T., Mundy, E. and Lopes, J. (2010) *Citizenship education in England 2001–2010: young people's practices and prospects for the future: the eighth and final report from the Citizenship Education Longitudinal Study (CELS)*, London: Department for Education.

Kroen, S. (2004) 'A Political History of the Consumer', *The Historical Journal*, vol 47, no 3, pp 709–36.

Loader, B.D. (ed) (2007) *Young Citizens in the Digital Age: Political Engagement, Young People and New Media*, London: Routledge, pp 1–19.

Maier, C.S. (1970) 'Between Taylorism and Technocracy: European Ideologies and the Vision of Industrial Productivity in the 1920s', *Journal of Contemporary History*, vol 5, no 2, pp 27–63.

Manning, N. (2014) 'The Relational Self and Young People's Engagements with Politics', *Journal of Sociology*, vol 50, no 4, pp 486–500.

Manning, N. and Edwards, K. (2014) 'Why has Civic Education Failed to Increase Young People's Political Participation?' *Sociological Research Online*, vol 19, no 1, p 5 [online] available at: http://www.socresonline.org.uk/19/1/5.html.

Marsh, D., O'Toole, T. and Jones, S. (2007) *Young people and politics in the UK: apathy or alienation?* Basingstoke: Palgrave Macmillan

Martin, A. (2012) 'Political Participation among the Young in Australia: Testing Dalton's Good Citizen Thesis', *Australian Journal of Political Science*, vol 47, no 2, pp 211–26.

Melucci, A. (1989) *Nomads of the Present: Social Movements and Individual Needs in Contemporary Society*, Philadelphia, PA: Temple University Press.

Mesežnikov, G., Gyárfášová, O. and Smilov, D. (eds) (2008) *Populist Politics and Liberal Democracy in Central and Eastern Europe*, Bratislava: Institute for Public Policy.

Micheletti, M. (2003) *Political Virtue and Shopping: Individuals, Consumerism and Collective Action*, New York: Palgrave.

Musgrove, M. (2006) Sweatshop Conditions at IPod Factory Reported, *Washington Post,* 16 June [online] available at: http://www.washingtonpost.com/wp-dyn/content/article/2006/06/15/AR2006061501898.html (accessed 3 June 2013).

Nielsen, R.K. (2013) 'Mundane Internet Tools, the Risk of Exclusion, and Reflexive Movements – Occupy Wall Street and Political uses of Digital Networked Technologies', *The Sociological Quarterly*, vol 54, no 2, pp 173–7.

Norris, P. (1999) *Critical citizens: global support for democratic governance*, Oxford: Oxford University Press.

Odone, C. (2012) 'What is it about Gorgeous George that gets the girls?' *Telegraph,* 3 April [online] available at: http://blogs.telegraph.co.uk/news/cristinaodone/100148867/what-is-it-about-gorgeous-george-that-gets-the-girls/ (accessed 4 May 2012).

Offe, C. (1985) 'New Social Movements: Challenging the Boundaries of Institutional Politics', *Social Research*, vol 52, pp 817–68.

O'Toole, T. and Gale, R. (2013) *Political Engagement Amongst Ethnic Minority Young People: Making a Difference*, Basingstoke: Palgrave MacMillan.

Park, A. (2004) 'Has modern politics disenchanted the young?' in A. Park, K. Curtis and C. Thompson (eds) *British Social Attitudes, the 21st Report*, London: Sage, pp 23–48.

Peace, T. and Akhtar, P. (2014) 'Biraderi, Bloc Votes and Bradford: Investigating the Respect Party's Campaign Strategy', *British Journal of Politics and International Relations,* DOI 10.1111/1467–856X.12057.

Peralta, E. (2012) 'Protesters At Apple Stores Demand "Ethical" Products', *NPR* [online] available at: http://www.npr.org/blogs/thetwo-way/2012/02/09/146657989/protesters-at-apple-stores-demand-ethical-products (accessed: 9 August 2013).

Pidd, H. (2012) 'How women won it for George Galloway', *Guardian*, 4 April [online], available at: http://www.guardian.co.uk/politics/2012/apr/04/how-women-won-it-for-galloway (accessed 4 May 2012).

Polanyi, K. (1957) *The great transformation,* Boston, MA: Beacon Press.

Polavieja, J.G. (2013) 'Economic crisis, political legitimacy and social cohesion', in D. Gallie (ed) *Economic Crisis, Quality of Work and Social Integration: The European Experience*, Oxford: Oxford University Press, pp 256–78.

Power Inquiry (2006) *Power to the People,* Report of Power: An Independent Inquiry into Britain's Democracy, London: Power Inquiry.

Putnam, R. (2000) *Bowling Alone: The Collapse and Revival of American Community*, New York: Simon and Schuster.

Print, M., Saha, L. and Edwards, K. (2004) 'Youth electoral study – report 1: enrolment and voting' [online] available at: http://www.aec.gov.au/about_aec/Publications/youth_study/index.htm.

Rabinbach, A. (1992) *The Human Motor: Energy, Fatigue, and the Origins of Modernity*, Berkeley, CA: University of California Press.

Rheingans, R. and Hollands, R. (2013) '"There is no alternative?" Challenging dominant understandings of youth politics in late modernity through a case study of the 2010 UK student occupation movement', *Journal of Youth Studies*, vol 16, no 4, pp 546–64.

Rose, N. (1989) *Governing the Soul. The Shaping of the Private Self*, London: Routledge.

Rueschemeyer, D., Huber Stephens, E. and Stephens, J.D. (1992) *Capitalist development and democracy,* Chicago: University of Chicago Press.

Scott, J.C. (1998) *Seeing Like a State: How certain Schemes to Improve the Human Condition Have Failed,* New Haven, CT: Yale University Press.

Sörbom, A. and Wennerhag, M. (2013) 'Individualization, Life Politics, and the Reformulation of Social Critique: An Analysis of the Global Justice Movement', *Critical Sociology*, vol 39, no 3, pp 453–78.

Stolle, D. and Micheletti, M. (2013) *Political Consumerism: Global Responsibility in Action*, Cambridge: Cambridge University Press.

Tarrow, S.G. (2011) *Power in Movement: Social Movements and Contentious Politics* (3rd edition), Cambridge: Cambridge University Press.

Theocharis, Y. (2012) 'Cuts, Tweets, Solidarity and Mobilisation: How the Internet Shaped the Student Occupations', *Parliamentary Affairs*, vol 65, pp 162–94.

Tilly, C. (2004) *Social Movements, 1768–2004*, Boulder, CO: Paradigm Publishers.

Torney-Purta, J., Lehmann, R., Oswald, H. and Schulz, W. (2001) *Citizenship and education in twenty-eight countries: civic knowledge and engagement at age fourteen*, Amsterdam: International Association for the Evaluation of Educational Achievement.

Touraine, A. (1971) *Post-Industrial Society*, London: Wildwood House.

Tyler, I. (2013) *Revolting subjects: social abjection and resistance in neoliberal Britain*, London: Zed Books Ltd.

US Census Bureau [no date] *Table 1. Reported Voting and Registration by Sex and Single Years of Age: November 2012*, [online] available at: http://www.census.gov/hhes/www/socdemo/voting/publications/p20/2012/tables.html (accessed 6 August 2013).

Van Biezen, I., Mair, P. and Poguntke, T. (2012) 'Going, going, … gone? The decline of party membership in contemporary Europe', *European Journal of Political Research*, vol 51, pp 24–56.

Van Zoonen, L., Vis, F. and Mihelj, S. (2010) 'Performing citizenship on YouTube: activism, satire and online debate around the anti–Islam video *Fatina*', *Critical Discourse Studies*, vol 7, no 4, pp 249–62.

Vicari, S. (2013) 'Public reasoning around social contention: A case study of Twitter use in the Italian mobilization for global change', *Current Sociology*, vol 61, no 4, pp 474–90.

Wagner, P. (1994) *A Sociology of Modernity: Liberty and Discipline*, London: Routledge.

Wattenberg, M. (2011) *Is voting for Young People?* (3rd edn), New York: Pearson Longman.

Whiteley, P.F. (2011) 'Is the party over? The decline of party activism and membership across the democratic world', *Party Politics*, vol 17, no 1, pp 21–44.

Young, I. (2003) 'From guilt to solidarity', *Dissent*, vol 50, no 2, pp 39–45.

Part One:
The changing landscape of politics

TWO

Does participation always have a democratic spirit?

Michele Micheletti

Introduction

Let's face it. We love it and think the more the better. Our ongoing passion for participation leads politicians and policy makers to cry out when it declines, and scholars of politics to track, trace and analyse the numerous ways in which individuals engage and disengage politically. Political scientists intensively debate *where* participation takes place – if it occurs only in parliamentary politics and government-oriented settings or also in other settings (van Deth, 2010; Stolle and Hooghe, 2006; McFarland, 2010; Scholzman, 2010; Stolle and Micheletti, 2013). Some scholars devise innovative theories, methods and materials to study emerging venues for citizen engagement outside government and commonly find that fears of participation's decay often are related to privileging certain forms of political activity over others. This insight helps to explain why politicians and policy makers in different countries target electoral participation among the youth, including suggesting compulsory first-time voting and lowering the legal voting age to 16 (for example, Swedish Save the Children Foundation's Youth Movement, 2006; IPPR, 2013). More general agreement coheres over the importance of the *who* of participation, a topic involving worries of whether or not pockets of participatory inequality exist, how and why they come about, and how they might be remedied (Brady, Verba and Schlozman, 1995; Verba, 2003; Stolle and Micheletti, 2005; Schlozman, Verba and Brady, 2012). Here scholars analyse the individual characteristics of participants and non-participants and ask whether gender, age, education, ethnicity, race, religion, income, social class and so on matter for who participates and who does not. The short answer is that they do. The general fear is that certain groups are better and others worse off at realising themselves in politics. Important concepts such as 'mobilisation of bias' (see below) and books like *The Unheavenly Chorus: Unequal Political Voice and the Broken Promise of*

American Democracy (Schlozman, Verba and Brady, 2012) reflect this concern.

Research on participation does not stop here. Scholars examine *how* participation takes place, that is, through which forms, tools and methods. Though somewhat related to the where question above, this one is more about bringing scholarship up to date with today's political world. For instance, scholars might ask how politically concerned individuals target the 'politics of products' of transnational corporations since these entities have gained more political power through contemporary economic globalisation. They even explore how people participate to solve problems created by economic austerity, governmental shutdowns and global climate change, or study how the online activities of a global political character are used in participatory activities (Stolle and Hooghe, 2006; Dalton 2008a, 2008b; Micheletti and McFarland, 2010; Bennett and Segerberg, 2011). Moreover, researchers investigate the *why* of participation in order to understand better the motivations, incentives, resources and networks that mobilise or draw political actors into politics (Conway and Feigert, 1968; Brady, Verba and Schlozman, 1995; Bäck, Teorell and Westholm, 2011). This focus is important because it helps us to understand the interests, values and norms underlying political behaviour as well as whether mobilisations of bias exist or not. Recently scholars have begun systematic studies of the *so what* of participation by evaluating whether and how effective different participatory activities are in bringing about societal change and well-being (Bosi and Uba, 2009; Stolle and Micheletti, 2013, chapter 7).

Participation scholarship greatly improves our understanding of political activity and assuages some worries about its decay. However, it also slights other important questions, particularly ones about how well it helps to grow democracy. The implicit assumption in scholarship has been that participation is good for democracy even when there is clear evidence to the contrary – from voting Hitler into office and boycotting Jewish merchants in the 1930s to contemporary protests of gay rights, public-dialogue forums that hinder free debate and special-interest mobilisation that thwarts global environmental problem solving. Hence the question: *Does participation always have a democratic spirit?*. This chapter contributes some thoughts and offers suggestions for how participation's democratic spirit can fruitfully be studied. It begins with a short overview of an insightful study that brings democratic theory and participation research closer together, suggests how citizenship research can be used to study this important question, briefly discusses how this approach might be applied empirically and then ends with a few final reflections on this question's importance for science and society.

Participation and democracy: some innovative insights

By revealing how normative democratic theory values participation, Swedish political scientist Jan Teorell (2006) identified important 'blind spots' in past research. He discusses how liberal, participative and deliberative democratic theory justify the role of participation in democracy and, in so doing, fills a knowledge gap on why participation is assumed to be important for democracy. For liberal democratic theory, participation offers individuals political voice – the foremost mechanism for interest representation in parliamentary politics – thus explaining why political equality and inequality (the who question) are important societal matters. For participatory democracy, the main value is hands-on involvement in decision making. It welcomes participation opportunities outside the parliamentary system, for they offer additional opportunities for self-governing and problem solving. For deliberative democracy, its core value is learning about and understanding politics by talking through the issues.

These theories generally assume, therefore, that participation is good for democracy, and thereby even accept the 'the more of it the better' thesis. For liberal and deliberative democracy, more of it by more people strengthens political equality and knowledge. For participatory democracy, participation and more of it implies wider and perhaps deeper community engagement. More participants and more participation are, furthermore, generally deemed to be better for political systems. For liberal theorists, a plurality of participatory forms and more of their use tends to 'make the system more responsive to citizens' needs and preferences', which promotes the equal protection of interests (Teorell, 2006, p 792) and enhances political equality. For participatory theorists, more participation fosters the individual's social and political capacities, which, it is assumed, also improves the quality of the citizens. The core value for deliberative theorists is accepting the political system's legitimacy (its political rules and decision outcomes). Here participation is envisioned as teaching how to be a good and understanding democratic loser if one's interests do not always prevail in decision making (so-called critical citizenship, see Norris, 1999). But as it is not always the case that participation in the real-life politics functions this way, should not scholarship recognise this?

Aside from this obvious additional blind spot, previous scholarship's point of departure has generally been to theorise from the perspective of the nation-state. This yesteryear's political context is typically collectivist in orientation. Here a central characteristic is its elite orientation through representative democracy and strong political agents able to screen the flow of ideas in and out of politics. Two prominent screening forces (gatekeepers) have been the traditional media (broadcast-network television and radio, traditional newspapers) and large membership organisations (particularly encompassing trade unions and political parties) that could function as strong socialising agents for informing and steering citizens into politics. In short, this era's participation was to large degree conducted in 'pre-packaged' involvement opportunities (compare Dalton, 2008b, p 93), offering strong suggestions about how to think and behave politically as well as about which political values to identify with. Elsewhere I have coined the concept of 'collectivist collective action' to characterise participation in this era and have identified it in pure ideal-typical terms as requiring that citizens accept the norms and rules of physical and territorially or nation-state-based structures whose numerical strength gave them the legitimacy to screen out undesirable (for them) political views and values. They could even convince prospective members to change their views and behaviours to fit better in the organisational mould and the identity politics expressed by its grand or semi-grand ideological narratives (Micheletti, 2010, pp 24–34). Table 2.1 provides details of this characterisation.

Today's political era is different and typically identified as looser, more flexible, open and vulnerable to many diverse influences, targets and values. Participation in it resembles more the pure ideal type of 'individualised collective action' (Micheletti, 2010, pp 24–34), theorising political actors as not primarily seeking a pre-packaged established political home, as in yesteryear, or trusting traditional authorities (political parties, broadcasting networks, unions and so on) to tell them what to think politically and how to behave in politics. Rather, political actors create their own political identity and express and act it out in real life. Today's political actors in many democracies also have much more freedom to create their own political identity and engagement in politics. They believe that their attempts to influence (liberal democracy's justification for participation), their desire for hands-on and Do-It-Yourself (DIY) involvement (participatory democracy's justification) and even their hunger to understand politics more fully (deliberative democracy's justification) can be achieved outside yesteryear's framework. Therefore, political activity can occur on a more individualised basis, for instance through less-organised and structured market-based activism (political consumerism) outside the parliamentary sphere or through social media. Self-development and self-governing can even imply life-style politics (Bennett, 1998) and life-style political consumerism (for example, veganism or simple living) (Micheletti, 2010, p 182–5; Stolle and Micheletti, 2013). This self-governing form of participation, requiring the demand for more active choice and rights on the part of individuals, differs considerably from those forms theorised by participatory democracy in the past (for example, the workplace) (Pateman, 1970). Table 2.1 presents yesteryear's and contemporary participation as pure ideal types. The terms 'participation 1.0' and 'participation 2.0', borrowed from the evolution of the World Wide Web from the more linear and static

Table 2.1: The ideal types of participation 1.0 and participation 2.0

Yesteryear's collectivist collective action Participation 1.0	Today's individualised collective action Participation 2.0
Political identity built from and with structures and social positions, unitary identity following life paths and role models	Political identity and social position not taken for granted, map out your own life path, be your own role model
Participation in established political homes (for example, membership-based interest groups and political parties)	Use of established political homes as point of departure to decide own preferences and priorities, creation and development of individualised political home (for example, via social media and life-style politics)
Participation in territorially based physical structures focusing on the government and political system	Involvement in various kinds of networks not based in any single physical territorial level or structure
Participation that is channelled through grand or semi-grand ideological narratives (traditional political ideology)	Involvement based on self-authored individualised narratives ('self-reflexivity')
Participation in representative democratic structures Delegation of responsibility to leaders and officials	Self-assertive and direct involvement in concrete actions and settings Responsibility is not delegated to leaders and officials but taken personally and jointly Self-actualisation, individualised responsibility taking, responsibilisation
Member interests and identity filtered, adapted, moulded to political preferences of these interest-articulating and aggregating institutions Loyalty to established structures, acceptance of organisational norms, values, standard operating procedures and so on	Dedication and commitment to urgent causes rather than loyalty to organisational norms, values, standard operating procedures and so on Individualised responsibility taking for urgent causes

Source: Adapted from Micheletti (2010, p 27)

Web.1 to the more socially interactive and flexible Web.2, are coined to reflect similar developments in participation, and also to underscore their significant ideal-theoretical differences. 'Participation 1.0' represents 'old school' yesteryear's collectivist and elite-dominated participation culture; 'participation 2.0' is the term for the new generation of participation with looser, more plural, elite-challenging and individualised elements.

Given its relative newness, much effort is devoted to explaining and even defending 'participation 2.0'. Scholars argue that this conceptualisation of participation brings research up to date with current realities and assuages panic about participation's decay. They identify globalisation, individualisation and privatisation as key processes spurring on 2.0 activities, venues and opportunities and find that its participatory formats are increasingly used (Dalton 2008a; Stolle and Micheletti, 2013). 'Participation 2.0' is found to occur more spontaneously and can, for instance, surge as swarms (Segerberg, 2010) or carrotmobs (Hoffmann and Hutter, 2012), be triggered by various new authorities on politics, take place in 'leader-less' networks of 'scattered individuals' (McFarland, 2010, pp 23–4) and be performed more anonymously. 'Participation 2.0' generates theoretical debates on creative participation,[1] new conceptions of how individuals participate in politics (individualised responsibility taking and responsibilisation[2]), but it is noteworthy that its democratic quality is also slighted in scholarship, though researchers are probing the value portraits of its users (see more below).

Some scholars and experts express worries about citizens' current ability to learn about politics and the value of participation in today's more multifaceted political world (Crick and Lockyer, 2010; Wattenberg, 2012). Among other matters, the role of self-interest in triggering and shaping participation and its contribution to democracy is intensively debated; scholars differ in their analysis (Burtt, 1993; Innes and Booher, 2004; Micheletti, 2010). Here the central question is whether the more individualised collective-action setting is evolving participation from engagements for the common good toward the individual good. Is the 'we intentions' of politics fizzling away and being replaced by a focus on self, self-interest and self-promotion as a political project? Is, so to speak, participation becoming a 'selfie', just like photographing has to a great degree become a more individual and individualised activity? Obviously these questions pertain to 'participation 2.0', but also even to '1.0' because traditional political agents increasingly appeal to self-interest to attract supporters, as when social citizenship is framed in terms of welfare pocketbook voting and established environmental associations evoke emotions to advocate and mobilise for their cause (Boström and Klintman, 2011; Stolle and Micheletti, 2013).

Another worry is what here is identified as the eventuality of a value divide between 'participation 1.0' and '2.0' and what this might mean for growing democracy. This implies that the two participation cultures might have different value portraits separating them from each other and drawing in interests and individuals (that is, mobilisation of bias) in particular ways. An insightful ethnographic study of a civic group associated with British labour, for instance, reveals an internal tension between participation via social networking sites ('participation 2.0') and participation drawing on the group's more collective political ethos ('participation 1.0'). '2.0 participants' were found to be more ego centred and focused primarily on self and forms of self-representation, thus leading the scholars Fenton and Barassi (2011, p 188) to conclude that the two participatory cultures do not 'sit easily' with each other. Other research reports similar findings indicating a value divide. A large survey of US citizen involvement in democracy shows, interestingly, that the individuals involved in certain '1.0' forms (voting, working for and in a political party) tend to have a restrictive view of how one should engage in politics and are more oriented toward the duty norms of democracy (duty citizenship, see Table 2.2 for definitions). In contrast, those individuals who participated more in signing petitions, lawful demonstrations, political consumerism, web activity and other looser, contentious or extra-parliamentary activities veering more toward the '2.0' ideal type tend to stress other citizenship norms, particularly solidarity and enlightened understanding (Table 2.2) (Dalton, 2008b, especially pp 72, 92). This research suggests the possibility that changing participatory norms lie behind the surge of the 'participation 2.0' culture. This might, therefore, imply that the changing norms determine in some way the where, how and who of political participation. Do these results reveal a worrisome mobilisation of bias that threatens the democratic quality of participation? A value divide between, say, voters and demonstrators might, for instance, have significant consequences for the future functioning and legitimacy of democratic society.

My review of research reveals additional blind spots in participation research and challenges scholars to find ways to assess participation's democratic quality. It also prompts a democratic audit of old authorities (political parties, trade unions and so on) and new authorities (for example, pop-culture celebrities and bloggers) as sources for understanding and acting out politics. Additionally, it calls for new ways of studying if and how participatory culture and different forms of participation socialise citizens into adopting certain democratic norms over others. For instance, does electoral politics, as suggested above, socialise into system loyalty and duty citizenship? Do other participation forms socialise more into elite-challenging norms and/or those associated with global and solidarity citizenship? Or might it be the other way around: that people holding certain democratic norms and societal values are drawn into particular forms of participation over others? Regardless of the direction of causation, the point here is that scholars should devote effort to assessing the democratic quality of 'new ideas about authority and new practices' (Dahl, 1990, p 1) that are emerging in many countries, and also even the democratic robustness of more-established authorities and practices.

Asking questions about what might be called the 'downside' of participation is crucial. Not only do they enhance and advance scholarship, they also can contribute to societal debates that help the general public to understand itself better, and to policy making and political investments in improving democratic society. Interestingly, similar questions arose from the flurry of concern over the decline of social capital in many countries around the world. Through scholarly pondering on whether or not social capital always makes democracy better (Adler and Kwon, 2000; Stolle and Hooghe, 2005; Warren, 2008) a more nuanced view of its democratic contribution emerged. Today scholars acknowledge two general forms of social capital and claim that they can have different potential effects on democracy. Bonding social capital is identified when people sharing similar characteristics (religion, ethnicity, age, gender, social class and so on) are brought together into networks. While the cosiness generated in such settings was applauded in the past for creating strong bonds of interpersonal trust, today scholars acknowledge the potential risks from the creation of exclusionary likeness networks that condemn otherness and difference, lead to 'sinister ends' and create 'negative externalities' (Putnam and Goss, 2002, p 11). Bridging social capital, the other form of social capital, draws together people with dissimilar characteristics and involves value-oriented mechanisms that can promote broad social solidarity, cross-cutting allegiances and toleration of difference. Yet bridging social capital can also have a democratic downside if its focus on creating allegiances and consensus translates into assimilation and consent, thus putting a damper on free debate, deliberation and the politics of difference. This chapter seeks to stimulate a similar discussion on the upside and downside of participation and the reasons and implications of governmental, non-governmental organisation (NGO) and private efforts to promote certain of its forms over others.

Assessing participation's democratic ups and downs

How well do 'participation 1.0' and '2.0' mirror and nurture the norms of democracy? How do attempts to influence politics, liberal democracy's justification for participation, promote the spirit of a common good? Is there a risk that self-governing efforts, so favoured by the proponents of direct and participatory democracy, might have the same problematic tendency as bonding social capital? Does deliberative talking together to learn about politics, decide what to think and legitimise the political system always evoke democratic norms? Or can it just as easily function as a thought police and turn into a value ghetto or training ground for adopting certain accepted (politically correct?) stances (see Cornwell, 2007)? Can it, therefore, be that the forms, structures or venues for exercising 'participation 1.0' and '2.0' fall short in mirroring, nurturing and maximising key democratic norms? How do they, in other words, function as general socialising agents for democracy; do they draw in (and encourage) participants with different value bases or not? In sum, the general question is whether 'participation 1.0' and '2.0' promote a form of mobilisation of bias (Schattschneider, 1960; Bachrach and Baratz, 1962), a participation downside, that pushes out certain individuals while pulling in others, encourages some democratic norms while suppressing others and considers certain value profiles more appropriate and perhaps better than others.

Sound far fetched? Perhaps, but studies in other research fields reveal, for example, how values and interests mobilise, organise and consolidate into institutional structures, with the end result being that they support, constrain and empower biases in the policy making of administrative institutions. This means that they are, therefore, able to create structural barriers that construct meaning, homogenise habits and distribute goals and duties (Hendriks, 2000). Conceivably in similar fashion, participation forms are infused with certain values, reflect and cultivate certain identity shaping and promote certain relational characteristics that are biased toward particular democratic norms over others. After all, they too are opportunity structures that 'constitute connections, channels and gates of entry, which influence the fate of problem definitions, policy options and concepts embraced by various actors and organizations in the public domain' (Hendriks, 2000, p 290). Another pertinent query alluded to in previous research is whether or not the participants and non-participants in the various forms differ on how they view the norms of democracy. Do they have different value profiles, and, if so, why?

To answer this list of key questions, investigations characterised by theoretical precision and empirical focus are necessary. Here an important literature that can contribute ideas is empirical citizenship study. This scholarship explicitly and systematically discusses a series of democratic norms about what it takes to be a good citizen. These norms or expectations, generated from democratic theory, focus on how political actors should behave and participate in politics if they want to practise good citizenship. Research based on this literature can, therefore, help to address the question about participation's downside by focusing on the values that typically characterise political actors drawn into certain participation forms, and also indirectly address the question of a worrisome mobilisation of bias. However, unfortunately and similar to the democratic theories reviewed above, this research is presently rather weak on investigating new citizenship norms or expectations formulated in newer citizenship theory. This newer theorising explicitly addresses the significance of the on-going processes of globalisation, individualisation and privatisation in the contemporary political world.

Updating this research by formulating operational definitions of the new citizenship expectations is, therefore, an important research task. Empirical citizenship study must, in other words, also probe the changing status, role and function of citizenship in multi-levelled governance systems both within and beyond the nation-state. Fortunately, newer citizenship theory formulates norms about cosmopolitan citizenship (Delanty, 2000), ecological citizenship (Dobson, 2003) and sustainable citizenship (Bullen and Whitehead, 2005; Lister, 2007). These theories jointly argue for a reconfiguration of citizenship that broadens its territorial reach and includes other arenas than the parliamentary sphere. They also ponder the democratic effect of enhanced freedom of choice (for example, in educational, pension, health, consumer culture and so on) for how we conceptualise self-interest and the common good as well as for how we perform citizenship. For some scholars these developments signify that citizenship must be practised in 'every waking minute of everyday' (Bullen and Whitehead, 2005, p 513). Thus, citizenship does not only have a public face. It is present in the informal private, community and family sphere.

Citizenship theory is then clearly important for a robust assessment of the democratic merit of participation. In the past, scholars have used it to formulate precise operational measures of several democratic norms believed to be important for participation. Collectively these norms are said to represent 'a shared set of expectations about the citizen's role in politics' and because they 'tell citizens what is expected of them, and what they expect of themselves' and 'shape citizens' political behavior' (Dalton, 2008b, p 78). This chapter calls these norms 'citizenship expectations'. Such expectations about participation can be found in public policies, international conventions and national constitutions. Even corporations apply them (see Micheletti and Stolle, 2012 for discussion of the Walt Disney Company's Corporate Citizenship Report).

Typically, citizen surveys ask about how important the respondents believe various expectations are for good citizenship. Therefore, these surveys seek information on subjective views of good citizenship, with questions about: duty-based expectations of the main political body (the nation-state); exercising civic, political and social rights in a responsible fashion that promotes political equality (social solidarity); and enlightened, reflective or critical citizenship that address general concerns from deliberative democratic theory. At times the surveys include expectations more directly reflective of newer citizenship theories, for example, when they ask about the importance of freely acting on one's own initiative rather than expecting government to solve problems for you (a 'participation 2.0' trait and individualised responsibility taking) or the importance of choosing environmentally friendly, ethically produced products even if they are not the best and/ or cheapest solutions for you personally (ecological and sustainable citizenship) (Petersson et al, 1989, 1998; van Deth et al, 2007; Dalton, 2008a, 2008b).

Table 2.2 presents in the first column the list of citizenship expectations as they appear in most surveys; the question formulation is included at the bottom of the table. Some expectations reflect the political culture of one particular country and are therefore not applicable in others.[3] Table 2.2 also shows how citizenship expectations that tap newer theorising on cosmopolitan, ecological and sustainable citizenship can be formulated. The last four expectations in the table are operational measures of the more-encompassing sustainable citizenship theory. 'Always try to treat people who are different than yourself in an equal way' adds other elements of identity and difference into the citizenship equation, thus broadening the focus beyond merely not discriminating against immigrants by not treating them 'worse than native' countrymen and women. 'Actively seek information on how corporations behave in [country name] and the rest of the world' focuses on the broader spatial perspective of citizenship beyond nation-state-oriented parliamentary politics. 'Be prepared to consume less to fight climate change' brings in consumer choice and behaviour as part of good citizenship and also blurs the conceptual boundary between the public ('politics') and private sphere ('non-politics'). 'Think about how your practices can affect the well-being of future generations' adds responsibility for future lives into the good-citizenship equation. These four citizenship expectations were measured in Swedish, and for the first time in the winter of 2012–13 and then again in 2014.

Table 2.2: Operational definition of citizenship expectations found in citizenship surveys/General categorisation as citizenship norms

Citizenship expectations	Categorisations as citizenship norm
Vote in general elections	Duty citizenship, participative citizenship
Never try to avoid paying tax	Duty citizenship
Develop your own opinions independently from other people's	Engaged citizenship, enlightened/reflexive citizenship
Always obey laws and regulations	Duty citizenship
Serve in the military when the country is at war	Duty citizenship
Report a crime that you may have witnessed	Duty citizenship
Serve on a jury if called	Duty citizenship
Stay well-informed about what is happening in society	Participative citizenship
Be actively involved in clubs and societies	Participative citizenship
Show solidarity with people in [country] who are worse off than yourself	Participative citizenship, solidarity citizenship, engaged citizenship
Show solidarity with people in the rest of the world who are worse off than yourself	Solidarity citizenship
Be prepared to break the law when your conscience requires it	Participative citizenship
Never commit benefit fraud	Duty citizenship
Don't expect the state to solve problems; instead, act on your own initiative	Enlightened/reflexive citizenship
Put others' interests before your own	Solidarity citizenship
To subject your own opinions to critical examination	Enlightened/reflexive citizenship
Try to actively influence societal issues	Engaged citizenship, solidary citizenship
Do not treat immigrants worse than native [country; for example, Swedes]	Solidarity citizenship

Choose environmentally friendly, ethically produced products even if they are not the best and/or cheapest solutions for you personally	Solidarity citizenship
Always try to treat people who are different than yourself in an equal way	Sustainable citizenship
Actively seek information on how corporations behave in Sweden and the rest of the world	Sustainable citizenship
Be prepared to consume less to fight climate change	Sustainable citizenship
Think about how your practices can affect the well-being of future generations	Sustainable citizenship
The survey question is: 'There are different views on what it takes to be a good citizen. In your personal opinion, how important is it to ...?' The respondents are given a scale from 1 to 5 with 1 representing not very important, 2 rather unimportant, 3 neither important nor unimportant, 4 rather important, 5 very important, and the opportunity to choose the answer 'unsure/don't know'. Not all surveys use these exact formulations.	

Sources: Petersson et al (1989, 1998); van Deth et al (2007); Dalton (2008a, 2008b)

These citizenship expectations also formulate a robust operational definition of what can be meant by the value portrait of 'good' participation and therefore can be explicitly and systematically used to assess participation's democratic quality. Aside from their obvious use in surveys to assess the citizenship expectations (or values) lying behind different forms of participation, they can be included in ethnographic studies observing and following the values involved in individual engagements in various causes and, using different participatory forms, in face-to-face interviews, in focus groups and to study how organisations and institutions understand and promote the role of participation in developing democracy (see Micheletti and Stolle, 2012 for examples of an institutional study). Such studies can complement and expand the general questions of the who, where, how, why and so what of participation by offering a fuller value portrait of participants and institutional efforts. They can be employed to study official documents from, say, education, youth or immigrant policy to reveal arguments (that is, the citizenship expectations) for supporting (certain forms of) participation, thus contributing to knowledge about whether some expectations are emphasised more than others and casting more light on the mobilisation of bias issue. The expectations can even be used to examine how political agents (NGOs, political parties, public agencies and so on) motivate the need for participation and if they use the expectations differently depending on whom they target (for example, youth, ethnic groups and so on) and the problem at hand. Such studies can map the value profile of different authorities as socialising and mobilising agents and contribute to knowledge about whether or not they emphasise certain expectations over others, how broadly they perceive the importance of participation in society today and how it should be performed.

Table 2.2 also lists how previous survey research has analytically categorised the expectations into different, more general citizenship profiles. Dalton (2008a, table 3, p 87) formulates two general sets of citizenship expectations – duty and engaged citizenship – in his study of good citizenship in the United States, while pioneering Swedish research that analysed survey results in more detail lists four sets (duty, reflexive, solidarity and participative citizenship) (Petersson et al, 1998; see also Petersson et al, 1989). The cross-national European comparative study Citizenship, Involvement, and Democracy (CID) identifies three general citizen types (critical and deliberative, law abiding and solidarity citizenship) (Denters, Gabriel and Torcal, 2007, p 100). Generally the surveys find widespread acceptance of the expectations about good (democratic) citizenship, but also that they are not completely or equally embraced by all groups of individuals and not equally across countries. Swedish surveys have administered this question on a number of occasions, thus also offering scholars the opportunity to conduct time-series analysis.

An additional benefit of citizen surveys is that they often include questions on actual political participation,[4] thus opening up opportunities for directly analysing the relationship between citizenship expectations (the 'oughtness' of citizenship) and real-life participation (the 'doing' of citizenship). The participation question might include items about: voting; political party involvement (passive and active member); donating money to political causes (political parties, NGOs and so on); participating in a NGO (for example, union, activist or local group); participating in a strike, demonstration or protest; taking part in an illegal protest action; displaying campaign material (for example, a campaign button); contacting a politician, an organisation, civil servant, judicial body, media actor and so on; expressing opinions in the press, radio or TV; using the internet for political purposes (visiting a website, forwarding a political e-mail and so on); contacting or trying to influence a company; boycotting products for political, ethical or environmental reasons; deliberately choosing ('buycotting') to buy certain products for political, ethical or environmental reasons; trying to influence the range of products in a store for political, ethical or environmental reasons (for lists see Petersson et al, 1998; van Deth et al, 2007; Dalton, 2008a, 2008b; Sustainable Citizenship, 2009, 2012, 2014). Again, some of these questions reflect specific political culture.[5]

Although empirical research on the implications of democratic norms (the citizenship expectations) for political participation is still in its infancy, some survey findings offer a few clues that help to answer this chapter's main questions. For example, Russell Dalton found that duty citizenship is significantly related to electoral activity (voting, working for a candidate, displaying campaign material, that is, 'participation 1.0') but not to contacting a political figure, donating money or working with a group (more 'participation 2.0'). It is noteworthy that his analysis shows a significant negative relationship between high duty citizenship and protest activities (signing a petition, legally protesting, boycotting, buycotting) and internet activism (visiting a website, forwarding a political e-mail and so on) that represent 'participation 2.0' culture. The expectations about engaged citizenship were found to correlate more closely with forming one's own opinion independently of others, supporting people who are worse off, being active in politics and in voluntary organisations. Thus it would appear that involvement in 'participation 1.0' and '2.0' reflects a value divide, and perhaps they contribute differently to developing and furthering democracy. This study also reveals that younger respondents show a stronger commitment to engaged citizenship than to duty citizenship and that older generations are more dutiful (Dalton, 2008a, especially pp 81, 146). Similar results are generated from other studies. A survey of Western Canadians found, interestingly, that a strong belief in 'community duty' had a negative effect on voter participation, a positive one on non-traditional activities (the more '2.0' form) and that a strong belief in 'duty to vote' was not related to non-traditional participation (Raney and Berdahl, 2009). Finally, a study of Danish, Finnish, Norwegian and Swedish adolescents concluded that the changes in commitment to citizenship expectations noted in research most likely have an effect on how individuals participate in politics and, therefore, should be studied, as in the case of social capital, in terms of their consequences for making democracy work (Oser and Hooghe, 2013, p 341). In sum, there appears, therefore, to be a clustering or relationship of attraction between certain citizenship expectations and certain participatory forms. This general finding further strengthens this chapter's claim about the need to study the eventuality of a value divide in participation and the role that participatory forms play in mobilising bias.

Some of this work has already begun. Dutch political scientist Jan W. van Deth (2010, p 165) deserves credit for asking 'Do people using specific modes of participation support specific normative positions?' He gave an answer through an analysis of CID survey responses on five forms of participation representing both participation '1.0' (party contactors, party activists, voters) and '2.0' (protesters, political consumers). He found that European party activists stand out on almost all expectations; protesters somewhat less on accepting certain duty citizenship expectations (especially the one about always obeying laws and regulations); and political consumers (a typical 'participation 2.0' form) lower on commitment to being active in organisations (van Deth, 2010, table 9.6, p 169). This study offers a glimpse into what seems to be a value divide between the '1.0' and '2.0' participatory cultures that reflects the overarching shift from collectivist to individualised collective action. In particular it signals what might be called a rebuffing of yesteryear's authorities (membership organisations, obeying the state) by individuals more contextualised in 'participation 2.0' settings. However, what this development implies for democracy is still an open question.

Though insightful and pioneering, this research cannot really offer a satisfactory answer about a worrisome mobilisation of bias or the structural downside of participation. Luckily, some studies comparing participants with non-participants offer a bit of help here. A Swedish study contributes some interesting differences between political consumers (that is, those who boycotted or buycotted) and 'non-political consumers' (those not having participated in boycotts or buycotts). In this analysis political consumers rank the importance of all three general expectations of duty, solidarity and information-seeking citizenship (roughly, enlightened or critical citizenship) higher. What particularly stands out is their commitment to solidarity citizenship (see measures in Table 2.2). Political consumer participants were found to be more committed and non-political consumers less committed to these expectations of good citizenship (Micheletti, Stolle and Berlin, 2012, table 3, p 156). However, there might even be value differences between those who only boycott and those who only buycott (Copeland, 2014). Obviously, more research effort should be put into deeply penetrating the data discussed in this section as well as generating new data so that we can improve our understanding of the value portraits that characterise 'participation 1.0' and '2.0' and to help us learn more about the dynamics of their mobilisation of bias. Yet they do demonstrate that the chapter's questions are germane and deserve more study.

Democratic deficits in political participation?

This chapter is provocative in tone and challenging in character. Its main argument is that society needs to consider the democratic quality of participation by asking why we should promote participation. The discussions above cast light on some blind spots in participation research by showing how scholars have tended to assume or simply just want to believe that participation reflects core democratic norms (see Thomassen, 2007). It offers brief telling examples from real life both then and now that show that participation neither always nor necessarily promotes democracy. The chapter also emphasises that we must consider how the shifts from more collectivist to more individualised political cultures affect the character and workings of participation. To stress this point I coin the term 'participation 1.0' to represent the more collectivist and pre-packaged participatory repertoire of yesteryear and the term 'participation 2.0' for the looser and more individualised one more characteristic of today's political world. The chapter reports research revealing value-profile differences between the two participatory cultures, which fuels the claim about the importance of democratically auditing them.

The discussion continues by suggesting ways to remedy the identified blind spots in participation research. Importantly, it discusses how insights from newer citizenship theories and empirical citizenship study can be employed to democratically audit participation. Together these approaches contribute to new citizenship expectations and necessary empirical rigour. For participation scholars, this especially means addressing the on-going processes of globalisation, individualisation and privatisation in their studies. The chapter discusses, therefore, how measures of good citizenship must also incorporate norms about citizenship responsibility in the broader spatial, temporal and material societal relationships now characterising the political world. It formulates four new expectations for empirical study. As discussed above, these additional expectations involve norms about the equality of difference (recognition and acceptance of various identities); the political role of corporations and private consumption; and the relationship between self-interest, private life and intergenerational justice. The newer citizenship expectations acknowledge the significance of spheres and institutions outside the parliamentary arena – most prominently the private sphere of personal life and the globalised economic sphere of transnational corporations – for good citizenship. It is, therefore, important that they are included in assessments of participation's democratic quality. The new expectations incorporate contemporary theoretical ideas (norms) about societal responsibilities within and across these spheres as central for growing democracy. For instance, the expectations of individual responsibility for contributing to a solution to climate change and for future well-being (intergenerational justice) reflect theorisation on ecological and sustainable citizenship, thus also offering a different take to the general worry about the role of the self and self-interest in politics today.

The chapter also reveals some worries deserving more systematic scholarly attention, particularly signs of a value gap between 'participation 1.0' and 'participation 2.0' cultures of political involvement. Its review of previous research reveals a value gap between highly committed duty citizens, on the one hand, and engaged citizens, on the other; citizens more committed to '1.0' forms (particularly party activity and organisational membership) were found to be associated strongly with duty citizenship and not so much with forms veering toward 'participation 2.0'. Does this matter for democracy? Most likely, yes, and for different reasons.

Traditional '1.0' participation has helped to develop and maintain the democratic system's stability and legitimacy, albeit differently across countries. It has, importantly, mobilised generations of citizens into participatory opportunities and given them solid advice about taking political stands through its strong ideological narratives. Its pre-packaged conceptions of good citizenship created the welfare state in many countries. Its ability to function as a screening filter for democratic thought by authorising certain viewpoints and involvements and dismissing others also helped to frame the parameters of political responsibility. Today many forms of 'participation 1.0' lack enthusiastic support and innovative creativeness: perhaps due to its strong soldiering of support for old authorities in the current era, which calls for more freedom of thought and more space for varying political action and which is characterised by the presence of new authorities with different ideas about decision making on complex problems at home and abroad. Another possible explanation concerns the widening gap between the formal institutions of parliamentary politics and the location of power in society. The Occupy and degrowth movements, whose main goal is to change the political-economic relations in society and to bring large corporations and financial systems under democratic control (Pickerill and Krinsky, 2012; Demaria et al, 2013), are good examples here. Therefore, 'participation 2.0' appears, in contrast, as more open, exciting, vibrant and future oriented, thus attracting individuals who view enhanced activated personal responsibility and strong solidarity with others unlike oneself both in and beyond the confines of the nation-state as important expectations for good citizenship. Of course, as 'participation 1.0' and '2.0' are pure ideal types and thus not expected to manifest themselves completely in real life, many individuals might be both '1.0' and '2.0' participants, though they might show varying enthusiasm and dedication for these two basic forms and engage in them for different reasons. Some citizens might show leanings to one or the other. But some might not, which is a challenge for the democratic or inclusionary role of participation in democratic society. Thus, the value gap between 'participation 1.0' and '2.0' also might possibly also be a divide on the who, where, how and why questions of participation.

The so what question is a different story. Scholars and societal actors are pressed to explain whether and how 'participation 1.0' can come to the aid of global climate change and the equal treatment of all across the world, mainly due to its nation-state format. Similarly, what role can the engaged and solidarity citizenship characteristic of 'participation 2.0' play in creating and maintaining long-term, legitimate, authoritative, collective solutions for complex problems (with climate change again as a key example)? Changing voluntarily one's meat-eating life-style to a vegetarian or vegan one most likely will not suffice. Or, as some environmentalists (green authoritarians) argue, does participation really support strong, resolute, green decision making (for a discussion see Doherty and de Geus, 1996)?

Finally, what mechanisms and actions are needed to avoid the potentiality of a developing steep value divide between 'participation 1.0' and '2.0'? This question appears crucial because the inklings of a value gap in survey results also tend to coincide with a divide among groups of citizens, which can threaten democratic growth if the divide implies exclusion and inequality. While older citizens are more active in 'participation 1.0' forms and more supportive of duty citizenship, younger ones are more enticed by 'participation 2.0' and committed to engaged and solidarity citizenship. Whether this divide reflects life-cycle effects (the influence of physical age on participation and citizenship norms) and can, therefore, change over time (as one gets older), or instead points to a generational shift that will not change over time, is a question worth pursuing further. Other similar value divides might even exist and separate ethnic, religious and gender groups into different participatory camps and cultures. Can it be that different assessments of good citizenship are involved in the gender gap in participation, with men generally participating more and in more ways than women? Perhaps underlying citizenship expectations might even figure into political-ideological leanings (Right, Left, Green, Libertarian, Authoritarian, Nationalist and so on), how the leanings are manifested in participation forms and, as suggested in a recent US study, used as cues for how we assess others in positive or negative ways (Iyengar and Westwood, 2014).

The basic point is that it is important for democratic society's future that groups of individuals with certain value profiles do not get put off from voting, that habitual voters do not automatically rebuff more 'participation 2.0' and that we believe that we can trust each other in general terms, irrespective of partisan stance or preferred participatory repertoire. Otherwise a dangerous divide might develop that not only leads to worrisome mobilisations of bias but that also threatens the legitimacy of representative democracy as a form of governance and, therefore, the democratic underpinnings of society. Social science has, indeed, a role to play in identifying and evaluating these mechanisms for politicians, policy makers and civil society actors so that they can deal with them in a responsible and unbiased fashion.

Notes

[1] Creative participation refers to situations in which (1) a large number of scattered individuals (2) share some common notion of the need for public action to attain or preserve some common good including a common perception of justice but (3) find that established political institutions do not provide a means for such public action. In this situation, individuals desiring such public action and participation must create their own means of participation (Micheletti, 2010; see also McFarland, 2010).

[2] *Responsibilisation* refers to current tendencies to economise public domains and methods of government. For individual actors it signifies that they as employees, welfare recipients, managers, civil servants, citizens, consumers and so on must more actively undertake and assume self-governing tasks, thus implying indirect techniques for leading and controlling individuals without being responsible for them. Instead of assuming that their rights will be respected, individuals must have good knowledge of their rights and demand that they are realised. *Individualised responsibility taking* is defined as reasonable individual choice involving considerations about the societal effects of one's actions. It includes two components. The first refers to a series of structural prerequisites that enable citizens to make reasonable choices that they believe are best for themselves and society. The second set of prerequisites is personal background characteristics that give individuals the capability and interest to make such reasonable choices in everyday life (see Stolle and Micheletti, 2013, chapter 1).

[3] For example, the question on military service and jury duty has been asked in the US but not in Europe, and the question on benefit fraud has, as far as is known, been asked only in the Nordic context.

[4] The typical question is 'Citizens can do various things to try to bring about improvements or prevent deterioration in society. In the last 12 months have you done any of the following?' and then follows a battery of different forms of participation, as those discussed above.

[5] The entry 'working for a political candidate' is asked in the United States and the ones about political parties asked in Europe, thus reflecting the differences in the two political systems.

Reference list

Adler, P.S. and Kwon, S.-W. (2000) 'Social capital: The good, the bad, and the ugly', in E. Lesser (ed), *Knowledge and social capital: Foundations and applications*, Boston, MA: Butterworth-Heinemann, pp 89–115.

Bachrach, P. and Baratz, M.S. (1962) 'Two faces of power', *American Political Science Review*, vol 56, no 4, pp 947–52.

Bäck, H., Teorell, J. and Westholm, A. (2011) 'Explaining modes of participation: A dynamic test of alternative rational choice models', *Scandinavian Political Studies*, vol 34, no 1, pp 74–97.

Bennett, W.L. (1998) 'The un-civic culture: Communication, identity, and the rise of lifestyle politics,' *PS: Political Science & Politics*, vol 31, no 4, pp 740–61.

Bennett, W.L. and Segerberg, A. (2011) 'Digital media and the personalization of collective action', *Information, Communication & Society*, vol 14, no 6, pp 770–99.

Bosi, L. and Uba, K. (2009) 'Introduction: The outcomes of social movements', *Mobilization: An International Quarterly*, vol 14, no 4, pp 409–15.

Boström, M., and Klintman, M. (2011) *Eco-standards, product labelling and green consumerism*, London: Palgrave Macmillan.

Brady, H.E., Verba, S. and Schlozman, K.L. (1995) 'Beyond SES: A resource model of political participation', *American Political Science Review*, vol 89, no 2, pp 271–94.

Bullen, A. and Whitehead, M. (2005) 'Negotiating the networks of space, time and substance: A geographical perspective on the sustainable citizen', *Citizenship Studies* 9 (5): 499–516.

Burtt, S. (1993) 'The politics of virtue today: A critique and a proposal', *American Political Science Review*, vol 87, pp 360–8.

Conway, M.M. and Feigert, F.B. (1968) 'Motivation, incentive systems and the political party organization', *American Political Science Review*, vol 62, pp 1159–73.D

Copeland, L. (2014) 'Conceptualizing political consumerism: how citizenship norms differentiate boycotting from buycotting', *Political Studies*, vol 62, no S1, pp 172–86.

Cornwell, A. (2007) 'Spaces for transformation? Reflections on issues of power and difference in participation in development', in S. Hickey and G. Mohan (eds) *Participation – from tyranny to transformation. Exploring new approaches to participation in development*, London: Zed Books, pp 75–91.2007

Crick, B. and Lockyer, A. (eds) (2010) *Active citizenship. What could it achieve and how?* Edinburgh, Edinburgh University Press.

Dahl, R. (1990) (1970) *After the revolution? Authority in a good society* (revised edition), New Haven, CT: Yale University Press.

Dalton, R. (2008a) *The good citizen: How a younger generation is reshaping American politics*. Washington, DC: CQ Press.

Dalton, R. (2008b) 'Citizenship norms and the expansion of political participation', *Political Studies*, vol 56, pp 76–98.

Delanty, G. (2000) *Citizenship in a global age: Society, culture, politics*, Buckingham: Open University Press.

Demaria, F., Schneider, F., Sekulova, F. and Martinez-Alier, J. (2013) 'What is degrowth? From an activist slogan to a social movement', *Environmental Values*, vol 22, pp 191–215.

Denters, B., Gabriel, O. and Torcal, M. (2007) 'Norms of good citizenship', in Jan W. van Deth, J.R. Montero and A. Westholm (eds) *Citizenship and involvement in European democracies. A comparative analysis*, London: Routledge, pp 88–108.

Dobson, A. (2003) *Citizenship and the environment*, Oxford: Oxford University Press.

Doherty, B. and de Geus, M. (eds) (1996) *Democracy and green political thought. Sustainability, rights and citizenship*, London: Routledge.

Fenton, N. and Barassi, V. (2011) 'Alternative media and social networking sites: The politics of individuation and political participation', *The Communication Review*, vol 14, no 3, pp 179–96.

Hendriks, F. (2000) 'The mobilization of bias revisited: Institutional design, cultural bias and policy-oriented learning', in D.W.P. Ruiter (ed) *Governance in modern society. Effects, changes and formation of government institutions*, Dordrecht: Kluwer Academic Publishers, pp 281–97.

Hoffmann, S. and Hutter, K. (2012) 'Carrotmob as a new form of ethical consumption. The nature of the concept and avenues for future research', *Journal of Consumer Policy*, vol 35, pp 215–36.

Innes, J.E. and Booher, D.E. (2004) 'Reframing public participation: Strategies for the 21st century', *Planning Theory & Practice*, vol 5, no 4, pp 419–36.

IPPR (Institute for Public Policy Research). (2013) 'Young voters should be required to vote first time round', 26 August, http://www.ippr.org/articles/56/10725/the-case-for-compulsory-first-time-voting. Accessed 5 November 2013.

Iyengar, S. and Westwood, S.J. (2014) 'Fear and loathing across party lines: New evidence on group polarization', unpublished paper, http://cess-web.nuff.ox.ac.uk/wp-content/uploads/2014/09/partisan_affect.pdf.

Lister, R. (2007) 'Inclusive citizenship: Realizing the potential', *Citizenship Studies*, vol 11, no 1, pp 49–61.

McFarland, A.S. (2010) 'Why creative participation today?' in M.Micheletti and A.S. McFarland, *Creative participation: Responsibility-taking in the political world*, Boulder, CO: Paradigm Publishers, pp 15–33.

Micheletti, M. (2010) *Political virtue and shopping: Individuals, consumerism, and collective action*, 2nd edition with epilogue, New York: Palgrave.

Micheletti, M. and McFarland, A.S. (eds) (2010) *Creative participation as responsibility-taking in the political world*, Boulder, CO: Paradigm Press.

Micheletti, M. and Stolle, D. (2012) 'Sustainable citizenship and the new politics of consumption', in Sustainable citizenship and the new politics of consumption', *The Annals of the American Academy of Political and Social Science*, vol 644, no 1 (November), pp 88–120.

Norris, P. (ed) (1999) *Critical citizens: Global support for democratic governance*, Oxford: Oxford University Press.

Oser, J. and Hooghe, M. (2013) 'The evolution of citizenship norms among Scandinavia adolescents, 1999–2009', *Scandinavian political studies*, vol 36, no 4, pp 320–46.

Pateman, C. (1970) *Participation and democratic theory*, Cambridge: Cambridge University Press.

Petersson, O., Westholm, A. and Blomberg, G. (1989) *Medborgarnas makt*, Stockholm: Carlssons. An English version is available in manuscript form at http://www.olofpetersson.se/_arkiv/skrifter/citizen.pdf.

Petersson, O., Hermansson, J., Micheletti, M., Teorell, J. and Westholm, A. (1998) *Demokrati och medborgarskap. Demokratirådets rapport 1998*, Stockholm: SNS Förlag.

Pickerill, J. and Krinsky, J. (2012) 'Why does Occupy matter?' *Social Movement Studies*, vol 11, nos 3–4, pp 279–87.

Puolimatka, T. (2002) 'Education for critical citizenship', *Philosophy of Education*, pp 271–3.

Putnam, R. and Goss, K.A. (2002) 'Introduction', in R. Putnam (ed) *Democracies in flux. The evolution of social capital in contemporary society*, Oxford: Oxford University Press, pp. 1–19.

Raney, T. and Berdahl, L. (2009) 'Birds of a feather? Citizenship norms, group identity, and political participation in Western Canada', *Canadian Journal of Political Science*, vol 42, no 1, pp 187–209.

Schattschneider, E.E. (1960) *Semisovereign people: A realist's view of democracy in America*, New York: Holt, Rinehart and Winston.

Schlozman, K.L. (2010) 'Creative participation: Concluding thoughts from the land of the the Boston Tea Party', in M. Micheletti and A. McFarland (eds) *Creative participation. Responsibility-taking in the political world*, Boulder, CO: Paradigm Publishers, pp 173–90.

Schlozman, K.L., Verba, S. and Brady, H. (2012) *The unheavenly chorus: Unequal political voice and the broken promise of American democracy*, Princeton, NJ: Princeton University Press.

Segerberg, A. (2010) 'Swarming: imaging creative participation', in M. Micheletti and A.S. McFarland (eds) *Creative participation as responsibility-taking in the political world*, Boulder, CO: Paradigm Press, pp 34–49.

Stolle, D. and Hooghe, M. (2005) 'Inaccurate, exceptional, one-sided or irrelevant? The debate about the alleged decline of social capital and civic engagement in Western societies', *British Journal of Political Science*, vol 35, no 1, pp 149–67.

Stolle, D. and Hooghe, M. (2006) 'Consumers as political participants: Shifts in political action repertoires in Western societies', in M. Micheletti, A. Føllesdal and D. Stolle (eds), *Politics, products, and markets: Exploring political consumerism past and present*, New Brunswick, NJ: Transaction Press, pp 101–25.

Stolle, D. and Micheletti, M. (2005) 'The gender gap reversed', in B. O'Neill and E. Gidengil (eds) *Gender and social capital*, London: Routledge, pp 45–72.

Stolle, D. and Micheletti, M. (2013) *Political consumerism. Global responsibility in action*, Cambridge: Cambridge University Press.

Sustainable Citizenship (2009) 'Consumption and societal issues national survey', available from the author.

Sustainable Citizenship (2012) Leksaker och medborgarskap riksundersökning (Toys and citizenship national survey), available in Swedish from the author.

Sustainable Citizenship (2014) Jeans och medborgarskap (Jeans and citizenship survey of teacher education students), available in Swedish from the author.

Swedish Save the Children Foundation's Youth Movement (Rädda Barnens Ungdomsförbund) (2006) *Bör rösträttåldern sänkas till 16 år?* Norrköping: Rädda Barnens Ungdomsförbund. http://rbuf.se/sites/default/files/dokument/demokratiforunga_0.pdf (accessed 5 November 2013).

Teorell, J. (2006) 'Political participation and three theories of democracy: A research inventory and agenda', *European Journal of Political Research*, vol 45, pp 787–810.

Thomassen, J. (2007) 'Democratic values', in R.J. Dalton and H.-D. Klingermann (eds) *The Oxford Handbook of Political Behavior*, Oxford: Oxford University Press, pp 418–34.

van Deth, J.W. (2010) 'Is creative participation good for democracy?', in M. Micheletti and M. McFarland (eds) *Creative participation as responsibility-taking in the political world*, Boulder, CO: Paradigm Press, pp 148–72.

van Deth, Jan W., Montero, J.R. and Westholm, A. (eds) (2007) *Citizenship and involvement in European democracies. A comparative analysis*, London: Routledge.

Verba, S. (2003) 'Would the dream of political equality turn out to be a nightmare?' *Perspective on Politics*, vol 1, no 4, pp 663–79.

Warren, M.E. (2008) 'The nature and logic of bad social capital', in D. Castiglione, J.W. van Deth, and G. Wolleb (eds) *The handbook of social capital*, Oxford: Oxford University Press, pp 122–49.

Wattenberg, M.P. (2012) *Is voting for young people?* (3rd edn), Boston, MA: Pearson.

THREE

Love always wins: All Out's campaign for equality everywhere

Andre Banks

Introduction

Andre Banks is co-founder and executive director of All Out (www.allout.org). The organisation was established in 2010 with Jeremy Heimans and works to promote equality for lesbian, gay, bisexual, and transgender (LGBT) people around the world. All Out uses online organising strategies to build a global membership that directly contributes power and resources to local organisations fighting against discrimination. All Out now has over two million members and has been involved in several high-profile campaigns, most recently using the Sochi 2014 Winter Olympic Games to highlight Russia's 'gay propaganda' ban.

For those whose work has a focus on practice, finding the time and space to down tools and write can be extremely difficult. Not to mention some of the cultural biases that operate to devalue writing and thinking relative to 'doing'. So it came to pass that Nathan interviewed Andre for his contribution to this collection.

Nathan: Can you provide some biographical details about how you came to be involved in activism and campaigning – maybe how you even got interested in politics?

Andre: Almost all of my interventions into politics have been through the lens of identity, as opposed to issues. I don't think I planned for that to be the case, but when I look back on my career a lot of it has been about identity-driven campaigning. And I think as a working-class, Black, gay American all of those identities have been a big part of why I got into organising and campaigning. [...]

I had been interested in politics and I had definitely been going through a period of trying to understand and read and think about what it meant to be a critically engaged Black person in America. Reading all the things that people of that age read when you're Black, like James Baldwin, and really trying to understand and make sense of this unique set of identities. I think that was how I got involved with the Black student union at Ohio State. It was kind of a social group but it was also pretty politicised; they'd done a lot of work in the previous year on the diversity plan on campus and making sure that Ohio State was a great place for students of all races and ethnicities. So there was a political element to the group which I think was what I was most attracted to. But we hadn't really done a big and substantial campaign since I'd been a part of the group.

The first campaign that I was involved with was to support the striking workers at Ohio State. It's the biggest employer in Columbus, one of the biggest in the state of Ohio and all of the food service, custodial, landscaping workers, thousands of people went on strike – they hadn't received a raise in 15 years. I was a part of the Black student union which joined up with the local labour union to show support for the striking campus workers. It was an opportunity to think about power and how you move institutions to change for the long term. And questions like, who has power? How do people mobilise and wield that power? One of the big things I learned in that campaign was to ask, who has the most power and who is incurring the most risk? I think one of the things we were able to do really well as student organisers was be aggressive and push really hard because kicking a freshman on the Dean's list off campus was much more difficult and looked a lot worse for the university than firing a worker who was on strike. So there were ways that we could, in coordination with the labour union, take on more risk and push for the common agenda.

Sort of out of nowhere I became a leader in that campaign. We won a huge victory that was one of the bigger victories for the union nationally that year and from there I got on the radar of some of the national labour unions. From that job I was recruited to work in Washington DC with the AFL–CIO (American Federation of Labor and Congress of Industrial Organizations) to run a national programme getting other students involved in these kinds of campaigns.

I think it was working in solidarity that had a lasting impression on me and really informs the work that I do now and the way that I do it. […] I came to economic justice and workers' rights organising through the Black student union, so identity was always my way in.

Nathan: So at that time did you see yourself as having a future in the labour movement?

Andre: There were some fantastic people there that I got to work with; I had some really great mentors, but you still are dealing with institutions that have a long legacy of structural racism. So, different unions are in different places on this: some unions were leaders in the civil rights movement, while you have others that aggressively campaign to keep Black people from having jobs and to save those jobs for white union workers. So there was that cultural history, but also remnants like what the leadership looks like, whose voices are empowered and the ways in which democracy does and doesn't happen in those institutions. That was all really challenging.

I was actually very lucky. As a young Black guy who didn't know very much about anything [laughs], when I was in my early twenties, I think I was actually given a lot of space to push that agenda and some people really supported me, which was awesome. And these are signs of the progress in the labour movement, but it was still a challenging environment.

I think I felt like I never had a future in the labour movement. I kind of felt like I had this really cool side project – it was kind of running in parallel to but never in the centre of the institution – it was a new thing, a new project. But I think I learned that I was never going to thrive in a giant bureaucratic institution of any form. I've had one big institutional experience and then, like, run in the other direction [laughs] and went to smaller and smaller organisations until I was actually just starting them up from scratch [laughter].

I think that had a lot to do with my personality and my skills and strengths. I wanted to try new things and that was quite frustrating in a large institution. I think culturally it wasn't a fit for me; it felt like a movement that was a lot older and culturally monolithic. I wanted to work somewhere where diversity was important, and I don't mean that in a superficial sense. I wanted to work with people who saw the world in different ways, people who were from different places, people who had different experiences, people who had many different identities. That was important to me and that was not happening in the labour movement at that time.

Nathan: Can you tell me about the relationship you had or have now with electoral politics?

Andre: It's interesting because my grandmother was the district chief of staff for a congressman for basically my entire life, for like 25 years or something. So I'd always been around electoral politics, but I didn't until much later really feel connected to electoral politics. I wasn't passionate about any candidates. You know, my sister is 10 years younger than me and her first experience was tabling on campus for Obama in 2008 – I never had any of that experience. I think that from a very early stage I got into politics in a more radical way and I was always kind of like, 'Electoral politics? That's what other people do. I want to push for big sweeping changes to the system.' So I wasn't really engaged with it until later when I began to see it as an important piece of a broader strategy.

From where I sat at that time, there weren't politicians that were speaking to me. There weren't people that I felt were trying to get me to vote for them or canvass for them – there weren't those entry points.

I think the thing that I've always been really possessed by is the feeling that when it comes to making change in the world – which I'm pretty obsessed about – to me it's about bringing more people to the table. So that's always been the focus of my work. It's not been, win this policy change or make this institution stronger, it's always been about more and new voices at the table who have access to power to help create the change we want. As a result I've always felt a bit of an outsider, even in liberal and progressive social movements because I think that often that is not their orientation. It's like let's get more of those people who are already having those conversations to have them, as opposed to getting new people to the table. I think that is really what got me involved in the technology side of this work. I'm more of a nerd than a geek, so it wasn't that I'm super techie, it was about trying to find new people and new places and find easier entry points for people who hadn't been able to get themselves engaged or have a voice in social movements. […]

The groups that I've been involved with – Colour of Change, All Out (less so with the union work) and some other things I've worked on – they've been groups that in terms of political ideology have been relatively big tent. People come to those groups from different ideological perspectives, ranging from the left to the conservative end of things. And I think that's been an interesting part of the work. How do you build something that can cross some of those traditional divides and still be powerful and be inspiring for the folks who are involved?

Nathan: Do you think the focus on identity makes it difficult to talk about issues of material inequality?

Andre: For me, no. I mean, maybe it makes it a little bit difficult. Perhaps I should clarify what I mean when I say organising around identity. To me part of it is about building a community that is identity driven, but I think the more important part is that the reason to build that community and make it visible is to actually give a new set of people access to the tools of politics and the ways to be involved and engaged in politics in a meaningful and powerful way.

I think this goes to the point about ideological differences. When I worked at Colour of Change (http://www.colorofchange.org/) the Black people on that list, we had some things in common but most things not. In terms of where we came from, our economic backgrounds, our political backgrounds and so on. But what we did share was a sense that the political system right now is not hearing a politicised voice that advocates for the interests of Black Americans and the only way that's going to happen is if a group of us come together to make it happen.

The biggest challenge for me as a campaigner and story-teller is how do you create a story about change that is resonant with people and makes them feel that they're a part of the story and a part of shaping that story rather than a side character? And often I think the way to talk about material issues and get people excited is by helping people understand the ways in which those things intersect with their identity, with who they are and where they are. And I think that people can see that and it's real.

Nathan: 'All Out' is a great, provocative name. How did it come about?

Andre: [laughs] Very painfully or painstakingly. We went through a long process of trying to select the name. I mean, it probably took us six months of actively thinking and looking for the name before we came to it. Part of the reason it took so long is that we actually did a bunch of multilingual research around the name. We knew that the brand was going to be global and we thought putting it in English immediately makes it seem very Western, so the thought was maybe we could choose a name that was resonant in some other part of the world that we could build a brand around in other languages. Obviously no matter what language you choose you're leaving out the majority of people on the planet, so we looked at Portuguese, French, Spanish, Swahili, Hindi, a whole load of languages. One of the things we found was that there's very little shared international language or even visual imagery that really connects the LGBT movement. But one of the ideas that we found that was very resonant everywhere we looked was pride, and also the idea of coming out. There was a similar phrase or an expression that had meaning in pretty much every region that we looked at. We kind of got in our heads that we would use an English phrase and that the 'out' would make people think of LGBT issues but also wouldn't be too in-group in the way that a word like pride is. So it would be something that connected cognitively to the idea of gay rights, but at the same time wouldn't be about, 'I'm being proud because I'm an LGBT person', it would be something open to allies.

 The way that the name actually came into being was after doing all this naming research we threw out all the names because they all sucked! Myself and Joseph Huff-Hannon, who was the first campaigner at All Out, got up on a Sunday and we decided we were going to come up with the name – no matter what. We went through about seven pages of brainstorming new names, throwing everything out, and eventually one of us said 'All In' and the other then said 'All Out', and as soon as we said it we circled it about 13 times and we immediately knew that was it. I think it was the *double entendre* of all of us being able to be who we are, but also the mobilisation aspect of it – we're going all out for the things that we care about. We're going all out for equality or against discrimination.

Nathan: Have you had any problems with people thinking that the organisation is insisting that all LGBT people should be out?

Andre: A couple of people in the early days thought the name meant we should all be 'out', but everybody else seemed to get that this was a much better way to brand the work that we were doing than to go to the alphabet soup model. I think one of the things people like about All Out the most is the brand.

The name can be read as if we're saying 'everybody come out right now!' [laughter] and that was meaningfully built into it. What we tried to do was wrap the inclusive, mobilising meanings around the name in terms of the visual identity and the other language that became part of our organisational voice, to make sure that it didn't lend itself to us being seen as a vanguard making everyone come out of the closet. In fact, we want everyone who believes in fairness, who believes people should be treated equally, who believe people should be able to love who they choose; we want all of those people to come out, to make those views known, to bring their friends to the table and to push for these things that we care about. We did think about how to push the brand in the right direction rather than the wrong direction and I think largely people have connected with it and we've had mostly positive feedback.

So, your initial thought about being 'All Out' is about everybody coming out, but then it takes you really quickly to all of us being out of the closet about our values on this issue that's very difficult to talk about in a lot of places.

That language is also really powerful not just with All Out members but also with decision makers and people that are making policy choices about these issues. In a lot of our campaigns we're rarely asking people to do something that they haven't already committed to either verbally or on paper. So often we go to a government and say, you already have this set of rules so if you believe in this set of rules then you need to believe in it for everybody and we need you to actually put some political capital on the table and make sure that all of your citizens are being treated equally.

Nathan: You seem quite comfortable talking about brands and that kind of commercial language. Is that how you think about positioning All Out in terms of marketing, commercial language?

Andre: The ideas behind a brand are things that are really important for social movements and things that social movements have been doing forever. That is, creating a shared sense of common interests and common desires that many people can connect to and articulating a system of values.

In a weird way it seems like we don't think enough about these things, which seem like very necessary questions to be asking when we're engaging with other human beings: how do we tell a story that actually reaches people? How do we put as much thought and energy and research and talent and time into that as we do on our policy positions? How do we actually make sure that our position reaches people in a way that they can actually use it? And that's how I think about the branding aspect of it.

Early on we really wanted to use all the things that make corporations really successful at getting people to buy things, we wanted to use a lot of that, or at least be informed by it and bring that into our processes. We didn't want to manipulate people – that was something we wanted to leave off the table. But one thing that companies and agencies do really well when they want to build a successful brand is they do a lot of research, so we did months of research with people all over the world, focus groups and surveys, getting feedback from the people we actually wanted to reach as opposed to a few of us sitting in our room coming up with this thing. So even though in the end Joseph and I came up with the name, the way that we got to it and the reason we knew it was right was because we'd gone through this long process and we'd talked to all these people and we'd developed a really good sense of what the brand should be about.

Nathan: Can you tell a bit about the beginnings of All Out?

Andre: All Out has several beginnings, actually. OK, so I'll tell you two stories about All Out: when we launched it and when we had our first successful campaign. We launched All Out on 3 December 2010 with a video that's on our YouTube site (https://www.youtube.com/user/AllOutorg). We went to LGBT activists all over the world, on every continent and I think 20 cities, and arranged for photographers to photograph them holding up signs. And we stitched together this video that was about what we envisioned the organisation to be. We were nothing! We were no people, zero members, we hadn't even launched the website yet, but the idea was this is the kind of community we want to build; this is the kind of tone we want to strike. I look back at that video now and there are so many things when you look back which feel like you really got them wrong, but I feel like that was one of the things where – sure the production values could have been better if we had more money and there were more of us – but we totally got it right in terms of the tone and the spirit and where we were going. And I feel like we've actually started to live up to that vision, which is very exciting. So that was launch number one and that was how we launched All Out to the world. We asked our friends and family, people we'd been working with around the world and funders to send it out to their networks and from that about 2,000 people signed up to be a part of All Out.

A month later in January, we were getting started but thought it would be a slow burn; we still had to build the real website. We ran a small social media campaign when the United Nations (UN) were considering a resolution about extrajudicial killings and basically they were going to strip LGBT people as a protected class – apparently some countries try to do this every year. Susan Rice, who was the US UN ambassador at the time, had put a stake in the ground and said the US State Department is going to make the rounds and convince people to get this right. We did a social media campaign where we asked our 2,000 members to like Susan Rice's Facebook wall and tell her to keep up the good work. It was amazing because it actually worked – they were already doing it, but it got to her office and they were so thankful for the positive feedback and that they were actually getting credit for doing this good thing. Usually these things at the UN are lost in the depths of the bureaucracy. When the resolution came through and the vote went the right way Susan Rice tweeted and made a Facebook post that said, 'I went All Out for equality, we did it, we won' and so on. And we were like, whoa, that was a bit of magic. It was a sense that having a community that can be mobilised at key moments really is important.

About a week after that came our first big campaign. We had a very small team at the time, there were only three of us and we had just had an intern start. One of our campaigners heard this story about a Ugandan woman, Brenda, who had been living in the UK for eight years going through the asylum process but was now about to be deported back to Uganda. She was claiming asylum as a lesbian; when she was in Uganda people burned down her house, threatened to kill her and attacked her girlfriend. But as she was going through the asylum process in the UK no one would believe her claim that she was a lesbian, it was impossible to substantiate it. There are documents from this case where judges are asking her for the names of the three most popular lesbian bars in the UK, as proof that she's an actual lesbian. This is a person who's been through some really traumatic things in her life and she's like, 'I don't really hang out at popular lesbian bars' [exasperated laughter]. They asked her about gay magazines, things that are really ridiculous, but it exposed this massive flaw in the asylum system where there is no process through which people's sexual orientation can be convincingly established without violating their human rights. Lawyers have gone so far as to submit sex tapes into evidence because that was the only way they could prove that their client is gay.

Then, David Bahati, who is an MP in Uganda and also the architect of the 'kill the gays bill', he did an interview where he talked about Brenda and said something like, 'we can't wait till Brenda comes back, we'll be there to meet her at the airport so that she can repent and be reformed', so there was this open threat that if she went back to Uganda she'd be in immediate danger. We decided to ask the 2,000 people on our list to e-mail Theresa May, the British Home Secretary, to stop the deportation and also to take steps to change the asylum system to fix this flaw in the law for people claiming asylum based on sexuality. We heard about Brenda's story on a Friday, we e-mailed our members on Monday and around that time we found out that Brenda had been booked on a plane bound for Kampala (Uganda) the following Friday. It became very real because her deportation was imminent.

From the e-mail to our 2,000 members, within three days we ended up with about 65,000 people signing the petition and sending an e-mail to Theresa May. All those people also became All Out members, so we went from having 2,000 members drawn from friends and family to about 65,000 people from around 100 countries across the world. Part of what helped our campaign was the news coverage about David Kato's murder; this horrific story of a leading human rights defender who'd been brutally killed in his house. That came together with Brenda's story to really elevate it and there was a lot of news coverage.

We were doing everything we could to prevent her deportation. We contacted her MP, he filed an early day motion to get other MPs involved and help change the asylum system. We called other Members of Parliament, people in the Prime Minister's Office – anything we could think of. We delivered the petition with a group of activists in the UK who were doing a vigil for David Kato and they also took a big version of our petition to Theresa May's office and we got some media attention around that. A couple of days later we found out that Brenda had been taken to the airport and was placed in a holding cell ready to be deported. We were terrified that it would all be for naught, so we kept pushing, trying to get more signatures, more news coverage and more action behind the scenes. At literally the last minute, a judge issued a stay in her deportation while she was on the plane to be deported. The immigration officers came and took her off the plane and she was released from detention and she got a fresh hearing of her case. So that was our first campaign, which was incredibly dramatic [laughing]. Going from the three or four of us with a little website and a big idea to 65,000 people in many countries participating; we were getting responses from the UK government, we were talking to Brenda and her lawyer on the phone and we actually managed to stop her deportation. As far as I know she is still in the UK.

We've now worked on a few cases like this and we keep taking them because we want to keep this issue in the news and keep pressure on the Home Secretary to actually make a change in the law. Often at All Out we're thinking about how are we telling a story and having a short term impact, but also doing that in a way that's laying the groundwork for a long-term impact. Often times people think you can only be doing one or the other, but we totally reject that idea and we're almost always trying to do both: we try never to be short sighted but we try not to be so structurally focused that we miss opportunities to win victories along the way to the big change that we want. There have probably been three or four asylum cases we've taken on and in each one of those we've gone back to the Home Secretary and told the story to the media about how the asylum system is broken and kept that dialogue going. After three years, the home Secretary has now called for and accepted a formal report on the asylum system and stated that the system is unfair and is currently taking recommendations about the changes that could be made to improve the system. In our most recent campaign we were saying that now that we've got you to look into this question and acknowledge that the system is broken, now you need to take the next step, which is to stop the deportations until you fix it because otherwise you're deporting people based on a system which you know is broken. So we've been helping individual people, helping them tell their story, helping them stay in the country and stay safe, but all the while thinking that over the long-term this is an issue we want to chip away at.

Part of this is about telling these stories in ways that take the issue out of a stuck bureaucracy and get other kinds of people involved and animated and inspired to push for this change; where otherwise they might have felt like 'this has nothing to do with me', or 'why would I ever think about this?' But now we have almost 400,000 members in the UK, all of whom have actively participated in these campaigns and so through story-telling we have built a constituency for this issue in the country: they're educated, they're ready to be organised and they're vocal about it when the opportunity arises.

Nathan: You've already hinted at this, but can you tell me about the kind of strategies you use at All Out?

Andre: We are a kind of interesting mix of things. I think our core, meat and potatoes, is this thing called online organising, like the MoveOn (www.moveon.org) GetUp! (www.getup. org.au/) model. To put it simply, at the heart of it is using e-mail-mediated campaigns to respond at moments of crisis and opportunity in ways that capture people's imagination, bring those people into the organisation and give us the opportunity to build them up across time to do more things and have deeper commitments on issues, and also help them bring the people in their networks into the cause. That's a big part of what we do. Nonetheless, I think that if you compare us to other online organising groups we are different for a couple of reasons. First, we have a really strong, creative, story-telling component: for the issue that we work on we don't only need to build political power or economic power, we also have to build a certain kind of cultural power to have the impact that we want. That is, for people around the world to be able to live openly, to not have to lose their freedom or their family because of who they are or who they love. These aren't changes that can be legislated; they aren't changes that necessarily come with wealth or resources. Instead we need a cultural shift and for people to believe a different story about who we are and where we belong in society. So one of the things that we've always focused on and can be seen in the launch video and our name is a visual identity around the organisation; having a strong creative and cultural component to the work that we do.

Second, we see our role as providing All Out members with two kinds of opportunities. The first is about helping individuals aggregate their voices to push decision makers to make decisions that are more in line with our values of fairness, justice and equality – that's pretty traditional online organising. The other opportunity that we try to create is helping All Out members have the inspiration, language and the cultural artefacts to also change culture and conversations about LGBT issues. For us every time a member posts something on their Facebook wall, it's not just about getting another petition signature, it's also about that person saying to their social network 'This is something I care about, I'm articulating it in a way that you can understand', and bringing others into a story about the issue that puts it on their radar in a way that it might not have been. And even in places where it is relatively easy to talk about these issues, the US, the UK or Australia, I still think it's very hard for people to post gay things to their Facebook wall without feeling somewhat intimidated – not all their Facebook friends know they're out, or they're afraid a colleague will see it and it might hold them back at work. People sometimes throw it away, like sharing things on Facebook is easy and trivial, but on this issue I feel like every time something is shared it's been articulated in such a way that it connects with people's values but also makes it possible to share it and talk about it and be a conversation starter. That's very powerful to me, especially given that at least 40% of All Out members are straight. So we're not just talking to the same people, we're bringing a lot of new people in. Among All Out members, something like 65% have never been involved in an LGBT organisation before, which amounts to about 1.3 million people new to LGBT politics organising in their community or giving money or keeping up with issues and that is part of what feels the most powerful and important to us.

Nathan: So, given what you're saying, does that mean you think because of the issues you work on, concerns about 'clicktivism' (for example, Karpf, 2010) are less relevant for All Out?

Andre: I think in any kind of organisation, whether you're digitally driven or not, I think the problem of getting people to deepen their engagement and stay involved is always difficult – that is your job as an organiser. I feel like the clicktivism debate is a debate about being shallow that's pretty shallow [laughter]. I've worked in organisations that are held up as these sacred, grassroots, deep-connections organisations and actually what's happening in a lot of those organisations running a chapterised model is somebody has taken over the chapter, rules it by actively keeping other people out and refusing to build or expand it, but keep their little fiefdom. And as long as they pay their dues the organisation is fine with it! I don't say that to be disparaging of other organisations or that model; it is always difficult to find ways to make an organisation dynamic, to create new opportunities for people to step into leadership, and to ensure that people's relationship with the organisation and the issue are growing deeper in substantive ways and in ways that bring more of themselves and more of their community into the work.

It is a challenge for All Out, but I think the clicktivism debate goes wrong when it ignores the ways in which genuine, deep connections with issues are made in a digital environment, and the amount of time and energy that people like me put into asking questions about strengthening participation and trying to address this challenge. For example, we've made a real effort in the last six months to try and increase the number of All Out members who have completed three or more actions. We've done this because our data suggests that those who have undertaken three or more actions are much more likely to organise their own event, tell friends about campaigns, to donate to us or another organisation. In the last six months we've more than doubled the number of people who've completed three plus actions, which means there's hundreds of thousands of people who signed a petition, perhaps on the Russia campaign, and have now gone on to support other campaigns like civil unions in Peru. For us this is important because it means people are moving from an interest in one issue to taking action and having a better understanding of issues internationally. It's also part of creating future leaders.

Nathan: Can you talk about the role of technology is All Out's work?

Andre: Our strategy with technology is that we try to reach All Out members where they are and in ways that they're used to being reached. This means we live on the internet, we are real on the internet, we are not tangentially using the internet – I think we are one of the few LGBT organisations that are digitally native. The theory behind All Out does not work without technology: using Skype to have conversations between our campaigners and organisers in every corner of the world, or having our staff communicate via e-mail and Google Hangouts and a whole range of other technologies that help our organisation run. We also rely on data-analysis tools which help us optimise our campaigns and reach vast numbers of people. But, at the moment, the technology that's being used to drive some of the most successful organising campaigns and social change campaigns is really only built to work in the US and parts of Europe. It's actually very difficult for us to find technology that helps us serve our membership internationally and takes this problem seriously. So for me it's important that we're not just giving those already in the debate new and more clever ways of contributing, but actually bringing new people to the table. To me that's why technology is exciting, not because it's faster or gets more signatures on a petition, it's about using technology to give people who have not had entry points access to doing this work and being the voices and faces of this movement.

Nathan: Do you see any separation between your online and offline activism/campaigning?

Andre: I see them as being part of one continuous trajectory. When we look at the numbers on how people participate, we see that there are some people who will never organise or go out to a demonstration – and we think that's kind of OK – and there are some people who will never be donors, there are some people who will never make a phone call, there are some people who only rarely sign a petition. But, for every one of those people, there's somebody who *only* wants to make phone calls, *only* wants to organise events, *only* wants to make donations. We see our job as serving up all of the opportunities, trying to serve up the right opportunity for the moment and making sure there's enough diversity in that across time so that all the different kinds of people can have all their different interests met at All Out. If you look back at what we've done in the last year we really push ourselves to be tactically creative because it helps us keep our full list engaged.

All of it is driven by the internet, in the same way that almost anything that you go to that is organised as an offline event is driven by the internet, because somebody has made a Facebook event or invited you via e-mail or sends you a text message to remind you to get there [laughs] – all of those things are the same things that we're using.

Nathan: What sorts of things do you think All Out does well?

Andre: I think one of the things we do well which is quite invisible is working with partners in difficult circumstances and bringing their voices and interests into the work that we do. There's never a campaign that we launch in any part of the world that is not done in consultation with an organisation or a local partner in that place. A huge chunk of an All Out campaigner's time is spent on Skype working through local issues, developing a nuanced understanding. Like, how do you phrase something so that it's compelling, but also isn't going to say, alienate some local leader who's really important for achieving change? Those kinds of things that are invisible to people reading the e-mails but so much work goes into that. It means our team have to be great strategists, great campaigners and also great diplomats and great communicators, to talk to people from all over and help them figure out how we can use All Out and our members to support the work they're doing.

I think we've also been good at taking issues which are very important, but largely overlooked and by force of will and effort, drive them into the mainstream. The Russian campaign is a good example of that. We had been working with Russian groups steadily for three years before Sochi (2014 Winter Olympic Games) came along and then, along with many others, we were able to help make that one of the biggest issues of the moment (Figure 3.1). So we've been able to drive issues well and take issues where people would have been somewhat isolated and help them get more attention and more resources and help them win.

Figure 3.1: All Out activists presenting a petition signed by over 300,000 people calling for the International Olympic Committee to speak up against Russia's anti-gay laws, Switzerland, 2013

The other thing we're really good at is winning [laughter]. Not for our own egos, but we think it's what keeps people reading our e-mails, it's what keeps people engaged and wanting to do more. We have to show that the theory behind All Out – that when we come together with a common cause we can create an impact that we couldn't do on our own – we have to show that that's true and we have to show it all the time, week after week, month after month, year after year. I think we've been able to do that; this week we prevented Lou Engle from speaking in Switzerland. Lou Engle is one of these Christian ministers from the US who goes around the world and tries to convince governments to create anti-gay laws and raise a lot of money for these kinds of activities. We've been running a steady campaign against his group and the US laws which allow such groups to raise and spend money on these nefarious activities pretty much with impunity; nobody has any records and they don't have to track it and we think it's a nightmare. So Engle was going to give a speech in Geneva and we ran a campaign asking the Swiss government to deny his visa and asking the venue to cancel his event. Within about a day he made a statement saying that there was a smear campaign by gay activists which forced him to cancel his visit. So we haven't upended the system of people exporting hate to other countries, but we did set him back and prevent him from raising further money in Geneva to do these nefarious things around the world. We see such victories as very important.

Another thing we do well is creating visual artefacts and providing a visual language that tell a story which can reach millions of people. I think the best example of that was our recent campaign for the International Day Against Homophobia and Transphobia. A very important day, but very difficult from a branding perspective [giggles], it's IDAHOT, not exactly the most memorable thing, but the idea is great; everybody doing something on the same day to raise these issues and help them get some currency. We wanted to focus on the fact that it's a crime to be gay in 77 countries; we wanted that to be the discussion on IDAHOT. We created a graphic, a pink square with the number 77 in it, and we posted it to All Out's Facebook wall (Figure 3.1). We then sent an e-mail to All Out members saying that we'd posted this number on our wall and that the next day, for IDAHOT, we'll announce that it's the number of countries in which it's a crime to be gay. It was about starting this conversation on IDAHOT and educating people what's at stake. It seems like the simplest thing, but it probably ended up being our most viral post ever. Between the first posting of the 77 and the one posted the next day we reached more than 5,000,000 people, they were shared more than 75,000 times. It was a useful way of taking these issues and breaking them out of whatever silo they might have been in – if you're reaching that many people in a day that means it's not the usual suspects. We don't have 5,000,000 people on All Out's list and we have about 100,000 on Facebook, so those are new people who heard about this and then also shared it.

Figure 3.2: All Out's infographic created for the International Day Against Homophobia and Transphobia, 2014

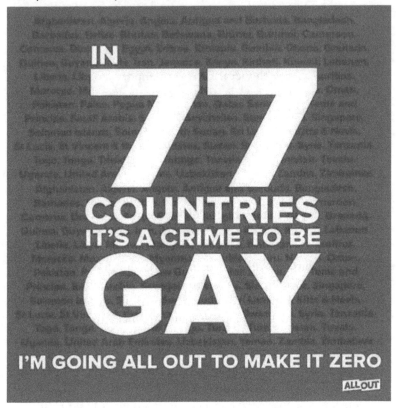

Nathan: The other side of that question is what sorts of things do you think All Out struggles with or could do better

Andre: Oh gosh, that's also a really long list! We're still a really small team and so it's still hard for us to move as fast as we would like and to have the breadth of relationships and coverage internationally that we would like. For example, we don't currently have a staff person in Asia, which is a major block for us, but we just have to get to a place where we have the size and the scope and organisational resources where we can invest in that. Having more staff in more places who are able to connect more deeply with more activists around the world is something that we're always aspiring to do better on.

We're currently trying to develop a more data-driven culture to sit alongside the creative side of All Out. We're trying to develop strong mechanisms for testing the work that we do, and doing a better job of using the data and tools that exist on the web so that we're better listeners as well as better campaigners. To understand the conversations that are happening, making sure we stay relevant to what's going on in the rest of the internet and not end up in this little All Out bubble, but be in the middle of the debate.

We're always working on this but I think we could do a better job of helping other groups understand who we are. The tendency is to believe that All Out is a Western or American organisation, which is kind of true in the sense that we started it from New York and I'm American, but our other co-founder (Jeremy Heimans) isn't American, he's Australian and our staff is not American – it's probably about one-third American and two-thirds international – our membership is actually more English than American, but more than a half of the membership is from everywhere else in the world. We're trying to be more global, to be able to present more globally; we've just added new staff to our offices in Paris and Belo Horizonte so we're really trying to make sure we're doing more in more languages in more countries.

Nathan: One of the other things I wanted to ask you, especially in terms of being a story-teller, I wondered about the shift from gay rights and the LGBT movement being about sex and sexuality towards more talk about love, which has been prominent in recent marriage-equality campaigns. Do you think that's a reasonable claim? Is that part of what's going on?

Andre: I think a lot about that; we could write a whole other book on that topic [laughter]. Two of the things that All Out really values, love is one of them, but the other thing that is slightly less obvious, but actually everywhere in our work, is self-determination. Part of love is love for self and the ability to define who you are, what you want to do, how you want to be and to be able to do that in whatever way you want. And we don't define love by being in a traditional-looking relationship, I think that's something we are really careful about and if I ever tried to define it in that way I think most of the staff would sail to New York and beat me up [laughter] because they would not believe in it. We push those two values because we believe that in a big tent they are ideas that a lot of people connect to, fundamentally understand and feel. From these two values we can actually go in a lot of directions: there are ways it goes toward sexual liberation and a lot of the work around decriminalisation, for example, is about sex. We're talking about laws that are about sodomy or buggery and we can say that these laws that make it a crime to be with the person you want to have sex with, the person you want, are not OK. And from those values these claims are not a big leap; even for people who maybe don't think of themselves as people pursuing their own sexual liberation necessarily, we've got them to the place where they can have that conversation in the context of these laws.

We've also used the love framing to talk about family in ways that are much broader than just marriage: it's about being able to be with the person or people that you want, being able to have the kind of family that you want, and to have that family treated equally and recognised. Even when we were doing the marriage-equality campaign in France, our slogan was 'every family is equal', and we held a big demonstration with a whole range of different kinds of French families participating.

As opposed to trying to normalise gay people through 'normal'-looking relationships, I think what we're trying to do is normalise difference, to create an acceptance of difference. A diversity of how people are and what they're like and to help people be able to tell the story of why it's OK and feel like there are other people on their side who also believe it's OK.

Nathan: What do you think All Out offers young people that makes them want to engage and participate which seems to be lacking in electoral politics?

Andre: I think it's less about what we offer and more that the younger you are the more likely you are to be close to somebody who is out or coming out or having a conversation about their sexuality. Those conversations are just much more prevalent among people who are 25 and under than they were ever for people of our generation, much less our parents or grandparents. I think a lot of the interest is driven by people's personal connection to what we're talking about. This doesn't feel distant to them, this is personal: my friend has to experience this kind of discrimination. I also think for many younger people part of their identity is that they're on the right side of these issues: I'm a person who is open to gay and trans people, I've got some language and education around that and that is part of who I am and it's important that people see me as that kind of person.

I also think that one of the things about All Out's work is that there are real possibilities for change and there are campaigns that are really interesting and exciting that need people's attention. So some of it is just that; we're creating interesting, impactful campaigns that are successful and I think that really resonates with people. They see the personal connection, they understand what's at stake, and then on top of that there are these life or death situations or campaigns where you could really improve the life of an individual or group and people really respond strongly to that.

I found my way to issues through understanding my identity and I think identity-driven movements can be really powerful because they are always to some extent about self-actualisation: it is about realising who I want to be in the world I want to be in. I think that's always part of why you get involved in things and when you get involved in an identity-driven movement it's about recognising what you want this identity to mean to you and other people and coming together with other folks to share that process. I think it's enormously powerful to be a part of such movements because they feel very personal and they can lead you into other important issues. We see that a lot at All Out. There are some campaigns that everyone's interested in and there are some issues that sections of the All Out membership are incredibly passionate about, but nobody else cares about [laughter]. If we do an education campaign there's some people who are like 'Yes! Kids in schools, bullying, they need a hotline; I am all over this all day and night!' while a lot of people are like 'Meh' [laughter]. People do find their way to understanding issues, understanding systems of power, unmasking decision makers and seeing them for what they are and how to influence them by movements that connect with who they are as a person and how they see themselves and their lived experience in the world.

Reference

Karpf, D. (2010) 'Online political mobilization from the advocacy group's perspective: looking beyond clicktivism', *Policy & Internet*, vol 2, no 4, pp 7–41.

FOUR

Social media and political participation: BBC World Service and the Arabic Spring

Marie Gillespie, Nesrine Abdel Sattar and Mina Lami

Introduction

European international broadcasters once enjoyed a privileged position in the global media sphere. For decades, the BBC World Service, Radio France International and Deutsche Welle, alongside their American counterpart Voice of America, have been among the most listened-to radio stations in the world.[1] Their broadcasts in Arabic have been an integral part of Middle Eastern news cultures, even if they have also been regarded with an ambivalent mixture of respect and suspicion (Partner, 1988; Vaughan, 2008). These European and American broadcasters now operate in an environment where they must compete with very popular news organisations such as Al Jazeera and Al Arabiya that attract large Arabic-speaking audiences not only in the Middle East but globally. As state-funded international broadcasters, they also have more or less explicit diplomatic functions: from projecting a positive national image on the world stage to directly communicating strategic interests and foreign policy goals to Middle East audiences; from instilling the virtues of informed citizenship to promoting the communication skills required for deliberative democracy. In the context of a highly uncertain and volatile geopolitical situation in the Middle East, funding cuts, shifts in governance, as well as technological and editorial challenges, these 'legacy' broadcasters are struggling to compete in former territories where they once thrived, and their missions are no longer clear or certain.

The foreign-language services of international broadcasters, like BBC Arabic, must find new ways to engage Arabic-speaking audiences who now have a plethora of media from which to choose, and who may baulk at the thought of consuming the news from old colonial powers. They are experimenting with using social media to attract and keep their audiences and, in order to fulfil their public service remit, to promote participation among citizens in political debate. BBC Arabic already has a long history of offering audiences opportunities to contribute to programmes via the telephone and e-mail but, with the advent of social media, the terms of engagement change (Gillespie, 2013). Producers employ real-time social media-monitoring tools to track user behaviour, make editorial choices, evaluate their work and satisfy funders, stakeholders and governments. The social media data gives producers useful insights into which topics are trending on Twitter or how Facebook groups debate political issues and events, but it also creates problems.

The use of social media-monitoring data to track trends and behaviour triggers tensions between empowering citizens to participate in political debate and monitoring news consumers to boost ratings, prestige and competitiveness. There is also the question of who sets the terms and topics of debate in the spaces of communication created by the BBC's Arabic Service. Is it the audiences or the BBC? Who participates? Do some countries or some social groups dominate? In this chapter we assess whether the integration of social media into news and current affairs programming actually furthers (global) engagement in political debates. We evaluate the rhetoric and the realities of claims about political empowerment via social media.

The chapter is based on a case study on the integration of social media in an interactive TV political debate programme broadcast daily by the BBC Arabic Service called Nuqtat Hewar (NH) or Talking Point. The project took place in 2011–12 – a momentous year for the Middle East that saw the rise and fall of the Arab Spring.[2] It follows a larger, interdisciplinary research project on the BBC World Service as a transnational contact zone – a space where citizens from around the world can consume and communicate via its 27 language services.[3] The empirical research for our NH case study was carried out by four researchers – two of whom were based at BBC Arabic in order to allow for our ethnography of news production to proceed alongside our analysis of the BBC's social media-monitoring data (to which we had privileged access). Discourse and image analysis was also conducted simultaneously and iteratively by the other two researchers in response to ethnographic and social media data. The aim was to evaluate how the BBC Arabic Service uses social media to engage audiences in a 'global conversation' (BBC Trust, 2007). The 'global conversation' is the concept used by the BBC World Service (BBC WS) to reflect its public service ambition to use digital and social media to empower audiences, in this case Arabic-speaking citizens, to engage in political debate, thereby making a contribution to a global public sphere based on established principles of communication in democratic polities – including equality, diversity, plurality, reciprocity.

The chapter examines the similarities and differences that can be observed between this ideal Habermasian conception of the public sphere and the empirical realities of political participation via social media in a rapidly and chaotically emerging digital public sphere (Gripsrud and Moe, 2010). We explore the tricky trade-offs that BBC WS producers face in their deployment of social media between: transparency and gatekeeping; immediacy and accuracy; subjectivity and objectivity; and public service values versus public diplomacy imperatives. Our aim is to offer a measured assessment of the opportunities and the constraints in adopting and adapting social media to engage overseas citizens in political debate and the implications for acquiring and deploying the communication skills required for political engagement in deliberative democracies – what we refer to as deliberative literacies.

The chapter begins with a brief overview of the theoretical literature and findings of recent empirical studies of participatory forms of journalism. It then outlines the political and policy context of the BBC WS. In particular, it sketches the BBC WS's changing relationship with its funder (until 2014), the UK Foreign and Commonwealth Office (FCO) and highlights the tensions between the public service aspirations and the public diplomacy imperatives that are embedded in the concept of the 'global conversation'. The main part of the chapter is based on our case study of NH, which is premised on principles of participatory journalism.

Our argument is that the BBC's traditional journalistic ethos is at odds with the social-media practices of Arab news audiences and, in the case of NH, that this creates huge difficulties for widening and diversifying participation on the programme and political engagement. However, although the empirical realities of user participation online and via social media are very far from a Habermasian ideal conception of the public sphere and the BBC's aspiration to foster 'a global conversation', there is plenty of evidence that a 'democratic deepening' is evolving alongside participatory forms of journalism (Heller, 2009), albeit, at present, among only a limited demographic stratum. New forms of deliberative and media literacy are developing among NH users and this is contributing to energising political communication (Coleman and Gøtze, 2012). But political communication is itself undergoing a sea-change, not least in the more varied places and spaces in which it occurs and as repertoires of political participation multiply and change.

Participatory journalism: opportunities and constraints

Participatory journalism represents a new trend in broadcasting, but the proliferation of terms used to describe developments in digital communication has tended to obscure our understanding of the nature and quality, scale and scope, and significance of new forms of mediated political participation. Whether we refer to 'produser-led' or 'peer-to-peer' production, 'user-generated content' or 'citizen journalism' or 'citizen producers', the underlying principles of open participation, democratic decision making, fluid heterarchy and ad hoc meritocracy are usually the same (Bauwens, 2005).

Bruns, for example, uses the term 'produsage' to signal the dual status of users as producers ('produsers'), arguing that the process itself is 'built on the affordances of the techno-social framework of the networked environment ... especially the harnessing of user communities that is made possible by their networking through many-to-many communications media' (Bruns, 2007). Benkler and Nissenbaum (2006, p 1) argue that peer-to-peer production, as a socio-technical system, has the potential to foster moral and political virtues – democracy, social justice, autonomy. Allen (2006) emphasises the way citizen journalism is associated with crises and catastrophes that compel people to bear witness and articulate their voice in the fight for democracy and dignity in many parts of the world. Uses of social media by citizen journalists, in particular, were instrumental in the organisation of the uprisings during the Arab Spring (Lotan et al, 2011). And following the protest movements among the indignados in Spain and the various Occupy movements, attempts at developing new theory to explain how digital media facilitate more 'personalised public engagement' and a 'logic of connective action' are opening up new avenues of understanding (Bennett and Segerberg, 2012).

These new trends in production are part of what Jenkins (2006) refers to as convergence culture – an unstable cultural process that catalyses a series of unpredictable interactions between different media systems and users (radio, television and online) capable of generating new forms of participatory culture and social and political organisation. Participation in politics depends on news media, and the digital public sphere affords new possibilities for democratic communication (Gillespie, 1995, 2007; Dahlgren, 2005; Gripsrud and Moe, 2010).

It would seem that participatory journalism or production is almost inevitably a positive development. But terms like 'citizen journalism' and 'participatory production' are highly contested notions that encompass diverse practices across multiple technologies, genres and formats.

An emphasis on the empowering and transformative opportunities, welcome as that may be, may serve to mask the inequalities, exclusions, silencing and surveillance aspects of digitally networked initiatives, for as 'power moves with the speed of electronic signals in the fluidity of liquid modernity, transparency is simultaneously increased for some and decreased for others' (Bauman and Lyon, 2013, p 12). If social media is used by citizen producers for their own purposes, how do international news organisations, transnational corporations and governments respond when those purposes oppose their interests? What happens when social media trails are used to track, trap and crack down on protesters? Clearly, social media projects are good at creating networks with weak ties, expanding participation and challenging power in the short term, but it remains to be seen if they have the power to effect enduring change and promote a strengthening of democratic development at national and international levels.

Citizen journalism and social media pose major challenges to established principles and practices of journalism. The informal rhetorical style of user-generated content (UGC) and social media has to be reconciled with 'factuality' and being 'on message'. Further problems surround the authority and credibility of traditional channels and formats when UGC is introduced. Working in real time requires rapid responses based on real-time media-monitoring data, but over-reliance on such data stifles creativity, while ignoring it may result in a failure to respond to the information needs and interests of audiences and a drop in market share. Problems of editorial control, gatekeeping, gate-watching, moderation, freedom of expression and the (self-) regulation of online communities proliferate.

Integrating online media with radio and television redraws hierarchies and roles in news organisations, shifting the boundaries between producers and consumers and blurring definitions between audiences as users, fans, citizens and publics. Terms change as fast as strategies in international broadcasting. Incorporating 'citizen journalists' in social media experiments might have been the BBC WS's strategy in 2010, but by 2011 it had disappeared from the lexicon of the BBC's corporate strategy as senior management recoiled at the idea that BBC professionalism and impartiality might be undermined by amateurs. The more neutral term 'user-generated content' became current. Moreover, a participatory project may be open to all but the result may not be inclusive. Projects with an overtly political thrust are particularly vulnerable to being hijacked by saboteurs of extreme ideological persuasion or by pranksters. So it is important not to presume outcomes but to understand, as we seek to do in this chapter, the structural qualities of participatory production, the organisational dynamics and the cultural as well as the political factors that constrain participatory practices.

Political participation and deliberative literacies

Modern democracies, in principle, combine three institutional features: first, citizen autonomy in the private sphere; second, citizenship based on the inclusion of free and equal citizens in the political community and communication processes; and third, a public sphere that operates independently of the state and acts as an intermediary between state and society (Habermas, 2006, p 411). Habermas' deliberative model situates discourse and negotiation at the heart of democracy. Listening as well as talking is essential to equal and reciprocal relations in fair and free debate (Dobson, 2014). In Habermas' view, deliberating citizens and their collective search for solutions to common political problems require some degree of publicity and transparency, inclusion and equal opportunities for participation, and also the expectation of reasonable outcomes. These are essential requirements for political engagement where deliberation is central to democratic decision making.

Deliberation often takes place in everyday rituals of interpersonal communication as part of the process of collaborative reception of broadcast news and is an inconspicuous form of communication, involving asking for and giving reasons (Gillespie, 1995 and 2007; Buckingham, 2000). With social media, collaborative deliberation becomes more conspicuous, observable and researchable, providing opportunities for research and for surveillance, raising difficult ethical issues. The notion of the 'global conversation' at the BBC WS embeds a lay version of the ideals of deliberative democratic communication and of global, even cosmopolitan citizenship, albeit one that operates in the UK's national interest – part of the UK's public diplomacy infrastructure and 'soft power' effect. But, as Habermas suggests, political communication can facilitate deliberative processes only if a self-regulating media system operates independently of its socio-political environment, and if anonymous audiences can voice their views between an informed elite discourse (of politicians and media pundits and intellectuals) and a responsive civil society.

The digital public sphere presents new possibilities for democratisation and empowerment via participatory forms of production (Gripsrud and Moe, 2010). However, empirical research on the introduction of participatory journalism and UGC in online newsrooms supports prior findings of this research team and urges caution (Jönsson and

Örnebring, 2011). Domingo's research, for example, shows that producers have to translate a very powerful myth of interactivity into their everyday working practices (Domingo, 2008). His ethnography of newsroom practices, like our case study of NH, found that traditional norms of journalism militated against innovation and creativity. So, despite progress towards greater opportunities for interactivity, successive studies identify a yawning gap between the rhetoric and reality of interactivity and bemoan the fact that we know very little about what actually goes on in online newsrooms – making it difficult to assess how participants are chosen and the extent to which their inputs are monitored or edited or censored (Deuze, 2004; Domingo, 2008).

Important as it is to understand interactivity, too narrow a focus on these interactional dynamics can detract attention from questions about the acquisition and deployment of cultural competences and new media literacies that are vital to deliberative political participation (Gillespie, 2013). The forums linked to the BBC WS are, for example, contributing to 'democratic deepening' in providing a space for vigorous, energetic transnational public debate (Herbert, 2012). Participation in such debates can develop deliberative skills such as engaging in reasoned argument and appreciating the value of plural perspectives. Even with little interaction, the mere juxtaposition of divergent individual posts on a topic of common concern may be of immense value in exposing users to communicative spaces in which a diversity of people with plurality of viewpoints are treated on equal grounds (Herbert, 2012, pp 214–15). Whether such deliberative practices contribute to cosmopolitan citizenship of the style envisaged by the BBC WS in concepts of 'global conversation' and by academics like Delanty (2000) remains to be seen, but clearly news media provide the resources for citizenship (Buckingham, 2000; Gillespie, 1995) and shape 'deliberative literacies' – or the communicative competences and skills required for effective forms of mediated political engagement. Deliberative literacies are a much-needed public resource in times of complexity, crisis and confusion such as the Arab Spring, where the lines between information and misinformation, propaganda and public relations, news and scaremongering become blurred (Coleman and Gøtze, 2012).

Fishkin and Luskin (2005) identify the following as features of deliberative democratic debate that indicate the kinds of deliberative literacies that are required for successful political engagement. The debate should be:

1. *informed and informative* – assertions and claims should be backed up with appropriate evidence;
2. *balanced* – opposing and alternative arguments should be presented;
3. *conscientious* – all participants should be treated equally with respect and civility and reciprocal exchange encouraged (rather than some people dominating debate);
4. *substantive* – arguments should be judged on their internal logic and substance, not on who is making them
5. *comprehensive* – a diversity of people and a plurality of views should be represented.

So we must now ask – how well do the social media debates that are integrated into the Arabic Service's outputs at the BBC WS reflect these normative principles? But first some important context is required.

The BBC World Service: public service vs public diplomacy

The BBC WS underwent a dramatic series of changes in its operational locations, deployment of staff, organisation, funding and governance between 2011 and 2014, and is now part of the World Service Group.[4] It is now funded by the UK licence fee, but for decades, and until April 2014, it was funded by the Foreign and Commonwealth Office (FCO) as one of its major public diplomacy partners. Its main purpose, from an FCO point of view, was "informing and influencing audiences overseas for the purpose of promoting the national interest and advancing its foreign policy goals" (Foreign Affairs Committee, 2012).

In contrast, the BBC's aspiration is for the WS to be 'the world's best known, most creative, and most respected voice in international news', as stated in the BBC Trust's Operating Agreement (BBC Trust, 2007, p 1), which requires that the BBCWS:

> should connect and engage audiences by facilitating a 'global conversation' – an informed and intelligent dialogue which transcends international borders and cultural divides; by giving communities around the world opportunities to create, publish, and share their own views and stories; and, thereby, enabling people to make sense of increasingly complex regional and global events and developments.

Our case study on NH set out to understand whether and how BBC Arabic fosters a 'global conversation' – how it uses social media to encourage debate and dialogue across national, religious, ethnic and cultural boundaries. The 'Arab Spring' presented unprecedented opportunities for BBC Arabic to mobilise and experiment with social media to engage audiences/users in political debate. Our prior research had highlighted an unresolvable tension that had to be managed between adherence to the public service values that were of primary importance for journalists and the imperatives of public diplomacy that were of paramount importance to the FCO (Gillespie, 2013).

The FCO had made a significant investment in launching BBC Arabic Service Television in 2008. It proved to be a highly controversial move, not least because 10 mainly Eastern European services were shut down so as to release resources to fund it. It was initially widely perceived by Middle Eastern audiences as a rather blatant public diplomacy venture, but then all news media in the Middle East are seen to reflect the views of their funders (Sreberny, Gillespie and Baumann, 2010). Nevertheless, it was clear that if the BBC WS was to survive in the Middle East, where TV is now the main platform for news consumption, it would have to move with the times. And the fact that the BBC Arabic Service already had a fairly loyal audience base because of its long-standing presence in the Middle East (it was the BBC's very first foreign-language radio service, set up in 1938 to counter Fascist propaganda in the region) meant that it enjoyed recognition, if not widespread popularity (Vaughan, 2008). In fact the Arab Spring actually served to boost the popularity of BBC Arabic; overall audiences rose by more than 50% to a record high of 33.4 million adults weekly – up from 21.6 million before the Arab Spring (Landor, 2011).

The BBC WS's public service remit requires it to contribute 'to sustaining citizenship around the world' by providing independent analysis of news events from an international vantage point. Unlike some of its European and North American equivalents, BBC WS does not aim to project a 'British perspective', at least not in principle. From an FCO perspective, social media can bring long-term diplomatic benefits to Britain by fostering 'digital diplomacy' (Gillespie, 2009). BBC WS broadcasters of course do not see themselves as agents of public diplomacy but as professional journalists working within a long tradition of public service broadcasting. They would deeply resent and resist any implication that their work directly serves diplomatic ends. Their editorial independence from government is cherished and at key moments of political crisis – such as Suez in 1956 and over the Israel–Palestinian conflict – it has been the subject of intense conflict between the BBC and the FCO (Philo and Berry, 2004; Gillespie and Webb, 2012).

Apart from at moments of crisis, the relationship between the senior management at WS and the FCO is also one that has long been conducted by 'gentlemanly agreement' rather than overt or direct pressure. It is a relationship in which the FCO has exerted considerable power (Gillespie, Webb and Baumann, 2008). Whether it will continue to do so under the new licence fee arrangements remains to be seen but it is unlikely that the traditions inherent in this very British relationship that were developed over 80 years will be overturned overnight. Moreover, the diplomatic relationship between the BBC WS and its audiences is a subtle one. In our prior research on debate forums at WS, for example, we found that the public diplomacy value of digital debates was in the form, nature and perceived quality of interaction rather than in its content (Gillespie, Herbert and Andersson, 2009; Gillespie, 2013). In other words, the didactic promotion and demonstration of skills and competences in deliberative literacies is the main public diplomacy benefit from an FCO perspective. Public service values enhance the WS's public diplomacy functions but, as we shall see, it is these very same traditional values and journalistic ethics that conspire against the uses of social media for the purposes of 'democratic deepening' (Herbert, 2012).

Social media clearly pose a risk to established journalistic practices. The BBC WS therefore closely monitors and evaluates the impact of new initiatives. Real-time media-monitoring tools, in particular, and the digital data analytics that are an automatic by-product of social media use, are integral to corporate processes of editorial decision making, strategy, governance and accountability. And yet, in the absence of a clear social media strategy and highly risk-averse attitudes at the top of the corporation social media are not yet fulfilling their potential for political engagement. Nevertheless, BBC Arabic, a service that has received substantial funding and FCO backing for its public diplomacy potential in the Middle East, is in the vanguard of social media development at WS.

Case study: Nuqtat Hewar

NH is BBC WS Arabic's flagship tri-platform [i.e. broadcast, online and social media] political talk show – a popular TV genre across the Middle East that has been described as a 'modernity academy' where, in the heated polemic of public debate, the meanings of modernity are contested (Kraidy, 2010, p 202). It was chosen as a case study since it prides itself in incorporating users' online and social media interactions within a live TV and radio debate show.

The one-and-half-hour programme is broadcast five days a week, simultaneously on TV and radio for an hour, followed by half an hour on radio only. The format includes live interactions with key guests, phone calls from the audience (largely prepared in advance) and a dedicated 'interactivity' segment that incorporates a selection of users' web and social media reactions on the given topic. Moreover, interactions on SMS and Twitter are moderated live in the gallery (the room from where editors view live TV screens) and used whenever possible. To initiate debates, the team posts a few debate topics every week on its dedicated NH page on the BBC Arabic website. The team shares the debate questions on Facebook, Google+ and Twitter accounts to elicit users' comments. Registered users are invited to share any suggested debate topics on the NH web page. The majority of UGC on the debate questions is found on the BBC Arabic website (NH section), followed by the NH Facebook page. Twitter and G+ remain very limited in users' interactions.

A team of 13 managed NH at the time of the study, with three members devoting part of their time to monitoring and moderating social media content on the three key social media outlets of the programme: Twitter, Facebook and Google+. The programme relies primarily on the web page, which has been a strong arm to its content since the programme's inception on radio in March 2003.

The research sought to answer the following questions: How does the BBC WS understand and evaluate its remit regarding the 'global conversation'? How does NH use social media to engage users in a 'global conversation'? Who is participating in the conversation with whom? What kinds of conversation are taking place and do such practices contribute to 'democratic deepening'?

The case study on NH involved a multi-disciplinary team of academic researchers who were granted full access to NH's production processes and to the BBC's social media-monitoring data on user practices. We adopted an integrated approach, combining ethnographic research on production and user engagement alongside 'big data' and discourse analysis. We analysed user data and the interactive features of the BBC Arabic's online forums, juxtaposing them with fine-grained discourse analysis of the social media conversations taking place within the NH programme. To achieve that, first, a quantitative analysis of users' profiles and behaviour was conducted in the period 15 November 2011 to 25 January 2012. Using the BBC's own social media-monitoring tools – Facebook insights, Sysomos Heartbeat and Site Catalyst – the research examined user demographics and behaviour on the main BBC Arabic and NH Facebook pages, the main Twitter account, and the NH web page. Insights about key influencers shaping conversations and key debates were also analysed. Second, a discourse analysis was conducted on the NH website and social media pages to understand the life cycle of debate topics as well as the quality and diversity of conversation. Five TV episodes of NH were analysed. The analysis examined the debate questions and the characteristics of debate (diversity, pluralism, nature and quality of conversation), as well as how users' online participation was integrated into the NH TV show. For each platform, certain categories of exposure and forms of active engagement were selected in order to develop as comprehensive a picture of users' preferences and communicative practices as possible.

To complement the users and content analyses, we also conducted ethnographic observations on the production contexts, looking at the dynamics of gatekeeping users' participation and the processes inside the newsroom. This included a total of 21 days of participant observation of NH in the period between mid-November 2011 and the end of January 2012, in addition to 18 semi-structured interviews with the editorial, management and social media team at both BBC Arabic and NH. It also included an extensive archival review of plans, records and technological artefacts used for managing and moderating debate (for example, TOPCat 2 news management system, the Jive moderating system). Such a mix of corporate and academic methods and data analysis, what we refer to as the 'social life of methods' approach, enabled us to evaluate the quality, nature, content and extent of the interactivity of the BBC's 'global conversation' forums. It also provided insights into how the BBC monitors its audiences and moderates the debates and how 'big data' analyses of audience behaviour are now incorporated into key corporate processes and decision making (Gillespie, 2013).

Evaluating BBC Arabic's 'global conversation'

Even though the BBC WS does not engage directly or formally in public diplomacy projects, one of its key public purposes is to engage overseas publics in a 'global conversation' via interactive media that will have public diplomacy benefits and outcomes. Yet, the vision of senior management at WS is different from the attitudes of journalists (senior and junior) at the BBC Arabic service; the latter believe that it is imperative to join the social media race fast, and that they 'cannot afford not to be there'. As the director of Online Journalism Service and Innovation at WS states "whether we like it or not, the audiences are using social media, so if we are absent, we are going to lose; we need to be there as soon as possible" (personal interview, 12 June 2012). Senior editors at BBC Arabic value social media as a source for content, a tool for news gathering and a distribution platform. The editor-in-chief of NH echoes what the wider Online Journalism Service team argues, that social media "make our choices easier and faster, because we can directly see online what interests people. It helps us in content development and in the distribution of this content" (personal interview, 22 May 2012).

Nevertheless, although most journalists have been asked to create Twitter accounts, traditional routines and attitudes still persist. For instance, 1 in 10 of the NH team did not have a personal Facebook account at the time of study, while 3 in 10 did not have a Twitter account. Moreover, only one quarter of those who owned a social media account were actually active on it. Also, 8 in 10 of staff over 45 years of age were not active on any social media platform. One senior Arabic staff member described the attitudes of several staff at the Arabic-language service, especially older members:

> "The position of social media is still not concrete enough. The concept is still new for many. Also, people are still looking at social media as a rival; sometimes journalists and managers look at it as a rival, or [as something that] is just 'good to have'; others question: 'is it the end of the BBC as a news organization?'" (Personal interview, 22 May 2012)

But the attitudes towards social media evinced by some of the journalists are not the only problem. The concept of the 'global conversation' is seen as unclear, remote and difficult to put into practice and impossible to evaluate. Despite the realisation by senior management of the potential role of social media and the rapid uptake by some (mainly younger and more junior) journalists, BBC Arabic is still grappling with the idea of audience 'engagement'. For instance, there are no clear, agreed definition or indicators to assess what the FCO or the BBC WS mean by 'engaging overseas audiences', and engagement in online and social media spaces also poses serious difficulties for audience researchers at BBC WS.

There is in fact no social media strategy and therefore it is difficult to know what is a success or a failure. For instance, while BBC WS defines 'engagement' as one of the key performance indicators, it measures it merely in terms of how users 'discuss with friends', or 'would recommend', or 'help to form opinions' around its news content. All the indicators used are quantitative and do not offer much insight into the qualitative aspect of users' engagement. Moreover, the understanding of how social media contribute to users' engagement and how one might assess their success is different in different parts of the organisation. The definition of 'successful' social media performance is measured based on different scales according to each team and according to different social media. One senior member of staff explains it thus:

> "Those who put [the social media] strategy into practice interpret it in their different ways. So they are not matching. Language Services have targets, and the Digital Future Media Team have their own strategy for social media. The Language Services social media management see the target as increasing engagement. Meanwhile, the Digital Team's 'perception' of success for social media is purely commercial: they want more traffic and more ads on the Arabic, Spanish and Farsi websites. So they [the Digital Team] assesses all languages now in terms of 'referrals' from social media and referrals from partners to the website; a completely commercial offer." (Personal interview, 7 June 2012)

This tension between the public service and the commercial criteria in evaluating uses of social media, and the problem of what precisely it means to engage Arabic-speaking audiences overseas, pose problems and create confusion when it comes to adopting social media.

Engaging audiences vs gatekeeping practices

Our production ethnography examined how the NH team sought to engage users in participatory debate via social media – Facebook and Twitter particularly. We also examined gatekeeping and filtering processes to assess how social media content was integrated in the actual TV episodes. Figure 4.1 illustrates the cycle of news production of NH and how contributions from users are linked in at each stage.[5] The NH cycle starts with the team posting a debate question on the NH web page and its dedicated Facebook and Twitter accounts. Then the preparation phase starts as team members observe users' contributions on each platform while at the same time following the BBC Arabic main website and other breaking news. Some of these users interactions are selected, aggregated and prepared for the episode. No Facebook comments posted live on the programme, but only Twitter feeds (together with SMS messages) are selected for real-time display. A dedicated producer interacts with users on Twitter and feeds selected users' responses into the live episode. Of course the selection process is crucial.

Figure 4.1: Cycle of news production and users' contribution to NH programme

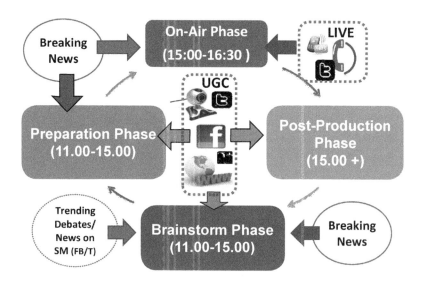

Although Twitter feeds were moderated and broadcast live during the episode, observation revealed that on average only six interactive tweets were selected, from which only one or two would be broadcast. During less popular episodes there were no Twitter interactions.

The gatekeeping of users' interactions in NH was done at two levels: choice of topic and of users' contributions to the episode (whether webcam video, poll, pictures, comments and other UGC, including social media posting). These choices happen on a daily basis inside the newsroom through a set of normative procedures and standard practices.

First, in terms of topic selection, different debate questions are posted on the NH Facebook page and the carousel of the NH website and the editorial team decides whether this topic will be the basis of an episode. However, precedence is given not to users' suggested topics but always to the news headlines on the BBC Arabic Service's website, which are strongly influenced not only by WS central news production but also by the radio and TV senior editors. With few exceptions the debate is news driven rather than user driven.

The second aspect of gatekeeping is the selection of users' statements or conversations that will feature in the episode. Users' comments on the NH Facebook page are post-moderated (that is, after they have been posted) throughout the day according to specific guidelines that prohibit obscenity, blasphemy, incitement to hatred and comments irrelevant to the debate question. The selection of comments for the live programme happens at the preparation stage by the interactivity producer of each episode, who (usually) picks a sample of comments that are deemed 'interesting' or seen as adding to the diversity of opinions. This selection is often based on epistemic values (of accuracy, veracity) and the news values of the BBC (newsworthiness, immediacy). Often, an aggregated numerical summary of the key views on the topic, rather than the verbatim of each comment, is presented by the interactivity producer in the middle of the episode. Only a handful of comments are quoted. Moreover, if there are any conversations (such as users talking to each other and in response to each other), they are not reflected, although efforts are often made to present all different views of the debate, regardless of their popularity.

As for Twitter, the selection of users' interactions is more proactive. The team follows tweets from a pre-set list of *influencers*, including active bloggers, politicians and intellectual celebrities. This list of the 100 most influential Arab Tweeters was put together by the social media team in the aftermath of the Arab Spring at the beginning of 2011. While this process seems to have included only the most 'outspoken' users, it poses questions of representational bias and underscores the structural hierarchies and inequalities that persist in the digital public sphere. It builds on earlier research that only 7% of Twitter users contribute to 90% of the entire content on Twitter, and selection excludes new or novice users, while vocal repeat users have more success in getting their voice heard (Hindman, 2009). Users' social media contributions do not form the majority of UGC on the live interactive TV and radio episode, although the NH web page contributions and guest-speaker telephone conversations do.

While moderating and censoring of social media content is guided by explicit rules, there are also implicit rules that the team adopts. For instance, cutting out any religious content, such as Qur'anic verses or sayings of the Prophet or Hadith, is a common practice, according to a broadcasting assistant who moderates comments: "We cannot proof them, and we claim at BBC to be non-religious, so we remove any [religious verses] comments" (personal interview, 21 November 2011). This example, one of many recounted to us during our research, indicates the tension between the BBC's editorial policy and the preferences of a targeted online audience. In the Middle East, a region characterised by religious tensions and the permeation of religious rhetoric in public life, such rules of engagement on BBC forums are too restrictive for the audience. This is especially so since the style of political debate in the Middle East talk shows is premised on the expression of political views in an emotionally and religiously charged register and idiom (Kraidy, 2010).

Observation of the NH team's monitoring practices showed that comments with grammatical problems are also often removed, privileging the voices of the intellectual and eloquent elite and denying representation to less literate sections of the public. Conversations submitted by users in English – on NH Facebook and web pages – are automatically deleted by the editorial team. According to the editorial team, the audience is primarily Arabic speaking, even though the BBC's and our own audience research showed that most Facebook users were bi-lingual (Arabic–English) and nearly half of users were based in diaspora (Andersson, Gillespie and Mackay, 2010). Explaining the rationale behind excluding English comment, one of the journalists stated that "we always delete any English [comments on Facebook], because we are mainly for Arabic people, so not everyone would understand the English" (personal interview, 21 November 2011). And when asked if he was aware of the large percentage of diasporic Arabs speaking English, he affirmed "Often they are Arabs, but even if they are, we don't know who would understand [English]" (personal interview, 21 November 2011). Moreover, no specific training was given to broadcasting assistants handling the moderation of content. Instead, most of the time the latter relied on asking each other or a senior journalist when a controversial comment arose – and in any case it is seen as low-status work.

Participation in the 'global conversation'

The study examined whether NH lived up to the ideals of a Habermasian-style public sphere as embedded in the notion of the 'global conversation' – specifically, the diversity of people and plurality of viewpoints represented across its three platforms in terms of gender, age and nationality.

Gender

Women's participation was considerably lacking in BBC Arabic debates. The debates and narratives were often determined and framed by men, who often spoke in the name of Arab women in debates. User participation on the BBC Arabic digital platforms was dominated by men in the 25–35 age group. The NH TV show featured on average only two female participants per episode, which reflected the low participation of women in the online debates that preceded the show. Women's participation was slightly higher on the Facebook page than on the website. A case in point was the debate question 'Why do you think matters escalated in Tahrir Square the way they did?' (NH, 20 November 2011), which received 420 comments on the website and 159 comments on the NH Facebook page. Only 12 of the comments on each platform were from women. This low participation by women was consistent across all the debate threads analysed.

More strikingly, women's participation did not increase when the debate topics were related to women's issues. An example of this was the debate question 'Do Arab cultures incite hatred against their women?' which was raised by the NH team on 27 April 2012. On the NH web page, the question received a total of 47 comments, all from men; and on the Facebook page it received only 2 comments from women participants out of a total of 34. This disparity could be attributed to structural inequalities and issues of digital exclusion – whether due to accessibility or technological competence. Further research is required to assess the key obstacles to women's participation in political and cultural debate in a variety of digital forums/public spheres.

Nevertheless, despite their small numbers, those women who did participate on the NH Facebook page were often very active, making detailed, well-informed comments that reflected a high level of education and political awareness. Careful examination of their contributions also showed that most of them held liberal views and strongly supported the Egyptian revolution and its youth. One active participant, Rabab Helal, for example, posted 11 comments to the debate 'What do you think of the rise of the *Salafis* in the parliamentary elections?' (NH Facebook page, 8 December 2011). Expressing her opposition to the *Salafi* current, she eloquently argued for the need to clearly differentiate between opposing a political party that is Islamic and opposing Islam, the religion. Similarly, the debate (25 May 2012) on the final results of the first round of Egyptian presidential elections, while receiving a large number of brief but poorly articulated comments, had a few exceptionally well-argued comments from women participants that enriched the thread with meaningful contributions.

Nation

National representation was wider than gender representation but still limited. Diverse nationals from 20 Arab countries, both residents in their home countries and in diaspora, actively took part in the NH online debates. Users often commented even when events were not related to their home countries. This brought a wide array of regional experiences and perspectives to the online debate. Yet, despite the diverse range of nationalities of participants in the online debates, the NH team often restricted its choice of participants who appeared on the TV show to nationals of the same country that was being discussed. A Syrian national was unlikely to be chosen to participate in a debate about Egypt. This editorial setting poses questions on the limits of participation and the plurality of (global) conversation to which the BBC WS aspires. Seventy-seven per cent of participants were from the home country under discussion (for more details see Abdel-Sattar et al, 2012). There was also a preponderance of Egyptian users, as Egypt received the highest share of debate topics raised during the research period. Complaints about the channels bias in favour of certain countries and topics over others were recurrent on the BBC NH page, especially among Maghreb users (Morocco, Algeria, Tunisia). It is important to point out, however, that the research was conducted during and immediately after the Egyptian parliamentary elections in November/December 2011, making this Egyptian focus more understandable.

Age

In general, online participants were younger than those taking part in the broadcast conversations. Contributors in the over-40 age category often participated by phone or were guests on the broadcast episodes. NH Facebook participants were predominantly in the 18–35 age group. The age profile of users as well as the medium itself shaped the quality of the debate. Facebook, for example, was mostly used for brief and informal input in colloquial Arabic. The NH debates that took place on Facebook, unlike those on the moderated BBC Arabic website, also reflected more polarised views, emotional comments and violations of BBC participation guidelines (such as swearing and profanity). Generally, participants expressed themselves in less-elaborate linguistic codes and idioms on Facebook. They displayed less-sophisticated rhetorical and discursive competence than their counterparts on the NH web page in communicating their political viewpoints (such as relying more heavily on conspiracy theories and expressing dogmatic, entrenched opinions rather than more open discursive styles (Aksoy, 2006).

The Facebook participants displayed fewer skills in 'deliberative literacy' than their more politically mature counterparts on the NH web page. This is of course a value judgement based on a set of criteria devised by the research team, drawing on previous research (Gillespie, 2007). Our more extensive report offers greater detail (Abdel-Sattar et al, 2012). However, this raises difficult questions about how we might evaluate deliberative literacies in digital public spheres more systematically, and whether or how we judge the quality of political discourse on Facebook.

The quality of conversation and plurality of viewpoints

The study examined the plurality of viewpoints among users and the NH moderation, and found that the BBC's policy of ensuring 'balance' was observed to a large extent. For instance, debates on the Egyptian elections and related events in Egypt showed very polarised views on issues, such as the success of the Islamic parties, the role of the Egypt's Supreme Council of the Armed Forces, and Tahrir Square protesters. Similarly, on the debate question 'What do you think of the rise of *Salafis* in Egypt?', posted on the NH website (8 December 2011), viewpoints expressed by users were equally divided: out of 50 comments examined, 17 expressed support for the Muslim Brotherhood, 17 expressed opposition to Islamist groups in general, 15 were neutral (in the sense of explaining or interpreting the results while withholding their personal opinion) and only 3 supported Salafi rule (that is, a stricter form of Islamic rule that is more literal in interpreting the Qur'an and Hadith). Rarely did a single view dominate the debate.

The social media platforms supported a much wider range of viewpoints and tended towards the more liberal and secular end of the political spectrum, as compared with those on the NH website, reflecting a younger, more politically Left cohort. For instance, support for the Tahrir Square protest (and its symbolism of resistance, protest and change) and calls to take to the square came much more frequently from Facebook participants.

Despite the plurality of views on NH digital platforms, there was little evidence of meaningful dialogue or reciprocal exchange among participants. Users often merely addressed the NH team in monologue style, or simply expressed their views and left, with no evident engagement with other users. In contrast, participants in the

NH TV episodes, given the interactive format and moderation of the programme, did not indulge in monologue. The TV programme brings UGC, phone callers and guests in the studio together to engage in a multi-platform dialogue that is facilitated through the skilful mediation of the presenters. This skilful mediation is vital to successful interactivity and dialogue that might approximate the ideal of a 'global conversation'.

Another facet of plurality was reflected in the different levels of participation on each platform. During the time of the research, social media platforms and their users received less individual credit on the TV show, compared to the more traditional means of participation: the phone-ins and the guests on the show. However, individual perspectives were aggregated and presented collectively as representing the different array of opinions on the topic.

Finally, related to topic selection and plurality was the BBC Arabic Service's coverage of events that were ignored or marginalised by its rivals Al Jazeera and Al Arabiya, given their own geopolitical agendas. This was the case in debates related to anti-regime protests among Shias in Bahrain and Saudi Arabia and by separatists in South Yemen. Despite the critical events surrounding the Egyptian elections and the rapidly escalating Syrian crisis during the research period, the three topics that received the highest levels of participation were those about separatist movements in South Yemen, Shia dissidents in Saudi Arabia and Shia protests in Bahrain. Topics like these, not covered or marginalised on rival channels, gave users an alternative platform on which to voice their opinions and their dissent. This has been found to greatly increase online participation. Nationals of these countries often commended the BBC Arabic Service for covering these topics, which they said were deliberately ignored by the Arabic media and press.

Conclusion

In this case study, production ethnography was combined with content and discourse analysis of social media discussions on BBC Arabic's NH political talk show to shed light on whether the integration of social media into news and current affairs programming actually furthers (global) engagement in political debates. We also re-analysed social media monitoring data to gauge patterns of use and interaction. Our research highlighted the gap between the rhetoric and realities of the BBC's 'global conversation' among BBC Arabic audiences during the Arab Spring in terms of four key aspects.

First, the inherent difficulties of translating the ideals of participatory journalism into practice result from the persistence of traditional newsroom routines and values based on a broadcast model of communication. As the case study of NH suggests, traditional journalistic standards and conceptions of audiences prevent newsrooms like BBC Arabic from fully embracing participatory forms of journalism. For instance, normative standards shaping gatekeeping practices constrain the diversity of people and the plurality of voices and viewpoints expressed. And although the aim is to enable intercultural dialogue among users, such practices obstruct the possibilities for developing a 'global conversation' of the kind defined by the Operating Agreement between the BBC Trust and the BBC WS. There are, then, deep tensions generated by the coexistence of broadcast and networked models of communication and associated practices and values that will take time to negotiate and resolve.

Second, the lack of a social media policy at BBC WS and of any benchmarks or criteria for clearly measuring and assessing 'engagement' or even what might constitute a 'global conversation' adds to the difficulty in attaining those public service ideals. Moreover, the BBC Arabic Service and the wider BBC WS adopt different definitions of such concepts, rendering any assessment of progress difficult. From a BBC Arabic perspective, the main goal is to increase audiences and engage them more effectively – building brand loyalty while remaining true to the BBC's journalistic ethos of impartiality and balance. Yet quantitative measures still predominate as the main indicators of success for the BBC's senior management to assess whether BBC Arabic performs well. Qualitative measures are also needed because the numbers engaging actively with social media are very small, as compared to audiences for radio and television, and therefore, to some senior managers, social media seem insignificant. This contributes to relegating social media to the bottom of the hierarchy in the newsroom, after TV and radio. Only the younger, less-experienced staff worked on social media systematically. But although early-career staff may have the best ideas for engaging social media users (who tend to be younger and better educated than audiences for traditional broadcast content), they have little power to express and execute their ideas, and their more experienced bosses may be less sympathetic to social media and may regard it as a threat to traditional journalism. This further inhibits the possibilities for political engagement via social media.

Third, in terms of diversity of people and plurality of voices and perspectives, social media-monitoring data and discourse and content analysis of interactions on NH social media and websites showed that NH participants were predominantly young men. Women's participation remained very limited. The TV audience for the show was also older than those using social media. These generational dynamics affected the nature of participation. Similarly, Arabic users using English were excluded and their comments were deleted. Given that one of the main reasons why users go to the BBC in the first place is that they either are Anglophiles or wish to become part of the global Anglosphere to augment their employment, travel or life chances, this strikes us as odd. It also suggests that perhaps bi-lingual platforms could help to advance political engagement across generations. During the Arab Spring, social media created generational gulfs in political communication, fragmenting the public sphere of deliberative debate. While social media may energise debate at critical moments, whether it created sustained and enduring political engagement in the long term remains to be seen.

Fourth, in terms of the quality of debate on NH Facebook page, there was little dialogue or reciprocal engagement in the conversations among users. Users were found to be talking 'at' each other rather than 'to' each other. Plurality in social media conversations was also an issue. While users presented a spectrum of views, the dependence on the most 'vocal' and articulate voices (often mature men) made for the repeated use of 'safe' participants, which skewed representation. There was also a tendency to create a strictly balanced debate of two opposing viewpoints rather than reflecting a wider, full spectrum of views.

Nevertheless, despite these constraints, there is evidence that social media is widening the repertoires of participation and the possibilities for political engagement via TV political talk shows such as NH. In the process, deliberative digital and plural literacies are being developed over time, albeit among mainly younger age groups. The development of deliberative skills and competences that contribute to high-quality, informed public debate as in the Habermasian ideal public sphere is a long-term process. Yet for BBC Arabic and its uses of social media it is likely to be the most important public diplomacy effect rather than any direct form of political influence.

The chapter has shed some light on changing repertoires of participation. The Arab Spring brought a significant increase in audiences for the BBC Arabic Service because citizens were able to debate topics that were taboo on rival channels and to use the BBC networks as a means of disseminating globally their personalised political actions and content. As such, the BBC Arabic Service and NH do provide an alternative platform of debate – albeit with different rules of engagement and discursive styles – to their competitors. They also act as a multiplier for the global dissemination of UGC. This adds to media pluralism in the region.

Despite this, BBC Arabic will struggle to survive in increasingly crowded media markets. The political and editorial constraints under which it operates limit its attractiveness to younger, internet-savvy youth in the region, while older demographics prefer radio and TV news. Competition with other, larger-funded regional news organisations like Al Jazeera, Sky Arabic and Al Arabiya also puts growing pressure on BBC Arabic to innovate in order to satisfy the growing needs of Arab audiences. And yet the hybrid nature of personalised digital networks linking up with large international organisations can be seen as astute tactic for projecting new forms of political participation on the world media stage.

Notes

[1] The names of these broadcasters have changed over time but there has been continuity in their remit as public service media and as integral to the diplomatic infrastructure of colonial and political power. Radio France International began as Poste Colonial in 1931; BBC World Service started as The Empire Service in 1932; Deutsche Welle started much later, in 1953; Voice of America started up in 1942. Other radio stations like Radio Free Europe, which was set up in 1949, were also important in the Cold War context.

[2] Gillespie, M. (2012) PI: *The Art of Intercultural Dialogue: Evaluating the Global Conversation at the BBC World Service*. AHRC Public Policy Fellowship. AHRC Translating Cultures Programme. www8.open.ac.uk/researchprojects/diasporas/news/public-policy-fellowship-at-the-bbc-world-service.

[3] Gillespie, M. (2007–10) *Tuning In: Diasporic Contact Zones at the BBC World Service*. AHRC Diasporas, Migration and Identities Research Programme. £496,476. Ref AH/E58693/1. http://www.open.ac.uk/socialsciences/diasporas/.

[4] The BBC World Service Group was formed in 2014 and includes the BBC World Service, BBC World News Television Channel, the BBC's international-facing online news services in English, BBC Monitoring Service, BBC World Service Group and BBC Media Action (the BBC's international development charity). It employs more than 2,500 journalists and support staff based in 113 countries, delivering over 83,000 hours of content per annum – see http://www.bbc.co.uk/aboutthebbc/insidethebbc/managementstructure/biographies/horrocks_peter.html.

[5] The full report on which this chapter is based can be read at: http://www.open.ac.uk/researchprojects/diasporas/publications/report/bbc-arabic-and-social-media-a-case-study-of-nuqtat-hewar.

References

Abdel-Sattar, N., Gillespie, M., Lami, M., Sayed, N., Wissam, M. (2012) *Social Media at BBC Arabic: A Case Study of Nuqtat Hewar*, http://www.open.ac.uk/researchprojects/diasporas/publications/report/bbc-arabic-and-social-media-a-case-study-of-nuqtat-hewar (accessed 29 July 2014).

Aksoy, A. (2006) Transnational Virtues and Cool Loyalties: Responses of Turkish Speaking Migrants in London to September 11 2001. Gillespie, M., ed. After September 11 2001: TV News and Transnational Audiences. *Journal of Ethnic and Migration Studies*, vol 32, no 6, pp 923–47.

Allen, S. (2006) *Online News: Journalism and the Internet*, Maidenhead: Open University Press.

Andersson, M., Gillespie, M. and Mackay, H. (2010) 'Mapping Digital Diasporas at the BBC World Service: Users and Uses of the Persian and Arabic Websites', *Middle East Journal of Culture and Communication*, vol 3, no 2, pp 256–79.

Bauman, Z. and Lyon, D. (2013) *Liquid Surveillance: A Conversation*, Cambridge: Polity Press.

Bauwens, M. (2005) ,The Political Economy of Peer Production', available at: http://www.ctheory.net/articles.aspx?id=499 (accessed 20 January 2014).

BBC Trust (2007) 'Operating Agreement: BBC World Service', available at: http://www.bbc.co.uk/bbctrust/assets/files/pdf/regulatory_framework/other_activities/world_service_op_agreement.txt (accessed 20 January 2014).

Benkler, Y. and Nissenbaum, N. (2006) 'Commons-based peer production and virtue', *Journal of Political Philosophy*, vol 14, no 4, pp 394–419.

Bennett, L.W. and Segerberg, A. (2012) 'The Logic of Connective Action', *Information, Communication & Society*, vol 15, no 5, 739–68.

Bruns, A. (2007) 'From Production to Produsage: Research into User-led Content Creation', available at: http://produsage.org/node/12 (accessed 20 January 2012).

Buckingham, D. (2000) *The Making of Citizens: Young People, News, and Politics*, London: Routledge.

Coleman, S. and Gøtze, J. (2012) *Bowling Together: Online Public Engagement in Policy Deliberation*, London: Hansard Society.

Dahlgren, P. (2005) 'The internet, public spheres and political communication: Deliberation and dispersion', *Political Communication*, vol 22, pp 147–62.

Delanty, G. (2000) *Citizenship in a Global Age: Society, Culture, Politics*, Maidenhead: Open University Press.

Deuze, M. (2004) 'What is Multi-Media Journalism?' *Journalism Studies*, vol 5, no 2, pp 139–52.

Dobson, A. (2014) *Listening for Democracy: Recognition, Representation, Reconciliation*, Oxford: Oxford University Press.

Domingo, D. (2008) 'Interactivity in the daily routines of online newsrooms: dealing with an uncomfortable myth', *Journal of Computer-Mediated Communication*, vol 13, no 3, pp 680–704.

Fishkin, J.S. and Luskin, R.C. (2005) 'Experimenting with a democratic ideal: Deliberative polling and public opinion', *Acta Politica*, vol 40, no 3, pp 284–98.

Foreign Affairs Select Committee (2012) Second Report. FCO Public Diplomacy: The Olympics and Paralympics 2012. Accessed at http://www.publications.parliament.uk/pa/cm201011/cmselect/cmfaff/581/58106.htm (27 July 2014).

Gillespie, M. (1995) *Television, Ethnicity and Cultural Change*, London and New York Routledge.

Gillespie, M. (2007) 'Media, Security and Multicultural Citizenship: A Collaborative Ethnography', *European Journal of Cultural Studies*, vol 10, no 3, pp 275–93.

Gillespie, M. (2009) 'Anytime, Anyplace, Anywhere: Digital Diasporas and the BBC World Service', *Journalism: Theory, Practice and Criticism*, vol 10, no 3, pp 322–6.

Gillespie, M. (2013) 'BBC Arabic, Social Media and Citizen Production: An Experiment in Digital Democracy before the Arab Spring', *Theory, Culture and Society*, vol 29, no 33, pp 92–131.

Gillespie, M. and Webb, A. (eds) (2012) *Diasporas and Diplomacy: Cosmopolitan Contact Zones at the BBC World Service 1932–2012*, Abingdon and New York: Routledge (CRESC Series).

Gillespie, M., Webb, A. and Baumann, G. (guest eds) (2008) Special Issue. The BBC World Service, 1932–2007: Cultural Exchange and Public Diplomacy. *Historical Journal of Film, Radio and Television*, vol 28, no 4, pp 453–58.

Gillespie, M., Herbert, D. and Andersson, M. (2009) 'The Mumbai Attacks and Diasporic Nationalism: World Service Forums as Conflict, Contact and Comfort Zones', *South Asian Diaspora*, vol 2, no 1, pp 109–29.

Gripsrud, J. and Moe, H. (eds) (2010) *The Digital Public Sphere: Challenges for Media Policy*. Gothenburg: Nordicom.

Habermas, J. (2006) 'Political Communication in Media Society: Does Democracy Still Enjoy an Epistemic Dimension? The Impact of Normative Theory on Empirical Research', *Communications Theory*, vol 16, no 4, pp 411–26.

Heller, P. (2009) 'Democratic Deepening in India and South Africa', *Journal of Asian and African Studies*, vol 44, pp 123–49.

Herbert, D. (2012) 'What Kind of Global Conversation? Participation, democratic deepening and public diplomacy through BBC World Service online forums: an examination of mediated global talk about religion and politics', in Gillespie, M. and Webb, A. (eds) 2012. *Diasporas and Diplomacy: Cosmopolitan Contact Zones at the BBC World Service 1932–2012*. Abingdon and New York: Routledge (CRESC Series) pp 211–30.

Hindman, M. (2009) *The Myth Of Digital Democracy*, Princeton, NJ: Princeton University Press.

Jenkins, H. (2006) *Convergence Culture: Where Old and New Media Collide*, New York: New York University Press.

Jönsson, A.M. and Örnebring, H. (2011) 'User-Generated Content and the News: Empowerment of Citizens or Interactive Illusion?' *Journalism Practice*, vol 5, no 2, pp 127–44.

Kraidy, M. (2010) *Reality Television and Arab Politics*, Cambridge: Cambridge University Press.

Landor, L. (2011) 'Arab Spring Helps BBC Arabic Audience Grow', http://www.bbc.co.uk/blogs/legacy/theeditors/2011/12/arab_spring_helps_bbc_arabic_a.html (Accesses 20 January 2014).

Lotan, G., Graeff, E., Ananny, M., Gaffney, D., Pearce, I. and Boyd, D. (2011) T'he Arab Spring: The revolutions were tweeted: information flows during the 2011 Tunisian and Egyptian revolutions', *International Journal of Communication*, vol 5, pp 1375–405.

Partner, P. (1988) *Arab Voices: The BBC Arabic Service 1938–1988*, London: BBC External Service.

Philo, G. and Berry, M. (2004) *Bad News from Israel*, London: Pluto Press.

Sreberny, A., Gillespie, M. and Baumann, G. (eds) (2010) 'The BBC World Service and the Greater Middle East: Comparisons, Contrasts, Conflicts', special issue, *Middle East Journal of Culture and Communication*, vol 3, no 2, pp 129–37.

Vaughan, J.R. (2008) 'The BBC's External Services and the Middle East before the Suez Crisis', in Gillespie, M., Baumann, G. and Webb, A. (guest eds) Special Issue. The BBC World Service, 1932–2007: Cultural Exchange and Public Diplomacy, *Historical Journal of Film, Radio and Television*, vol 28, no 4, pp 449–515.

Part Two: Contemporary political (dis)engagements

FIVE

Feeling politics: the importance of emotions for understanding electoral (dis)engagement

Nathan Manning

Introduction

A range of emotions are routinely invoked and represented in public discussions of politics. Recent examples abound: President Obama's 2008 campaign motif of 'hope'; the outpouring of anger and indignation expressed through the Occupy movement in many countries across the world (for example, Langman, 2013); the joy and excitement in Egypt as Mubarak was overthrown (Ali, 2011); anger at Tony Blair from families of British military personnel killed during the Iraq war (Lewis and Dodd, 2010); the shame evoked by President Bush's response to hurricane Katrina (Cornwell, 2010); the catharsis as Australia's prime minister formally apologised to Australia's indigenous peoples. In addition, there is also a body of academic literature that documents widespread electoral disengagement, low levels of trust and high levels of cynicism about politics and politicians (Dalton, 2004; Stoker, 2006; Hay, 2007; Fox, 2012). Thus, popular connections are made between emotions and politics, and surveys frequently point to citizens' dissatisfaction with politics; but social science, and sociology in particular, seldom considers the role and importance of emotions for electoral politics.

This chapter seeks to highlight the importance of emotions and feelings for understanding electoral (dis)engagement. Social research and analysis has long ignored the role that emotions may play in electoral politics, but recent work highlights the value of an emotionally attuned approach. Moreover, the decline of class as an organising framework for politics means that emotions may play an increasingly important role in citizens' (dis)engagement with electoral politics. The displacement of class means that as people rely less on habitual behaviour or social structure to guide action emotional reflexivity (Holmes, 2010) becomes more important in deliberating and negotiating politics. The emotional turn in politics emerges out of the infectious egalitarianism of mass democracy and manifests itself in an expectation that politicians should present themselves as connected to 'ordinary people' and everyday life. Affinity – and lack of it – is thus a major way of engaging with the polis in an increasingly complex world (see Manning and Holmes, 2014 for a detailed discussion). While high levels of dissatisfaction and electoral disengagement have been registered, many people do still engage with politics, if not through voting. This is happening affectively amid the demise of a grassroots base to party politics (Webb et al, 2002; Whiteley, 2011) and an undermining of the regulatory and identificatory purchase of social institutions like class that previously played central roles in organising citizens' political participation. This chapter will first explore why the social sciences have broadly ignored emotions when examining electoral politics. It will then be argued that social changes may have increased citizens' reliance on emotions and feelings to negotiate an increasingly individualised electoral politics. This will be followed by a discussion of recent qualitative research on the political (dis)engagement of white working-class people in the north of England. The research highlights the potential of taking seriously the role of feelings and emotions in electoral (dis)engagement. The chapter concludes by calling for a more sustained focus on the role of emotions in electoral politics and for future work to examine the ways in which citizens interpret and respond to a politics that is increasingly mediated and pitched at individuals rather than social groups.

Emotion and politics: strange bedfellows?

Before discussing the benefits of researching the role of emotions in political (dis)engagement and deliberation it is important to develop an understanding of why social science has to date broadly ignored their intersection. Several key reasons are discussed below.

For many, emotions and politics, particularly electoral politics, should not mix. At the outset it ought to be recognised that emotion and politics are often understood as dichotomous terms, which points to further binaries (Lloyd, 1984) – man/woman, mind/body, emotion/ reason. Emotion is frequently understood as aligned with nature and belonging to a realm other than politics, perhaps reflecting a broader division in modern societies between public and private. With industrialisation, politics became associated with a public world that is dominated by men, bureaucracy and impersonality; a self-interested world of work, commerce and competition. At the same time a counterweight is imagined for the private sphere of the household and family. These constructions of the private operated to bind women to the realm of nature through a timeless home of nurture, sympathy, benevolence and reproduction (Pateman, 1988; Tronto, 1993). To borrow Lasch's memorable phrase, a *Haven in a Heartless World* (1979). As such, emotions and feelings should be contained within the household and not be allowed to contaminate a public sphere that should be characterised by civility and rationality. Here, 'emotional needs' are understood as primitive barriers to enlightened, rational political decision making (Marcus, 2002). In a somewhat similar argument, emotions are understood as something to which only the masses are susceptible – 'Emotions are seen as irrelevant to the actions of elites' and power more generally (Ost, 2004, p 230).

Advocates of the separation of emotion and politics often point to the manipulation of emotions by politicians and public figures, drawing upon populist and fascist politics as an example of the dangers of mixing politics and emotions. In their influential study, Berelson et al (1954, pp 314–15) argue that a lack of 'passion' or 'affect' for politics is a good thing for the functioning of democracy, as it provides for compromise and resolution of political problems (see also Lipset, 1963; Yeo, 1974; Ost, 2004).

Of course, what lies behind such accounts of fascism is the binary of emotion and politics. Fascism is thought to appeal 'not to rational self-interest, but to emotional needs – often to the most primitive and irrational wishes and fears' (Adorno et al, 1950, p 10). The assumption that fascism is 'irrational' has been powerfully countered by Bauman (1989) in his account of the brutal efficiency of bureaucratic rationality in the final solution. Frankfurt School work like Adorno et al's reinforces the reason/emotion split partly through adherence to Freudian psychoanalysis, producing assumptions that people are ignorant and confused, barely repressing their irrationality under mass-produced conventional opinions. This renders individuals as lacking in any real agency and assumes that reasoning and deliberation are unemotional.

Implicit in such accounts of the effect of emotion on politics is that reason is weak relative to emotion (Marcus, 2002). Concerns about the ability of 'the masses' to exercise reason in political engagement have a long history (for example, Yeo, 1974; Keane, 2010, pp 78–84) and fears about the capacities of particular groups (for example, young people) continue to be raised periodically. Beyond questions of *capacity* for reason, emotions are typically understood as dominant forces too strong for individuals to resist (for example, Le Bon, 1896). Indeed, emotions are often described as powerful, as responses that overwhelm us – 'I was overcome with rage or grief' (see Burkitt, 2014). Emotions well up from within and are described as 'needs', 'impulses' or 'drives'; natural or biological responses that we struggle to control. The anxiety that reason is weak and in need of bolstering can be seen in the range of devices used, and reforms called for, to promote reason in politics: citizen summits and juries, televised leaders' debates, various restrictions on the media, town hall-style meetings with candidates or calls for a digital civic commons (for example, Coleman and Blumler, 2009). Therefore one of the key reasons why emotions have largely been overlooked in social research on politics is because they are understood as a powerful corrupting or contaminating force upon our ability to exercise reason in political participation. According to this perspective it is the dispassionate, reasoned citizens who keep their emotions in check that are best placed to engage in politics.

Beyond a desire to separate emotion and politics, another factor in overlooking the role that emotion may play in politics relates to methodology and disciplinary divisions. For many in the social sciences, emotions suggest something too nebulous and elusive to be the subject of empirical enquiry: how might emotions or feelings be measured? Emotions may also be understood as being firmly within the purview of a discipline like psychology. Furthermore, the study of politics is typically divided up between sociology and political science, with sociology having a focus on social movements and political science covering electoral politics and the operations of government. Indeed, recent sociological work has begun to explore questions of emotions in social movements (for example, Goodwin et al, 2001; Holmes, 2004; Flam and King, 2005; King, 2006; Gould, 2009; Benski and Langman, 2013). In contrast, more sociological approaches pay scant attention to emotions in electoral politics (but see a few chapters in Thompson and Hoggett, 2012; see also Ost, 2004; Coleman, 2013; Demertzis, 2013; Manning and Holmes, 2013, 2014). While electoral politics traditionally falls within the purview of political science, for many, the dominance of positivism and behaviourism curtails a meaningful engagement with questions of emotions. The ascendancy of these epistemologies within political science also tends to mean that the scale of analysis does not lend itself to the study of emotions. Population-based surveys designed to yield generalisable data are not the best tools for a nuanced exploration of the role that emotions and feelings may play in political (dis)engagement and deliberations.

In recent years political scientists have indirectly shown an interest in the role of emotions through work on electoral disengagement and dissatisfaction (see Putnam, 2000; Dalton, 2004; Stoker, 2006; Hay,

2007). Recent research from the UK even refers to the public feeling 'Disgruntled, Disillusioned and Disengaged' with British politics (Fox, 2012, p 877). While the contours of political dissatisfaction have been mapped, often in considerable detail, we have very little data in citizens' own words about why they are increasingly less likely to vote in elections or why they feel so fed up and disappointed with contemporary politics and politicians.

This situation has meant that the study of electoral politics and emotions has been neglected. One discipline has developed an interest in questions of emotion and politics and has the methodological resources and expertise to follow these, but tends to ignore electoral politics. Another relevant discipline is interested in electoral politics, but lacks the interest and methodological traditions to make the most of research in this field. But what is at stake here? Is this just one of many gaps in the knowledge base or does the role of emotion in electoral politics have broader significance than as an academic curiosity? Might there be other pressing reasons to examine emotions and electoral politics? For example, with a nuanced understanding of why people feel disgruntled and disillusioned with politics, reforms could be suggested to address declines in political trust and participation. A fuller understanding of how citizens feel about electoral politics could be part of improving democracy and creating a politics that people want to be a part of. Perhaps more significantly, there may be reason to think that the role that emotion and feelings play in citizens' deliberations about politics has increased.

As class has been expunged from the public lexicon and politics increasingly addresses individuals, social class no longer organises citizens' relationship to politics as it did in the past. In place of a politics organised by class, might emotions and feelings be increasingly drawn upon as citizens negotiate a mediated and individualised electoral politics? The section below argues that emotional reflexivity and feelings of affinity and its lack have become more important in contemporary society and have come to play an augmented role in electoral (dis)engagement.

The increasing importance of emotion in reflexive modernity

The period of 'organised modernity' (Wagner, 1994) between the late 19th century and the early 1970s involved relative political stability, with voting behaviour firmly aligned with social class position (Butler and Stokes, 1969). Governments of this time reconfigured society to minimise uncertainty and impose control after a period of great social, political and technological change. This restructuring was driven by the conventionalisation and homogenisation of practices, including the establishment of mass political parties; Taylorist and Fordist modes of production that also extended and normalised consumption; and the introduction of social security (and later the welfare state), ensuring material security but opening family life to disciplining and homogenising forms of 'scientific' state surveillance (Rose, 1990). This period was characterised by optimism about the future and society's ability to harness the power of science, technology and rationality to ensure the continuation of the prosperity enjoyed during the final decades of this era (Maier, 1970; Harvey, 1989; Rabinbach, 1992).

The period following 'organised modernity' was characterised by increasing uncertainty about the future and the breakdown of the newly established practices. It has variously been described as postmodernity (Lyotard, 1984), *Liquid Modernity* (Bauman, 2000), late modernity (Giddens, 1990) or reflexive modernity (Beck et al, 1994). Reflexivity gains importance as processes of industrialisation and detraditionalisation manufacture a range of unforeseen hazards and side-effects to which societies must respond (Beck, 1992). Beck argues that these catastrophes and on-going risks undermine our confidence in the ability to scientifically control nature, society and the economy, thereby politicising risks. At the same time, the structuring role of traditional institutions becomes obscured and this demands decisions from individuals, or at least that individuals assume responsibility for such decisions. While Beck is clear that individualisation does not mean people are increasingly atomised or alone, he argues that the shift to reflexive modernity accompanies the breakdown of social class as a central concept for organising society. In contrast, I would argue that class continues to shape social outcomes and is an important part of many people's identity (for example, Skeggs, 2004; Reay, 2005; Furlong and Cartmel, 2007). Nonetheless, the organising effects of social structures like class have become obscured from view for many individuals and in a field like politics the language of class has been purged from the rhetoric. Accordingly, social class has declined as a means of organising politics.[1] Social change weakens the hold of class over politics and vote, opening up space for the mediatisation and 'personalisation of politics'.

The argument is that feelings and emotions have seeped into the gap left by the decline of an electoral politics based on identity (see also Manning and Holmes, 2014). In particular, class identity faded as an institutionalised foundation of electoral politics in conjunction with the development of other identity politics, especially around new social movements from the 1960s. For example, the women's movement, civil rights, black power and gay/lesbian movements were based on notions of identity resting on shared experiences as members of an oppressed group. This chapter explores how citizens might construct their needs and interests in (inter)action or, indeed, inaction and disengagement. Instead of vote and class position being closely aligned, I argue that citizens relate to a mediatised politics in a context of detraditionalisation wherein feelings and emotions are useful for understanding the on-going ways in which citizens experience (dis)engagement with politics and politicians.

Thus, social class may not organise politics as in the past, but it remains culturally and personally important for many people and plays a key role in how citizens relate and connect to electoral politics and politicians (see Anderson, Yang and Heath, 2006; Heath et al, 2009). Precisely how citizens do this in reflexive modernity remains under-researched. To elaborate on this is to recognise people's critical and agentic judgement of politics and politicians. There is no doubt that various factors like policy, leadership, demographics and economics impact on election outcomes. Yet the shifting of structures that previously oriented people to politics requires new ways of relating to and interpreting politics, policies and politicians. Feelings and emotions appear important in such (dis)connections, drawing emotions into citizens' reflexive deliberations about politics.[2]

Understanding the role of feelings and emotion in people's reflexive engagements with politics requires a concept of reflexivity attuned to an emotional register. Beck and Giddens have promoted a predominantly cognitive model of reflexivity, situating the project of self within an emerging social need to monitor, calculate and respond to new risks or to the impact of detraditionalisation (Giddens, 1991; Beck, 1992). Lash and Urry (1994; Beck et al, 1994) have extended this model through their notion of aesthetic reflexivity, which involves the interpretation of aesthetic symbols, images and allegory. This moves us towards a more embodied notion of reflexivity, but the role of emotions in these accounts is distinctly lacking.

The need to emotionalise reflexivity

As outlined above, the shift to reflexive modernisation unleashes great uncertainty and diminishing confidence in our ability to tame and control the future. Giddens has focused on processes of detraditionalisation and explored the ontological insecurity that emerges under these conditions, where knowledge is constantly revised and there are no firm foundations upon which to base action; in the words of Beck and Beck-Gernsheim (2001, p 26), 'there are no historical models for the conduct of life'. For Giddens (1990), trust therefore becomes central to sociality and people increasingly rely upon abstract systems and experts, while Beck and Beck-Gernsheim have discussed the experimentation of do-it-yourself biographies (2001). These strategies do not account for the need to make decisions in the face of conflicting truth claims or for the part that emotions may play in constructing experimental biographies. In contrast, I draw upon a notion of reflexivity that holds emotions as central to the way people relationally interact with the world around them and reproduce the social. Emotional reflexivity is an embodied, cognitive and relational process in which social actors have feelings about and try to understand and alter their lives in relation to their social and natural environment and to others (Holmes, 2010). It is about how emotion[3] 'infuses' our perceptions of the world, others and oneself (Burkitt, 2012, p 458). In the context of this chapter, emotional reflexivity means recognising how feelings are part of citizens' (dis)engagements with politics.[4]

Clearly, research exploring citizens' emotional relationships with politics and politicians is very limited, but we do have some broad indications of the kinds of emotional responses citizens may have. As noted above, survey-based research suggests that British citizens feel 'disgruntled', 'disillusioned' and dissatisfied, and the widespread electoral disengagement identified in numerous established democracies support such accounts. Given this context of electoral disengagement, it seems likely that, when provided the opportunity to express their views in their own words, citizens will emphasise feelings of a lack of affinity between themselves, their daily lives and concerns and those of their elected representatives. Feelings of frustration, resentment and anger at the perceived disconnection of the political elite are also likely. Going beyond a quantitative mapping of electoral disengagement to explore the key emotional drivers lying behind this withdrawal is important, as it will help us to better understand how to create a politics that people care enough about to want to be involved.

The findings of the study reported below take a small step towards uncovering some of the ways in which *citizens* use feelings and emotions in their (dis)engagements with politics. In contrast to the dearth of research on citizens' emotional relationships with electoral politics, there are numerous examples of the ways in which politicians performatively use emotions, particularly as a means of gesturing at connections with everyday life and the general public. They attend popular sporting events or profess interest in popular culture; domestic imagery and context is used to 'humanise' them as parents and spouses (Langer 2010, 2012). In Australia, politicians (including prime ministers and opposition leaders) routinely sit in the front seat of chauffeured vehicles to avoid charges of snobbery (FitzSimons, 2012). US presidents choose inexpensive wrist watches while in office;[5] or British Tories were reportedly instructed not to drink champagne at the 2010 party conference when the government was about to introduce severe public spending cuts (Hope, 2010). We know much less about how these performances and the other communication strategies of politicians are *interpreted* by citizens and the role that feelings and emotions may play in their political deliberations.

The study

To help substantiate my argument about the value of examining the role emotions may play in electoral politics, I will draw upon material collected for a project on political dissatisfaction among members of the white working class in northern England (see Holmes and Manning, 2013; Manning and Holmes 2013). Fieldwork involved 12 semi-structured interviews with white participants doing semi- or unskilled work for low wages in Yorkshire and the North West (Barnsley, Burnley, Doncaster, Hull) prior to the 2010 UK general election. This was exploratory work that drew on a relatively small sample, but quantitative research conducted around the same time echoed some of the key findings (see Chappell et al, 2010).

Cold canvassing was used to identify and recruit participants from appropriate businesses in the towns selected. A few participants were referred to us by others. Waiters, bar staff, hairdressers, warehouse assistants, a courier and a bookkeeper for a trade supply firm and an administrator participated. This sample was broadly 'white working class' in background, most having no education beyond high school, and those who did (including the administrator) were still working in low-paid and mostly semi-skilled jobs. Only two participants (the bookkeeper and the courier) earned over £20,000, but they did not earn over £30,000 (roughly the national average) and had no higher education (Holmes and Manning, 2013).

Semi-structured interviews of about one hour's duration were used to explore participants' feelings about politics, politicians and parties. Questions were asked about why participants thought people were upset by the Westminster Members of Parliament (MPs) expenses scandal,[6] and what they thought were the most important problems politicians should be addressing. The latter question included prompts about whether those problems were evident in their local area or what the pressing problems in their local area were. The interviews were audio-recorded and took place in participants' homes, workplaces (cafes/pubs, warehouses and hairdressers) or nearby cafes. Anonymised audio files were professionally transcribed and thematically analysed by the researchers, separately in the first instance. An iterative process of immersion in the data and discussion between the researchers generated the final themes. Participants were not apathetic, as in simply uninterested, but were actively cynical about politics (Bhavnani, 1991), expressing this in terms of doubt, scepticism and critique. Their active rather than apathetic disengagement was also evident in expressions of frustration and resentfulness, as seen in the following sections covering the key themes.

'Ordinary people' struggling for connection

Respondents generally felt cynical towards politicians, viewing them as wealthy elites unlikely to be interested in the concerns of 'ordinary people'. Doreen,[7] a retired nurse from Barnsley, articulated this when she said of David Cameron: "Oh well he's a, he's snooty 'im" and "[h]e'll not be really interested in ordinary, what I class as ordinary people". Similar cynicism about the ability of elites to represent 'ordinary' people was voiced by others when respondents were asked how they felt about the upcoming 2010 election. As Mick, a cook in his twenties from Doncaster said:

> "take David Cameron for instance, you know, he weren't just born with a silver spoon in his mouth, he had the whole damn cutlery tray in his mouth, you know what I mean, how can that guy, how can that guy, you know, represent me? He can't, it's impossible, do you know what I mean, that guy will not be able to know what I, what I want from my local community ..."

Josh, who is in his mid-twenties and works in a bar in Doncaster, echoed this sense of disjuncture from privileged politicians.

> "I think, without being too crude, they're a bunch of jumped-up ponces that don't really know – they were all born with silver spoons in their mouth. And I sound really bitter about that but it's just I don't think, if you, you could

put any one of them in a room with say a bunch of my friends because there'd be nothing in common, they'd [sic] be no grounds to, grounds for common interests; it'd just be totally uncomfortable I think."

Richard, who is in his fifties and a bookkeeper for a tool company in Burnley, also thought David Cameron would face significant challenges in connecting with 'ordinary' people:

Interviewer: What about David Cameron? As a, as a leader of the Conservative Party what do you, how do you feel about him as a leader?

Richard: Well not too much in favour of him, he's a, well, he's a, like a rich guy so, although Tony Blair's enriched himself as Britain's prime minister, I wouldn't say he'd be my choice as the next prime minister if he does become so, I'd prefer William Hague myself but and as a Yorkshire man … Plus he seems more down to earth, like David Cameron went to Eton, which is nothing against him personally, I'm sure he didn't choose to go to Eton but it's that sort of, that is, in its own way doesn't identify him with the ordinary working man because really it's, it's the ordinary working man sort of varying between voting for the Labour Party and voting for the Conservatives that makes a difference as to which party comes to power really …

Participants indicated their suspicions about the ability of politicians to understand their local situation, but also emphasised the importance of politicians showing a connection to local conditions, as suggested above. The mention of the local almost always came spontaneously when participants answered questions on how they felt about the party leaders and other politicians. Richard and Doreen highlight local connections when they talk about politicians they like. Doreen says she likes Nick Clegg "cos he's from Sheffield … Oh aye, he's Yorkshire born. I like him, yeah … I like his, way he comes across." While Richard says, "I'd prefer William Hague [for Prime Minister] myself … as a Yorkshire man." They do not explain why they like people from their own locale; it seems that it is thought to be obvious. Although most respondents are reflexive about the problems of their local communities, unlike some (for example, Putnam, 2000), they blame disengagement on politicians not on citizens' failing to participate in civil society. Participants charged politicians with being unable to reach out and communicate across social divisions and understood this as a driver of their political disengagement.

On the other hand, some participants drew upon examples of politicians who showed 'passion' or conveyed knowledge, and suggested that these traits helped their engagement and undermined cynicism. Elizabeth, a Hull courier in her fifties, thought Margaret Thatcher had something that present politicians do not, which she explained when asked whether she thought that the Conservatives 'care about the concerns of people like you'.

> "Well they'll say they will, won't they, to get into power? I mean I went through the Maggie Thatcher years as a, as a lot younger than I am now obviously, and not a lover or a hater, some policies you like and some you didn't. You got the feeling she cared, that she was passionate about her country; not sure I get the same feeling about people in now but that was her as a personality coming through wasn't it?"

Elizabeth did not always like her policies but expressed admiration for Margaret Thatcher as someone who 'cared'. She valued Thatcher's 'passionate' approach; in contrast to contemporary politicians she was able to be convincing in her performances through her emotional engagement and conviction (see Stearns, 1997). Similarly, Mick, who was a staunch Labour supporter, indicated that politicians who convey sound knowledge are appealing even when they belong to other political parties:

> "I do like some of the, Vince Cable, that's the one, Liberal Democrats, […] But that guy should be, you know, make him prime minister because he, every time I hear him speak that guy knows what he's talking about."

From these responses it is clear that participants are not apathetic, they are willing to listen, but they are typically unsatisfied by politicians' attempts to talk to them. Moreover, their responses lay the blame for dissatisfaction and disengagement at the feet of politicians. Unlike accounts that view declining political participation as part of a broader downward trend in social capital (for example, Putnam, 2000), respondents see politicians' elite backgrounds, cynical performances, lack of genuine 'care', 'passion' and interest and understanding for 'ordinary' people as responsible for disengagement.

Frustration, resentment and indignation: politicians' ignoring economic disadvantage

Participants in this study were not apathetic but critical and felt frustrated and indignant towards politics and politicians. Labour was described by several as particularly disappointing. John, who worked in a warehouse in Burnley, thought Labour should be advocating for working people but instead "talk[ed] down" to 'ordinary' citizens. Others also thought Labour had abandoned its role as the party that fights for social and economic justice. Mark, a waiter from Doncaster, explained his frustration with the Labour Party's shift to the centre Right and its courting of the financial sector:

> "The Tory party are pretty much really the same as they ever were, it's, the disappointment is the Labour Party have gone closer towards the Tory party, you know, which is frustrating because, you know, you'd expect Labour party to sort of look out for working people, you know, but it seems like, like the way they treat, the way they dealt with the City and the way they sort of liberalised the City followed on what the Tories did and sort of said we can live on the wealth of the City while the good times go and then when it all blows up in your face they're like, they were partly to, they, they did nothing to sort of regulate the banks."

The sense of 'disappointment' and frustration with there being no one in politics to 'look out for working people' was expressed by many participants.

Questions about the Westminster expenses scandal also drew very clear criticisms. Participants' comments revealed feelings of moral outrage, hurt and disappointment at politicians' appropriation of public money for private gain, and also at the way politicians failed to appreciate their privilege relative to the socioeconomic deprivations and precarity of life for 'ordinary' working taxpayers (Standing, 2011). As Tom, a waiter in Burnley, expressed it in this exasperated comment: "Well, expenses is one thing, but daylight robbery is another, you know [laughs]." He went on to say:

> "You know, the working man in the street who puts these people into power is – has always, but more now in the present climate – is struggling to put food on the table, struggling to make ends meet. You know, I'm one of those

people ... life isn't easy, it's not fun, it's very difficult. You know, I barely have enough money to buy food, socialising has stopped completely. So, if I can't afford to do that, why should somebody who I've put in power – you know with the money that's taken from me in tax – then make their life rosier? I think that's pretty much the bottom line, isn't it."

Richard, like others, drew a clear distinction between legitimate, work-related expenses and those claimed dishonestly for personal gain:

"The, the idea is that generally speaking like the MP for Burnley would ideally be a Burnley person, [...] he or she would be expected to spend a great deal of time in London obviously and would need somewhere to live and the expenses is to cover that necessity and shouldn't really be done to sort of increase your salary from an MP's salary, which, which to me is a wonderful salary. To claim on top of that legitimate living expenses for living in London, fine, but anything other than that to, for these ridiculous things are, you know, like downright dishonesty where people have been claiming like mortgage interest on mortgages that have been already redeemed and finished with, that's just theft isn't it?"

Richard's moral outrage is clear in his comments about claiming for "ridiculous things" and the "dishonesty" of abusing the claims system. Such indignation was shared by most participants and also led to feeling demoralised and a sense that people had lost respect for politicians, as seen in the comments first from Josh and then from Elizabeth:

Josh: I just think it's ridiculous and I'm glad they've all been made to pay back and I'm glad half of them have had to resign over it because I just think it's ridiculous and the amount of money that they do get paid to then take advantage of the system I think is out of order and again disheartening.

Elizabeth: So I think they deserve [to be caught and exposed], and paying it back and saying sorry doesn't wash because [...] they've got the money to do it and then they expect everything to carry on as if nothing had happened, it just seems a bit shallow and if they can behave like that in, in that small area it makes you wonder when there's something of a bigger, bigger question they're trying to, you know, deal with and answer, does their character then not allow them to be honest within that bigger picture of things? You know, I don't know, you don't know do you, you don't know what type of people they are [...] I just think it's deceitful. I think a lot of people now, I'd say yeah, the respect's gone.

Participants viewed politics as an occupation for wealthy people and they were cynical about them using it for their own advancement. Andrew, a clerk from Doncaster, said:

"One of the main problems with our political system is it costs money to be in politics and that stops ordinary people from going into politics. If you look at the make-up of all the politicians we've got, they're all lawyers, bank managers, all these, you know well-off people in the first place, who go into politics. And it doesn't do their image any good when you have one of these expenses scandals happens on top of that [laughs]."

The Westminster expenses scandal dramatically highlighted just how disconnected many politicians are from 'ordinary' citizens. When talking about the scandal, John explained how it showed that politicians had no comprehension of their privileged position:

"Well I mean I look at that that some of them, their expenses is more than I earn in a year, a lot of them have haven't they? Somebody, was it today on the news saying that they've paid back forty-five thousand pound? One woman MP, she's had to pay forty-five thousand pound back. I mean that's twice what I earn in a year.... I mean it's the amount of money that was involved, you know, when people, there's other people, I mean I'm on twenty-odd thousand a year but there's other people who are struggling along on twelve thousand a year, you know, and they can't afford to do anything and then somebody's claiming for a floating duck house and a moat to be cleaned, several thousand pound and, you know, they can't even go on holiday."

John paints a stark picture of socioeconomic inequality and corruption. His comments, and those of other participants, are inflected with moral outrage and resentment at the misappropriation of public money for private benefit by privileged people in privileged positions. For other participants like Amy, a young hairdresser from Doncaster, this case also highlighted the way one set of rules seems to apply for politicians while another is used for regular citizens:

> "I think because obviously we, if we did it we'd get done, wouldn't we? You know, us sort of general public – and they're getting away with it."

Below, Mick also powerfully indicts the moral integrity of MPs and argues that the expenses scandal further reinforced a lack of affinity between 'rich' politicians and struggling working people:

> "[I]t just stinks, you know, they just abuse the system that because it's been abused for so long, it's like well that's all right then, you know, they haven't sort of looked past their own ignorance and stupidity, do you know what I mean? Just because somebody's been doing it wrong before, you know, two wrongs don't make a right […] You know, that's why people were so, and rightly so, aggrieved about it, you know. […] So the reason that people were so annoyed at the expenses because everyone was losing their jobs and nobody had any money and then we had all this sleaze about them getting extra money on top of the, you know, ridiculous amounts that they're already getting and the, you know, people saying well it's, it's all right, it's like, no, no, hang on, it's our money, you know, I know it's not our money because we pay taxes for a reason but, you know, that's our taxpayers' money, you know what I mean?"

Like other participants, Mick was trying to lead a 'decent' life by working hard and paying taxes. In the fall-out from the financial crisis he and others worried about the future of their jobs and watched friends and family members lose theirs, while their elected representatives were earning "ridiculous amounts" of money and failing to convey any genuine comprehension of the circumstances of 'ordinary' citizens. The expenses scandal was a rare moment wherein the gross inequalities between many citizens and their political leaders were revealed and received sustained attention in public debate. Participants were clear in their criticisms of the socio-political conditions that allowed such things to happen and profoundly dissatisfied with electoral politics as a whole.

The participants in this study were, like others, implicated in the individualisation of politics (Manning, 2013), but not in the ways often suggested. The collective and class-based nature of electoral politics has all but disappeared, and yet for these participants at least, the sense of shared material inequality persists (although this did not always extend across lines of ethnicity, see Holmes and Manning, 2013). Instead of looking to politicians to draw them together as workers exploited by capitalism, they desired politicians who showed some kind of affinity with themselves and their lives; to connect with politicians and feel as though they understood and cared about 'ordinary' people and everyday struggles. As clearly expressed above, for this group of participants politicians fall short of their expectations by a wide margin. They find it difficult to connect to politicians who are increasingly drawn from narrow, elite social backgrounds (House of Commons Library, 2010; Sutton Trust, 2010). Participants are critical of politicians' inability to talk across social divides, and interpret their communication styles as disingenuous and patronising. For these participants, political dissatisfaction and disengagement arises in part from the dynamics of affinity politics itself – politicians' attempts to perform connection with 'ordinary' citizens and everyday life are routinely perceived as false and inauthentic. Understanding political (dis)engagement in this way helps to reveal the critical work and actual engagement and critique required by a cynical political stance. Instead of apathy, participants articulated criticisms of a political system that embodies and reproduces privilege and fails to address the gross inequalities manifested in British society. The question of whether these participants vote, and are thereby considered politically engaged, is secondary to their sense of isolation from a political system that does not seem to be for "the likes of us".

Concluding remarks

This chapter has demonstrated some of the ways in which citizens continue to make demands of their political leaders via an affective interpretive frame. Citizens are not completely atomised (compare Bauman, 1999), electoral politics is not simply characterised by emotionless rational calculation of interests. Citizens' relationship with politics is often reduced to a kind of loathing,[8] but as the research outlined above shows, our emotional engagement with politics and politicians is much more complex than feelings of 'hate' alone.

A qualitative approach attuned to the emotional dimensions of citizens' engagements with electoral politics helps to shift the debate about political disengagement away from the failures of individual citizens, who apparently no longer possess the knowledge or moral fortitude to participate, towards the failings of a political system that embodies and reproduces inequalities. Nonetheless, it is difficult to see how power relations may be altered by these critiques, given the individualised context in which they occur. It is the demise of a politics organised by class that provides for emotional reflexivity to play a larger role in citizens' political engagements, but this shift has also seriously undermined the potential for collectivism to change politics. Social class has largely been expunged from the public and party-political lexicon, and in its absence citizens are frequently parcelled up into small electoral niches, despite any continued cross-cutting salience of socioeconomic deprivation to their lives. Running in parallel with the decline of collectivist political forms, the grassroots basis of mass political parties has also all but disappeared. While emotions may be an important basis for citizens' critiques of a mediatised, professionalised politics, it is a poor substitute for a party system with a vibrant grassroots base, genuine participation and links to local communities.

Being attuned to the emotional dimensions of electoral (dis) engagement can help to challenge the common assumption that disengaged citizens are necessarily individualised and apathetic by highlighting the critical work of citizens and the failures of political elites to meaningfully connect. Exploring the role of emotion in electoral politics unsettles divisions between emotion and rationality and offers a fruitful line of inquiry into how feelings and emotions are part of reasoning, reflexivity and agency (see also Burkitt, 2014). Furthermore, following Ost (2004, p 229), such a programme of research should also be about revealing the ways in which elites, electoral politics and power in general are intimately involved with emotions rather than understood as coolly unemotional and simply concerned with 'rational calculation of interest'.

Further empirical work is required to qualitatively flesh out the role of emotions in people's deliberations about politics and the ways in which feelings and emotions are drawn upon in political (dis) engagements by different social groups. A wide range of emotions are part of electoral politics and sustained scholarly investigation of the role of emotions in people's political (dis)engagements is long overdue. Sociology has a key role to play here, with its broad range of methodological and theoretical tools. Perhaps more consequentially, applying the sociological imagination (Mills, 1959) to give voice to and link up individualised criticisms of electoral politics into a public issue about the failings and inadequacies of our political system should form part of a critical, committed, public sociology (Burawoy, 2005).

Notes

[1] Nonetheless, I would not want to argue that contemporary politics is defined only by the politicisation of risks, post-materialist agendas or the abandonment of emancipatory politics. Cohort and generational dynamics have a role to play here, but so too do socio-economic conditions. Much of Europe is currently engaged in bitter battles to retain social services and some semblance of state welfare provision. The Occupy movement also provided a dramatic example of how materialist agendas retain relevance in contemporary politics. Indeed, the research discussed below highlights the on-going salience of socioeconomic inequality and social immobility.

[2] Affective strategies are available to both citizens and politicians and the question of whose affective allegiance politicians and parties seek will be important for future empirical work. For example, are specific groups, like young people or ethnic minorities, ignored at both a policy and affective level?)

[3] Burkitt helpfully distinguishes between feelings and emotions by arguing that feelings may be vague and amorphous until clearly identified and named as a specific emotion (Burkitt 2002).

[4] However, politics is just one sphere of society in which emotional reflexivity is increasingly necessary (Holmes 2010).

[5] Clinton famously wore an inexpensive American watch when in office, but has since developed a reputation for collecting luxury watches (Buchanan, 2008).

[6] This scandal had been brewing but erupted when, in May 2009, the *Telegraph* newspaper published leaked information detailing MPs' abuses of expenses claims.

[7] All names used are pseudonyms.

[8] Hay (2007) draws upon the cultural currency of these depictions in the title of his book *Why We Hate Politics*.

References

Adorno, T.W, Frenkel-Brunswik, E, Levinson, D.J. and Sanford, R.N. (1950) *The Authoritarian Personality*, New York: Harper & Brothers.

Ali, T. (2011) 'Egypt's joy as Mubarak quits. *The Guardian*, 11 February. Available at: http://www.theguardian.com/commentisfree/2011/feb/11/egypt-cairo-hosni-mubarak (accessed 5 March 2013).

Anderson, R, Yang, M. and Heath, A.F. (2006) 'Class Politics and Political Context in Britain, 1964–1997: Have Voters Become More Individualized?', *European Sociological Review*, vol 22, no 2, pp 215–28.

Bauman, Z. (1989) *Modernity and the Holocaust,* Cambridge: Polity Press.

Bauman, Z. (1999) *In Search of Politics,* Cambridge: Polity Press.

Bauman, Z. (2000) *Liquid Modernity*, Cambridge: Polity Press.

Beck, U. (1992) *Risk society: towards a new modernity*, London: Sage Publications.

Beck, U. and Beck-Gernsheim, E. (2001) *Individualization: Institutionalized Individualism and its Social and Political Consequences*, London: Sage.

Beck, U, Giddens, A. and Lash, S. (1994) *Reflexive Modernization: Politics, Tradition and Aesthetics in the Modern Social Order,* Cambridge: Polity Press.

Benski, T. and Langman, L. (2013) 'The effects of affects: The place of emotions in the mobilizations of 2011', *Current Sociology*, vol 61, no 4, pp 525–40.

Berelson, B, Lazarfeld, P.F. and McPhee, W. (1954) *Voting*, Chicago: University of Chicago Press.

Bhavnani, K. (1991) *Talking Politics,* Cambridge: Cambridge University Press.

Burawoy, M. (2005) 'For Public Sociology', *American Sociological Review*, vol 70, no 1, pp 4–28.

Burkitt, I. (2002) 'Complex emotions: Relations, feelings and images in emotional experience. In: Barbalet, J. (ed) *Emotions and Sociology*, Oxford: Blackwell, pp 151–67.

Burkitt, I. (2012) 'Emotional Reflexivity: Feeling, Emotion and Imagination in Reflexive Dialogues', *Sociology*, vol 46, no 3, pp 458–72.

Burkitt, I. (2014) *Emotions and Social Relations*, London: Sage.

Butler, D. and Stokes, D. (1969) *Political change in Britain: forces shaping electoral choice,* London: Macmillan.

Chappell, L, Clifton, J, Gottfried, G. and Lawton, K. (2010) 'Exploring the roots of BNP support', an Institute for Public Policy Research briefing paper, available from: http://www.ippr.org.uk/publication/55/1766/exploring-the-roots-of-bnp-support [Accessed 21 April 2013].

Coleman, S. (2013) *How Voters Feel*, Cambridge: Cambridge University Press.

Coleman, S. and Blumler, J.G. (2009) *The Internet and Democratic Citizenship*, Cambridge: Cambridge University Press.

Cornwell, R. (2010) 'Hurricane Katrina: The storm that shamed America', *The Independent*, 20 August. Available at: http://www.independent.co.uk/news/world/americas/hurricane-katrina-the-storm-that-shamed-america-2057164.html (accessed 5 March 2013).

Dalton, R.J. (2004) *Democratic Challenges, Democratic Choices: The Erosion of Political Support in Advanced Industrial Democracies,* Oxford: Oxford University Press.

Demertzis, N. (ed) (2013) *Emotions in Politics. The Affect Dimension in Political Tension*, Basingstoke: Palgrave.

FitzSimons, P. (2012) 'Has Newman got life back to front?' *Sydney Morning Herald*, 15 April. Available at: http://www.smh.com.au/opinion/politics/has-newman-got-life-back-to-front-20120414-1x043.html (accessed 15 November 2012).

Flam, H. and King, D. (2005) *Emotions and Social Movements*, London: Routledge.

Fox, R. (2012) 'Disgruntled, Disillusioned and Disengaged: Public Attitudes to Politics in Britain Today', *Parliamentary Affairs*, vol 65, pp 877–87.

Furlong, A. and Cartmel, F. (2007) *Young People and Social change* (2nd edn), Maidenhead: Open University Press.

Giddens, A. (1990) *The Consequences of Modernity,* Cambridge: Polity Press.

Giddens, A. (1991) *Modernity and Self-Identity: Self and Society in Late Modern Age,* Cambridge: Polity Press.

Goodwin, J, Jasper, J.M. and Poletta, F. (eds) (2001) *Passionate Politics: Emotions and Social Movements,* Chicago: University of Chicago Press.

Gould, D. (2009) *Moving Politics: Emotion and ACT UP's Fight against AIDS*, Chicago: University of Chicago Press.

Harvey, D. (1989) *The Condition of Post-Modernity: An Enquiry into the Origins of Social Change*, Oxford: Blackwell.

Hay, C. (2007) *Why We Hate Politics*, Cambridge: Polity Press.

Heath, A, Curtice, J. and Elgenius, G. (2009) 'Individualization and the Decline of Class Identity', in M. Wetherell (ed) *Identity in the 21st Century: New Trends in Changing Times*, Basingstoke: Palgrave Macmillan, pp 21–40.

Holmes, M. (2004) 'Feeling Beyond Rules Politicizing the Sociology of Emotion and Anger in Feminist Politics', *European Journal of Social Theory*, vol 7, no 2, pp 209–27.

Holmes, M. (2010) 'The emotionalization of reflexivity', *Sociology*, vol 44, no 1, pp 139–154.

Holmes, M. and Manning, N. (2013) '"Them that runs the country don't know what they're doing": Political Dissatisfaction Amongst Members of the White Working Class', *The Sociological Review*, vol 61, pp 479–98

Hope, C. (2010) '"No champagne please – we're Tories!" Party tries to set sober tone for annual conference', *The Telegraph*, 2 October. Available at: http://www.telegraph.co.uk/news/politics/8036803/No-champagne-please-were-Tories-Party-tries-to-set-sober-tone-for-annual-conference.html (accessed 19 November 2012)

House of Commons Library (2010) *Social background of MPs*. SN/SG/1528: 14 December. Available at: http://www.parliament.uk/briefing-papers

Keane, J. (2010) *The Life and Death of Democracy*, London: Pocket Books.

King, D.S. (2006) 'Activists and emotional reflexivity: Toward Touraine's subject as social movement', *Sociology*, vol 40, no 5, pp 873–91.

Langer, A.I. (2010) 'The politicization of private persona: Exceptional leaders or the new rule? The case of the UK and the Blair effect', *International Journal of Press/Politics*, vol 15, no 1, pp 60–76.

Langer, A.I. (2012) *The Personalisation of Politics in the UK: Mediated Leadership from Attlee to Cameron*, Manchester: Manchester University Press.

Langman, L. (2013) 'Occupy: A new social movement', *Current Sociology*, vol 61, no 4, pp 510–24.

Lasch, C. (1979) *Haven in a heartless world: the family besieged*, New York: Basic Books.

Lash, S. and Urry, J. (1994) *Economies of Signs and Space*, London: Sage.

Le Bon, G. (1896) *The Crowd: A Study off the Popular Mind*, New York: Macmillan.

Lewis, P. and Dodd, V. (2010) 'Families of Iraq war dead voice anger at "smirking" Blair', *The Guardian*, 29 January. Available at: http://www.theguardian.com/uk/2010/jan/29/tony-blair-iraq-war-inquiry1 (accessed 5 March 2013).

Lipset, S.M. (1963) *Political Man*, New York: Doubleday.

Lloyd, G. (1984) *The Man of Reason: 'Male' and 'Female' in Western Philosophy*, London: Methuen.

Lyotard, J.-F. (1984) *The Postmodern Condition: A Report on Knowledge*, Manchester: Manchester University Press.

Maier, C.S. (1970) 'Between Taylorism and Technocracy: European Ideologies and the Vision of Industrial Productivity in the 1920s', *Journal of Contemporary History*, vol 5, no 2, pp 27–63.

Manning, N. (2013) '"I mainly look at things on an issue by issue basis." Reflexivity and Phronêsis: Young Adults Conceptualisation and Practice of Politics', *Journal of Youth Studies*, vol 16, no 1, pp 17–33.

Manning, N. and Holmes, M. (2013): 'He's snooty 'im': exploring 'white working class' political disengagement', *Citizenship Studies*, vol 17, no 3–4, pp 479–90.

Manning, N. and Holmes, M. (2014) 'Political emotions: A role for feelings of affinity in citizens' (dis)engagements with electoral politics?' *Sociology*, vol 48, no 4, pp 698–714.

Marcus, G.E. (2002) *The Sentimental Citizen. Emotion in Democratic Politics*, University Park, PA: Pennsylvania State University Press.

Mills, C. Wright (1959) *The Sociological Imagination*, New York: Oxford University Press.

Ost, D. (2004) 'Politics as the Mobilization of Anger: Emotions in Movements and in Power', *European Journal of Social Theory*, vol 7, no 2, pp 229–44.

Pateman, C. (1988) *The sexual contract*, Cambridge: Polity.

Putnam, R. (2000) *Bowling alone: the collapse and revival of American community*, New York: Simon and Schuster.

Rabinbach, A. (1992) *The Human Motor: Energy, Fatigue, and the Origins of Modernity*, Berkeley: University of California Press.

Reay, D. (2005) 'Beyond consciousness? The psychic landscape of social class', *Sociology*, vol 39, no 5, pp 911–28.

Rose, N. (1990) *Governing the Soul: The Shaping of the Private Self*, London: Routledge.

Skeggs, B. (2004) *Class, Self, Culture*, London: Routledge.

Standing, G. (2011) *The precariat: the new dangerous class*, London: Bloomsbury Academic.

Stearns, P.N. (1997) 'Emotional Change and Political Disengagement in the Twentieth-Century United States: A Case Study in Emotions History', *Innovation*, vol 10, no 4, pp 361–80.

Stoker, G. (2006) *Why Politics Matters: Making Democracy Work*, Basingstoke: Palgrave Macmillan.

Sutton Trust (2010) *The Educational Background of the Members of Parliament in 2010*. Available at: http://www.suttontrust.com/research/the-educational-backgrounds-of-mps

Thompson, S. and Hoggett, P. (eds) (2012) *Politics and the Emotions: The Affective Turn in Contemporary Political Studies*, London: Continuum.

Tronto, J.C. (1993) *Moral boundaries: a political argument for an ethic of care*, New York: Routledge.

Wagner, P. (1994) *A Sociology of Modernity: Liberty and Discipline*, London: Routledge.

Webb, P, Farrell, D. and Holiday, I. (2002) *Political Parties in Advanced Industrial Democracies*, Oxford: Oxford University Press.

Whiteley, P.F. (2011) 'Is the party over? The decline of party activism and membership across the democratic world', *Party Politics*, vol 17, no 1, pp 21–44.

Yeo, S. (1974) 'On the uses of "apathy"', *European Journal of Sociology*, vol 15, no 2, pp 279–311, doi: 10.1017/S0003975600002940

SIX

UK Uncut: direct action against austerity

Tim Street

Introduction

Over the last few years my involvement in UK Uncut has taken several different forms. For example, I have regularly participated in its actions and protests, written articles and blogs about the campaign, given interviews to the media as a spokesperson and was a director of UK Uncut Legal Action, whose work I discuss below. I thought it would be worthwhile to write this chapter to reflect on what Uncut has achieved so far, and the strengths and weaknesses of its model of activism. This model has mainly involved people taking direct action in their local communities against the Coalition's public spending cuts by occupying branches of tax-dodging companies and demanding that the government make these companies pay their fair share. Such grassroots action not only motivated many more people across the country to organise their own protests, but connected strongly with the public at large by presenting a clear and strong message about why the government's reckless austerity agenda had to be stopped and how this could be done.

I begin by discussing how the movement got going, before touching on its use of mainstream and social media and the different tactics and forms of action used to protest against austerity and highlight the alternatives. I put these actions in context, looking at the social movements Uncut grew out of and how it relates to other political groups and issues. Finally, I describe some of Uncut's protests from my own perspective, considering the movement's overall significance and the importance of direct action as a tool for achieving social and political change.

How UK Uncut started

UK Uncut was born on 27 October 2010, just one week after Chancellor George Osborne announced the deepest cuts to public spending since the 1920s (Guardian, 2010). Around 70 people ran along Oxford Street in London, entered Vodafone's flagship store and sat down to protest at the company avoiding billions in tax (Murphy, 2010). Three days later a second day of action took place, with protesters claiming to have closed 'at least twenty-one' Vodafone stores across the UK (UK Uncut, 2010b). A few months later, and UK Uncut actions had spread to up to 50 towns and cities and several tax-dodging targets. Everyone from 'pensioners to teenagers, veterans to newbies' took part in actions in towns 'from Aberdeen to Aberystwyth' (UK Uncut, 2013a). Something was in the air – a mood and atmosphere built on deep feelings of anger and a need for meaningful resistance to austerity.

I'd heard about the idea for the first action through a friend who had started an e-mail discussion with several activists, many of whom knew each other from university or previous campaigns and protests. The plan was to meet at 9.30am prompt on the day of the action outside The Ritz. People were told in the call-out for the as yet unnamed group's action to 'Look for the orange umbrella. The Ritz is not our target. The target and plan will be revealed at the meeting point and then we'll be on the move very quickly so please, please be on time' (UK Uncut, 2010a). These lines capture something of the energy around Uncut's initial actions – protesting was being made adventurous, bold and exciting by a new generation of activists.

Yet behind the buzz and bravado, these young protestors were out to make a serious point. They were taking action to show that there was an alternative to austerity and to oppose the government's mantra that the UK was broke and that 'we are all in this together'. Such statements were shown to be falsehoods by the fact that the poor, vulnerable and marginalised were being made to pay for an economic crisis caused by the banks while rich individuals and corporations were dodging huge sums in tax. For example, at the same time that Osborne introduced a further £7 billion in welfare cuts, news had emerged that Her Majesty's Revenue and Customs (HMRC) had let Vodafone off paying £6 billion in tax. *Private Eye* had published a story by journalist and former tax inspector Richard Brooks detailing how HMRC (backed by Gordon Brown's Labour government) had taken Vodafone to court to recover the £6 billion. HMRC had won after a lengthy legal battle, only for George Osborne to let Vodafone escape paying what it owed (Shackle, 2011).

As more people took part in the actions and the media caught on to the level of public support for the protests, more stories of tax dodging came to light. Multi-billionaire businessman Sir Phillip Green was found to have dodged £285 million, leading to flashmob protests in branches of Topshop – owned by his Arcadia group. In 2005 Green awarded himself £1.2 billion, the biggest pay cheque in British corporate history. This dividend payout was channelled through a network of offshore accounts, via tax havens in Jersey, and eventually to the Monaco bank account of Green's wife's (Taylor et al, 2010). Since then, stories of well-known high street names engaged in tax dodging have snowballed, with new revelations regularly coming to light as the media began to dig deeper (Schlesinger, 2012; Financial Times, 2013; Whittell and Dugan, 2013a).

Tony Smith, one of the activists involved in starting UK Uncut, outlines how the first protest also filled a perceived void in organisation and action. Smith and his friends had attended a rally organised by trade unions and other left-wing groups outside Downing Street on the day (20 October 2010) that the cuts were announced by George Osborne. Smith recalls the feeling of 'disempowerment' and 'depression' that such events, though well meaning, created. A sense of failure regarding the 2003 protests against the invasion of Iraq – a defining political experience that radicalised many from this generation – lingered on. It was clear to Smith's circle of friends that they had to think about how things could be done differently. 'We realised that nobody else was really organizing at that moment. So there was a need to get this battle started early' (Sinclair, 2013, p 307–8).

At the start of UK Uncut's fight against austerity, social media platforms such as Twitter, Facebook and blogs proved particularly useful. Sam Baker, UK Uncut activist, pointed out how these tools 'ignite the potential of bypassing hierarchies and mass rallies in favour of a more decentralized, democratized, spontaneous model of protest' (Sinclair, 2013, p 310). UK Uncut partly borrowed and developed this model of organising and communicating from the UK's vibrant environmental movement – especially groups such as Climate Camp and Plane Stupid. UK Uncut activists had developed vital knowledge and skills by previously taking part in these groups' regular protests, meetings and social events. The anger that motivated anti-austerity activists to take to the streets was therefore channelled through innovative methods of organising. Non-hierarchical, participatory and democratic forms of direct action were developed to create a dynamic and genuinely grassroots mobilisation.

Getting online, getting organised and getting out on the streets

UK Uncut has provided a broad framework for participation through organising regular one-off protests and national days of action against the cuts. Since the start of the group, national days of action have almost exclusively taken place on a Saturday – in the late morning or early afternoon – to allow more people to join in. These events have been promoted on the UK Uncut website, a key tool in boosting public involvement and fostering a sense of unity among participants. Anyone can organise a UK Uncut action and list it on the group's website, so long as it involves 'civil disobedience against the government's austerity agenda' (UK Uncut, 2013b).

While political parties and trade unions have suffered from a general and sustained decline in membership, there has been a notable proliferation of pressure groups and, more recently, online activism. Examples of the latter phenomenon include Avaaz and 38 Degrees, which use online petitions to quickly harness their members' energy around topical concerns, raising awareness and influencing decision-makers. One of the main differences between traditional and newer campaign groups is the changing meaning of membership. Progressive pressure groups today tend to be less rigid and formal, focusing on particular issues rather than on grander narratives, such as class struggle. Membership of such groups is thus a much looser and more fluid experience, with people moving in and between campaigns and causes. UK Uncut members engage with each other online, but principally in order to get out onto the streets. This provides a sense of immediacy and empowerment, based on a DIY ethic where participants can quickly see the results of their actions. Pressure groups like Uncut cannot replace the history, stability and large networks of established campaign organisations and, in particular, trade unions. As I shall explore further below, it therefore makes sense for such groups sharing values and interests to work together and pool their comparative advantages whenever this is mutually beneficial.

A direct action network like UK Uncut relies on volunteers' enthusiasm and commitment rather than on paid staff and bureaucracies. As Armine Ishkanian and Marlies Glasius (2013, p 24) point out in their report on social movements 'Reclaiming Democracy in the Square?' many people involved in such groups bring a wide range of talents from their professional work to their activism. My own interest in working with Uncut came from a desire to give expression to my political ideals more freely, away from the – at times – constraining world of non-governmental organisations (NGOs), with their established modes of working and tightly defined mission statements. Through collaborating with Uncut I have certainly gained a great deal of experience in many areas of campaigning that I otherwise would not have been able to. Such voluntary protest groups can therefore provide a space where more radical and spontaneous political action may erupt, though potential allies are sometimes hesitant to engage with non-hierarchical organisations, owing to their unfamiliar methods.

Strategy and tactics for the anti-cuts movement

UK Uncut, as we have seen, began with an ambitious goal – to kick-start a popular social movement that could stop the government's spending cuts. Thus, as well as needing to create accessible, exciting and meaningful spaces where people could meet, exchange ideas and take action, it also had to develop clear and strong messaging in order to connect with and inspire the public at large. To achieve this the group argued that there was an alternative to austerity by highlighting the £25 billion lost annually through tax avoidance by wealthy corporations and individuals (Murphy, 2008). Uncut based its arguments on principles of equality and justice to show that the government's line 'We're all in this together' as part of a 'Big Society' was a deception, not least because the Coalition was directly benefiting from, encouraging and rewarding those who avoid tax (Solomons, 2012).

A key asset in this fight was that the group was able to draw on the in-depth tax expertise of people such as John Christensen of the Tax Justice Network, Richard Murphy of Tax Research UK, Martin Hearson of Action Aid and Nicholas Shaxson, all of whom had produced important research on both the UK and global tax systems. Their work explained clearly how the rich have avoided paying their fair share for many years by creating tax havens (through which half of global trade now flows) and other exclusive financial tools that circumvent tax laws and democratic controls (Shaxson, 2011). The secrecy and lack of accountability surrounding these systems means that most citizens are never aware of their existence. This dire state of affairs has occurred as a result of national governments being captured by private, pro-business interests and 'unelected oligarchies' (Beetham, 2011). Both Labour and Conservative governments facilitated the economic dominance of corporations and financial institutions by creating an environment of 'light touch regulation', as celebrated by then Chancellor Gordon Brown in his 2006 Mansion House speech (Brown, 2006).

Of course, not everyone agreed with the tactics or arguments of Uncut, for example, right-wing think-tank the Institute for Economic Affairs (IEA) portrayed the group's work as 'wholly misconceived' (Worstall, 2011, p 4). The real agenda behind the IEA's criticisms was a belief that it would be better if corporation tax were abolished and the UK were 'turned into a tax haven' (Littlewood, 2013). The Coalition government is clearly in tune with such thinking, given that the rate of corporation tax will have been reduced from 26% in 2011 to 20% by 2015 (HMRC, 2013). At the same time as fighting tooth and nail to protect the interests of the wealthy and privileged elite, David Cameron and his cabinet of millionaires (whose combined wealth is estimated to be £70 million), shifted the economic burden onto the shoulders of working people through regressive changes to the tax system (Reed and Horton, 2010; Hope, 2012). On top of this assault on the poor, real wages continue to decline sharply, so that the UK's record is among the worst in Europe and the minimum cost of living has increased by 25% since 2008 (BBC, 2013; Joseph Rowntree Foundation, 2013).

Yet, despite the severity of the government's austerity measures and the lack of an electoral mandate for them, the Coalition had successfully pushed the idea that the UK had spent beyond its means, so that immediately after the 2010 spending review most voters (52%) thought that the cuts were necessary (ComRes, 2010). The government was more easily able to do this because it could draw on the support of powerful establishment allies to back its ideological project. These included the International Monetary Fund (IMF), sections of the media and business leaders, with the latter joining together to argue that Osborne's cuts would 'strengthen Britain's economy by allowing the private sector to generate more jobs' (Adderley et al, 2010; Aldrick, 2010; MSN Money, 2010). Furthermore, the lack of any real opposition from Labour, who, as Owen Jones (2012) pointed out, 'from workfare to NHS privatization ... laid the groundwork for much of this Government's agenda', made life much easier for the Coalition. Despite this, according to Nigel Stanley's (2011) – TUC Head of Campaigns and Communications – analysis of YouGov opinion polls, by the start of 2011 most were 'worried about the impact, speed and scale' of the cuts and 'no longer thought they were fair'.

UK Uncut capitalised on the opportunity that this evolving public mood presented by repeatedly linking the unjust nature of austerity with the unjust tax system, whereby the rich could minimise their bills in ways that the poor could not. As a 2004 US study entitled 'The Crisis in Tax Administration' suggested, governments fear that if ordinary people (the 99%) see the rich elite (the 1%) playing by their own rules, they will seek to join them in illegally evading or legally avoiding tax (Aaron, 2004). The Coalition government was no different, with senior cabinet ministers, including David Cameron and George Osborne, forced to publicly denounce tax avoidance in early 2012 as 'morally wrong' and 'repugnant' (Hodges, 2012; Houlder, 2012). However, according to research by Christian Aid (2012), these fine words did not seem to convince the British public. Its August 2012 survey found that just two in five respondents believed that the government 'is genuine in their desire to combat tax avoidance'. Moreover, according to a report by think-tank British Future (Jolley, 2013, p 27), in 2013, 32% of people surveyed thought that 'tension between tax payers and tax avoiders' was one of the top two or three issues 'causing most division in British society as a whole today'.

UK Uncut helped to catapult the issue of tax avoidance onto the front line of political concerns by dramatising the subject through direct action and using simple language to explain a subject affecting every citizen in this country. These tactics played to the group's advantages while exploiting the weaknesses of its opponents. For example, the main strengths of the UK Uncut movement include: (i) its ability to create simple, replicable actions, mobilising groups of people in multiple locations against similar targets, (ii) to do this in ways that are confrontational and disruptive to power and (iii) that utilise clear, topical and poignant messages that are communicated widely. If any one of these components is missing from an action, then the overall likely impact of the action will be diminished. Tactically speaking, the weakness of several of the tax-dodging corporations is that their stores provide numerous targets for protest. There are also branches of these stores in almost every one of the UK's identikit high streets.

The most common type of UK Uncut action has therefore been a protest in or outside a high street tax dodger (UK Uncut, 2013c).[1] Judging by reports from activists and local media, these may involve on average between 10 and 50 people, last for two or three hours and may involve direct action or civil disobedience (UK Uncut, 2013d). Broadly speaking, the direct action that UK Uncut uses may be defined as a form of political protest where participants use their physical presence to confront a problem (such as public sector cuts) and highlight an alternative (for example, raising revenue through ending tax avoidance). Direct action may thus be used when other forms of political expression and engagement (such as petitions, government consultations, voting) have been tried but have not had the desired effect.

UK Uncut's brand of direct action has emphasised fun, creativity and inclusivity, so that spaces are transformed, with banks being turned into a public service that is being cut – such as a crèche or library, for example. Importantly, an April 2011 poll by YouGov found that 73% of people believed that 'peaceful civil disobedience (such as people staging sit-ins or occupying shops) ... was an acceptable way of protesting' (Paskini, 2011). Such findings lend legitimacy to Uncut's approach and also provide important breathing space for the campaign, particularly given the potential for heavy-handed and intimidating police presence at protests.

Figure 6.1: UK Uncut protesters outside a Barclays Bank branch

A rough estimate of the total number of people who have participated in a UK Uncut protest over the three years it has been in existence might place it in the tens of thousands. In comparison to the average trade union demonstration, such as the TUC's 2011 March for the Alternative in London, which gathered 500,000 people and lasted all day, this appears to be quite a low figure. But it is an error to gauge the relative success or failure of a direct action on a purely quantitative basis. Of far greater importance are qualitative factors relating to the dynamics between the protesters and the target (for example, a tax-dodging corporation and the government) and what these reveal about the morality of the situation. UK Uncut has shown that shutting down a tax-dodging shop requires only a small number of people in order to make a political and moral point. Besides this, mobilising thousands of people not only takes time and resources but presents its own logistical problems and can be less secure if the target of an action needs to remain secret in order to ensure protesters can stage a sit-in or occupation.

Critics of UK Uncut, such as David Allen Green (2011), who argued that the group should be protesting 'outside the Treasury' because companies have 'no choice' but to 'comply with the relevant tax regime' therefore misunderstand the reality of the situation on a political and tactical level. Firstly, corporations and their accountants – specifically the Big 4: Ernst and Young, Deloitte, KPMG and PWC – devote much of their time to lobbying for a tax system that minimises the contribution from business. Journalist Tamasin Cave (2013) has examined how the Big 4 are now 'embedded' in government and are 'earning hundreds of millions of pounds a year in government business, loaning their staff to government departments and the political parties, advising on everything from tax law to privatisation programmes'. Similarly, Felicity Lawrence (2012) has explained how representatives of tax-dodging businesses and banks, like Vodafone and Barclays, sit on exclusive corporate working groups at the heart of government, crafting policies entirely for their own benefit.

Not only are such companies actively setting the regulatory framework for tax, but also there are now numerous examples of how they have employed aggressive strategies to circumvent the tax system (Fernie, 2012; Gainsbury et al, 2013; Whittell and Dugan, 2013b). For example, as a director of UK Uncut Legal Action I was involved in the campaign (largely funded by public donations) to take HMRC to court in order to have its decision to let Goldman Sachs off at least £10 million in interest on an unpaid tax bill ruled unlawful. Since the 1990s Goldman Sachs, had – according to David Leigh of the *Guardian* (Leigh, 2011) – fought 'tooth and nail' to avoid paying national insurance on huge bonuses for its bankers. By 2010, according to a public judgement, the unpaid bill with accumulated interest had risen to £40 million. In December 2010 Dave Hartnett (then HMRC tax chief) caved in and forgave the banking giant the interest on the bill. The government was not going to get its full £40 million, but only £30 million (UK Uncut Legal Action, 2013). While we did not win our case, this 'dodgy deal' garnered significant publicity and outrage as the truth came to light, illustrating the degree to which public officials can be bullied by powerful businesses. Such cases should send a clear message that the British public demands that the government and HMRC take strong action to ensure corporations pay what they owe, when they owe it.

Returning to Green's (2011) assertion about where to direct one's anger, even though government buildings have rarely been the target of UK Uncut's protests, the government's austerity agenda is undoubtedly its main focus. This is made clear in the range of materials that Uncut produces for actions, in particular, the 'call-out' announcing the action, the press releases for media, the tweets and Facebook updates and the flyers and other promotional output – all of which are available online. In these materials, Uncut has also responded to the frequent assertion that while tax avoidance may be immoral, it is nonetheless legal, by arguing for a change in the law and has recommended a series of measures that could improve the UK's tax system, drawing on the knowledge of the experts mentioned above (UK Uncut, 2012d).

Spread the message: there is an alternative

From a tactical point of view, occupations of high-profile shops were also a very effective means of getting a platform from where to promote Uncut's ideas – simply because the act was so novel and difficult to ignore. Indeed, given the enthusiastic media response to such actions it soon became clear for Uncut members that if occupations almost guaranteed coverage, then that was a clear opportunity to draw attention to the damage caused by the cuts and discuss alternative policies that might not otherwise be heard. In this sense direct action was a blunt instrument – people sat down in tax dodgers and banks to point their finger at the real cause of the economic crisis and the real gap in public finances. This was done purposefully to counter the government's propaganda campaign for austerity, which had misdirected public anger towards blaming both the previous Labour government for overspending and the people receiving welfare benefits (Jones, 2012). Crucially, Uncut activists therefore invested significant time and energy before, during and after protests in engaging with mainstream media (such as traditional print and broadcast outlets) and social media (for example, Twitter, Facebook) in order to amplify the impact of their actions.

Figure 6.2: UK Uncut holding a sit-in at Lloyds Bank

UK Uncut's relationship with and use of mainstream and social media is mainly driven by two goals: (i) the need to amplify, in the most efficient and effective way possible, the group's key messages and (ii) the need to publicise and increase participation and engagement in the group's protests. In both of these the target audience is the public, given that, as outlined above, UK Uncut's central strategic aim is to mobilise opinion in favour of alternatives to austerity.

Mainstream and social media provide quite distinct, though related, opportunities for campaigners seeking to communicate with the public. Each is a different tool with unique applications, strengths and weaknesses. For example, while the messages produced by the traditional, corporate media can reach millions of people and are generally respected, they are controlled by remote hierarchies and may take some time to be transmitted. In contrast, social media platforms allow the user more control and flexibility over format and content, which may be immediately transmitted, but its reach is generally more limited and the information shared is not always trusted or verifiable.

Uncut's campaigns have therefore been crafted in ways that will get the most from each of these mediums. With the mainstream media this has meant being in constant contact with journalists, providing press releases and quotes for publication and having a team of well-rehearsed spokespeople available for interview. For social media, it has meant building an interactive online community through regular updates, commentary, announcements and the dissemination of ideas and opinions, allowing the anti-cuts movement to converse and organise. This has resulted in UK Uncut's actions gathering consistently strong mainstream media coverage across print and broadcast formats and its social media platforms having significant reach, with over 54,000 Facebook members and over 66,500 followers on Twitter.[2]

Building the anti-cuts movement and empowering people through direct action

As well as spreading its message far and wide through mainstream and social media, Uncut activists have also sought to engage with and learn from people suffering from the consequences of the cuts. While UK Uncut is perhaps best known for its occupations of high street tax dodgers, working with a wider range of people led it to develop more diverse tactics, focused on different targets, to fight austerity and highlight the alternatives. This was in large part a conscious decision, following the initial success of the group, in order to expand the message and demands of Uncut beyond the media's narrower focus on tax avoidance. While discussions on tax were central to the group's gaining a voice in the national political conversation, it was important that the real causes of the economic crisis and the impact of the cuts on people's lives were given full attention. This often meant working with those directly impacted by the cuts to develop campaigns according to their needs and struggles for justice.

In February and May 2011 Uncut therefore targeted branches of Barclays, HSBC, RBS and NatWest to protest against the fact that these banks had played a central role in causing the financial crisis, yet, having received huge state support, were carrying on with business as usual (Greenham, 2010). The call-out for the Barclay's action justified the action by singling out the bank's annual profits of £6 billion, and 'enormous bonus pool of £3.4bn, with a personal bonus for the CEO Bob Diamond of £9 million' (UK Uncut, 2011a). These actions emphasised how the occupations would transform banks and financial institutions – accurately described by Lord Turner in 2009 as 'socially useless' (Monaghan, 2009) – 'into something that people need, but will be cut', such as libraries, crèches and health services (UK Uncut, 2011a).

The symbolism employed here would become an important feature of future actions, as it enabled protesters to tell a story about the damaging impact of the cuts in a creative, imaginative way, often using humour or irony. These qualities of UK Uncut actions are important for several reasons. For example, Uncut has prioritised inclusivity in its actions – both in terms of making them accessible for families and children so as to ensure that spaces are fun and welcoming and by providing access for disabled people wherever possible. This has ensured that audiences can see people they can relate to taking action to protect public services. Efforts to vilify protesters are thus made more difficult and police may have to consider the public relations impact of any attempt to make arrests or use force. The mass arrest in March 2011 of 138 UK Uncut protesters for aggravated trespass while occupying Fortnum & Mason's was just one example of political policing aiming to deter and criminalise non-violent direct action (UK Uncut, 2011b; Malik, 2011).[3]

The need to prioritise inclusivity stems from the fact that people may feel uncomfortable about 'stepping into action' and moving into a protest situation outside of their past experience. Activist training groups, such as the Seeds for Change co-op, provide briefings and support on these issues to UK Uncut and others, building awareness of how to overcome the perception that direct action is for an activist elite. Other groups, such as Green and Black Cross, provide important legal advice on protesters' rights and offer legal observers to monitor police actions at protests.

Over the course of 2011 Uncut activists began to make more connections with activists and groups across the anti-austerity movement and beyond. This led to a series of informal partnerships with local activist groups across the UK as well as the NHS and health groups (for example, Keep Our NHS Public) and disability groups such as Disabled People Against Cuts (DPAC). Uncut has also consulted with established NGOs (e.g. False Economy, Move Your Money, New Economics Foundation, Robin Hood Tax), and unions (e.g. Public and Commercial Services, Unite, GMB) that have occasionally provided resources and materials, while Uncut members have organised solidarity actions on strike days and during marches (UK Uncut, 2011d).

As described above, in early 2011 Uncut had begun to make cuts to healthcare central to its messaging around bank occupations. This led to one of Uncut's largest and most spectacular demonstrations in September 2011, when Westminster Bridge was occupied to protest against the Health and Social Care Bill (UK Uncut, 2011c). By blocking the bridge to traffic, activists symbolised the need to block the passing of the Bill from parliament, across the Thames, to St Thomas' hospital on the South Bank. Uncut would also deploy similar tactics alongside DPAC in several actions in 2012, where disabled activists blocked busy public spaces, including Oxford Circus, Trafalgar Square and ATOS HQ (responsible for the despised Work Capability Assessments) to protest against the Welfare Reform Bill (UK Uncut, 2012a; 2012b; Taylor and Van Steenbergen, 2012).

Actions such as Block the Bridge serve several important functions. Not only do they send out important messages of resistance, but they can bring a movement together so that people can meet and exchange ideas and information and enjoy comedy and music performances. Moreover, Occupy London's first general assembly took place at the Block the Bridge action and the decision to occupy the London Stock Exchange was taken at this meeting (Indymedia London, 2011). Members of Uncut continued to support and organise with Occupy thereafter, including organising a march from St Paul's to the Treasury to demand HMRC chief Dave Hartnett's resignation (Cloake, 2011). Alongside shop occupations and larger public direct actions Uncut also began to target 'architects of austerity' – the very politicians who had created the cuts. Activists staged a street party outside Deputy Prime Minister Nick Clegg's house in May 2012 'over his role in supporting the coalition's cuts to public spending' (UK Uncut, 2012b; Taylor, 2012) and mock evictions at the houses of Welfare Minister Lord Freud and Work and Pensions Minister Iain Duncan Smith in April 2013 to demand an end to the 'bedroom tax' (Symonds, 2013).

Increasingly, within the Uncut movement, many of those who take action are directly affected by the cuts. The group has aimed to increase their participation in its work and to learn more about their struggles through networking and skill-shares. All UK Uncut members have either been affected personally or know close friends and relations who have been directly impacted on austerity. One member told me how her brother, who is autistic, had his Disability Living Allowance cut and their mother, who worked for the NHS, lost her job in the first round of cuts. The joint actions with DPAC have therefore been particularly important because at these protests Uncut worked with disabled activists who have previously felt invisible and powerless when taking action. Following joint planning, DPAC members led these actions, with Uncut providing interpreters for deaf people and offering accessible transport to protests.

Perhaps UK Uncut's most successful protest in terms of overall participation and impact was the 'Refuge from the Cuts' action in branches of Starbucks, with over 40 actions taking place in December 2012 (UK Uncut, 2012c; BBC, 2012). Starbucks is one of the largest coffee chains in the UK, and the second-largest cafe or restaurant chain in the world after McDonald's. Yet, between 2009 and 2012 it paid no corporation tax at all, despite making sales of £1.2 billion. Over the last 14 years Starbucks had paid only £8.6 million in corporation tax (Bergin, 2012). This action was named in recognition of the cuts to services affecting women (including healthcare, childcare, rape crisis centres and refuges) and the fact that low-paid women with families will be hardest hit by the cuts (Women's Budget Group, 2012). Protesters therefore staged sit-ins, transforming Starbucks into refuges, crèches and homeless shelters. For this action Uncut consulted with women's groups and organisations such as Go Feminist! and Southall Black Sisters on messaging and branding. Uncut's protests have thus seen women at the forefront of actions, promoting equality and women's rights, which are often side-lined and ignored in the corridors of power. This is a particularly vital task at present, given that, as the Counting Women In coalition's 2013 report *Sex and Power: Who Runs Britain* (Counting Women In, 2013, p 5–6) found, the UK remains a country largely governed by men, with women 'routinely excluded from decision-making roles in society as a whole'. As the report rightly points out, this exclusion of women from positions of power 'damages the interests of both women and men, as well as the country as a whole'.

Conclusion: resisting the government's lies and promoting alternatives for the 99%

The Coalition government, led by a patriarchal elite representing pro-business interests, is recklessly pursuing an unjust and unnecessary austerity agenda. This is part of a long-standing ideological project to reshape the state so that there is welfare for the rich and on-going pain for the poor, with vulnerable and marginalised people relentlessly targeted and demonised. The social contract in the UK is being broken as society becomes more unequal and people are increasingly fearful for their future. Meanwhile, powerful corporations use their significant influence to shape laws benefiting their interests alone, dodging their responsibilities to society whenever necessary, so that they do not pay their fair share of, or indeed any, tax. Without the rich paying what they owe, when they owe it, there will be no welfare state and no democracy.

UK Uncut has argued that we must transform Britain's economic and political system. The interests of the majority must be at the centre of decision making so that we invest in and protect our vital public services. In order to contribute to this goal, Uncut works to reshape and revive political engagement through direct action, employing a variety of tools and spaces for organising, and simple but effective strategies and tactics, so that we can spread our message and build an inclusive movement. Uncut's experiences will also, hopefully, add to the bank of knowledge that other social movements and political activists can draw on when developing their own campaigns.

Overall, Uncut deployed direct action as a tool to lever out undemocratic and unaccountable private and corporate influence from public spaces in order to empower the public so they can have their voices heard and, more importantly, make the decisions. Only by continuing to strengthen democratic and egalitarian forces in the UK will the fight-back against austerity be successful and sustainable economic and political models, providing for the well-being and dignity of the majority, be created.

Notes

[1] For example a branch of Barclays, Boots, HSBC, Lloyds, NatWest, Tesco, Topshop, Starbucks or Vodafone.

[2] Figures correct as of November 2013.

[3] Fortnum & Mason's parent company, Wittington Investments, has a 54% stake in Associated British Foods (ABF). According to the UK Uncut website, 'Some time between 2005 and 2008, ABF set up a holding company in Luxembourg. It then sent large sums of money – interest free – from ABF PLC and Primark (Ireland), also owned by ABF, into this holding account, from which it was sent straight back, this time with interest charges. According to tax experts, this has meant ABF's annual tax avoidance amounts to at least £10m through offsetting interest payments on profits.'

References

Aaron, H.J. and Slemrod, J. (eds) (2004) *The Crisis in Tax Administration*, Washington, DC: Brookings.

Adderley, W. et al (2010) 'Osborne's cuts will strengthen Britain's economy by allowing the private sector to generate more jobs', www.telegraph.co.uk, 18 October.

Aldrick, P. (2010) 'IMF backs austerity plan, UK on the mend', www.telegraph.co.uk, 27 September.

BBC (2012) 'UK Uncut protests over Starbucks "tax avoidance"', www.bbc.co.uk, 8 December.

BBC (2013) 'UK wages decline amongst worst in Europe', www.bbc.co.uk, 11 August.

Beetham, D. (2011) *Unelected Oligarchy- Corporate and Financial Dominance in Britain's Democracy*, Liverpool: Democratic Audit.

Bergin, T. (2012) 'Special Report: How Starbucks avoids UK taxes', uk.reuters.com, 15 October.

Brown, G. (2006) 'Gordon Brown's Mansion House speech', www.theguardian.com, 22 June.

Cave, T. (2013) 'Who really runs this place?', www.spinwatch.org, 17 June.

Christian Aid (2012) 'Majority of British adults say tax avoidance is "morally wrong"', www.christianaid.org.uk, 16 August.

Cloake, M. (2011) 'HMRC boss targeted by tax protesters', money.aol.co.uk, 24 October.

ComRes (2010) 'Poll Digest- Political- BBC Daily Politics CSR Poll', www.comres.co.uk, 21 October.

Counting Women In (2013) *Sex and Power 2013: Who runs Britain?* London: Fawcett Society.

Fernie, F. (2012) 'George Osborne's new plans to tackle tax avoidance', www.bbc.co.uk , 28 March.

Financial Times (2013) 'Great Tax Race', www.ft.com/indepth/great-tax-race.

Gainsbury, S., Ford, J. and Houlder, V. (2013) 'Pre-takeover Cadbury's aggressive tax avoidance exposed', www.ft.com, 20 June.

Green, D.A. (2011) 'The daftness of UK Uncut', www.newstatesman.com, 19 February.

Greenham, T. (2010) *Where did our money go? Building a banking system fit for purpose*, London: New Economics Foundation.

Guardian (2010) 'Spending review: The work of a gambler', guardian.co.uk 20 October.

HMRC (2013) 'Corporation Tax Rates', www.hmrc.gov.uk.

Hodges, D. (2012) 'David Cameron joins UK Uncut over Jimmy Carr's taxes', www.telegraph.co.uk, 21 June.

Hope, C. (2012) 'Exclusive: Cabinet is worth £70million', www.telegraph.co.uk, 27 May.

Houlder, V. (2012) 'Osborne tackles 'morally repugnant' tax abuses', www.ft.com, 21 March.

Indymedia London (2011) 'Block the Bill + Occupy London Assembly', london.indymedia.org.uk, 9 October.

Ishkanian, A. and Glasius, M. (2013) *Reclaiming Democracy in the Square? Interpreting the Movements of 2011–2012*, London: London School of Economics.

Jolley, R. (ed) (2013) *State of the Nation: Where is bittersweet Britain heading?* London: British Future.

Jones, O. (2012) 'If trade unions don't fight the workers' corner – others will', www.independent.co.uk, 2 March.

Jones, O. (2013) 'The Welfare Bill: A government of millionaires just made the poor poorer – and laughed as they did it', www.independent.co.uk, 9 January.

Joseph Rowntree Foundation (2013) 'The living standard squeeze tightens as minimum cost of living soars by 25% since downturn', www.jrf.og.uk, 28 June.

Lawrence, F. (2012) 'Britain's tax rules – now written for and by multinationals', www.theguardian.com, 19 March.

Leigh, D. (2011) 'Goldman Sachs let off paying £10m interest on failed tax avoidance scheme', www.theguardian.com, 11 October.

Littlewood, M. (2013) 'We should turn Britain into a tax haven', www.thetimes.co.uk, 23 May.

Malik, S. (2011) 'Cuts protesters claim police tricked them into mass arrest', www.theguardian.com, 28 March.

Monaghan, A. (2009) 'City is too big and socially useless, says Lord Turner', www.telegraph.co.uk, 26 August.

MSN Money (2010) 'What the papers thought of the budget', money.uk.msn.com, 23 June.

Murphy, R. (2008) *The Missing Billions: The UK Tax Gap*, London: TUC.

Murphy, R. (2010) 'Vodafone's tax case leaves a sour taste', www.theguardian.com, 22 October.

Paskini, D. (2011) 'Poll: 73% fine with #UKuncut style protests', www.liberalconspiracy.org, 4 April.

Reed, H. and Horton, T. (2010) 'Osborne's tax changes are regressive (not "progressive")', www.leftfootforward.org, 22 June.

Schlesinger, F. (2012) 'Fay Schlesinger', www.thetimes.co.uk.

Shackle, S. (2011) 'The orange umbrella that revolutionised dissent', www.newstatesman.com, 3 February.

Shaxson, N. (2011) *Treasure Islands: Tax Havens and the Men who Stole the World*, London: Vintage.

Sinclair, I. (2013) *The march that shook Blair: An oral history of 13 February 2003*, London: Peace News Press.

Solomons, M. (2012) 'Get the tax dodgers to pay for the cuts', www.politics.co.uk, 26 June.

Stanley, N. (2011) 'What I said to Netroots UK about the cuts campaign', www.touchstoneblog.org.uk, 8 January.

Symonds, T. (2013) 'Anti-cuts protesters block Lord Freud's road', www.bbc.co.uk, 13 April.

Taylor, M. (2012) 'Nick Clegg's house targeted by UK Uncut campaigners', www.guardian.com, 26 May.

Taylor, M. and Van Steenbergen, M. (2012) 'Disability rights protesters bring Trafalgar Square traffic to a standstill', www.guardian.com, 18 April.

Taylor, M., Lewis, P. and Gabbatt, A. (2010) 'Philip Green to be target of corporate tax avoidance protest', www.guardian.com, 29 November.

UK Uncut (2010a) 'Anti-Cuts Direct Action- Wednesday 9.30am', www.theircrisis.wordpress.com, 24 October.

UK Uncut (2010b) 'A Day of Action: Vodafone Stores Closed Across the Country', www.ukuncut.wordpress.com, 30 October.

UK Uncut (2011a) 'UK Uncut plans weekend of bank protests', www.ukuncut.org.uk, 18 February.

UK Uncut (2011b) 'Why Fortnum & Mason?', www.ukuncut.org.uk, 28 March.

UK Uncut (2011c) 'Block the Bridge: Block the Bill', www.ukuncut.org.uk, 21 September.

UK Uncut (2011d) 'November 30th: show some solidariTEA!', www.ukuncut.org.uk, 24 November.

UK Uncut (2012a) 'Message from the Invisible: scrap the Welfare Reform Bill!' www.ukuncut.org.uk, 20 January.

UK Uncut (2012b) 'The Closing ATOS Ceremony', www.ukuncut.org.uk, 14 August.

UK Uncut (2012c) 'CALL OUT! 8 Dec. Refuge from the cuts – target Starbucks!' www.ukuncut.org.uk, 11 November.

UK Uncut (2012d) 'UK Uncut's Alternative Autumn Statement', www.ukuncut.org.uk, 5 December.

UK Uncut (2013a) 'About UK Uncut', www.ukuncut.org.uk.

UK Uncut (2013b) 'List an action', www.ukuncut.org.uk.

UK Uncut (2013c) 'Targets', www.ukuncut.org.uk.

UK Uncut (2013d) 'Gallery', www.ukuncut.org.uk.

UK Uncut Legal Action (2013) 'Why Goldman Sachs?', www.ukuncutlegalaction.org.uk.

Whittell, R. and Dugan, E. (2013a) 'Eurobonds scandal: The high street giants avoiding millions in tax', www.independent.co.uk, 23 October.

Whittell, R. and Dugan, E. (2013b) 'The other energy scandal – power giants use loophole to cut their own tax bills', www.independent.co.uk, 27 October.

Women's Budget Group (2012) The Impact on Women of the Budget 2012, London: WBG.

Worstall, T. (2011) UK Uncut Unravelled, London: Institute of Economic Affairs.

SEVEN

Doubly disillusioned? Young Muslims and mainstream British politics

Parveen Akhtar

Introduction

If participation in mainstream politics is taken as a hallmark of engagement with the democratic process, then evidence shows an increasing disenchantment with democracy in the UK. Indeed, the path of mainstream politics is one less travelled not only by the British people; it's a trend prevalent in mature democracies across the world. Increasingly, people are not voting, joining political parties or volunteering their help at election campaigns as 'foot soldiers'. Disillusionment is more pronounced among certain groups, including young people. Muslim young people, like their counterparts in wider society, are sceptical about the effectiveness of mainstream politics and politicians. But, unlike their non-Muslim contemporaries, many young Muslims live in constituencies where the practice of biraderi, or kinship-based politics, is a feature of political life. The hierarchical and patriarchal structure of kin-based politics results in the effective disenfranchisement of young people and women. In turn, this creates a second layer of disillusionment for politically interested British Muslims. While the focus of this chapter is on the ways in which young British Muslims are disenfranchised from electoral politics, elsewhere I have shown how young Muslims are seeking out alternative forms of political engagement as an antidote to electoral exclusion (Akhtar, 2013). O'Toole, too, in this volume, shows some of the ways in which minority (including Muslim) young people are active in extra-parliamentary forms of political participation. The chapter begins with a discussion about some of the general concerns around declining participation in mainstream politics; this is followed by an examination of the more marked decline among certain demographics, in particular, young people and ethnic minorities. Next, British Muslim communities and the role of biraderi politics, especially the impact of biraderi on the political engagement of young British Muslims, are examined. The chapter draws on embedded ethnographic research, including informal interviews and participant observation with the Pakistani Muslim community in Birmingham over an extensive time frame (2005–14) for a project on British Muslims and political participation (Akhtar, 2013).

Decline in mainstream political participation

Participation in electoral and other mainstream forms of political engagement is in decline across many of the industrialised democracies. In the UK, this is in part due to a deep cynicism towards politicians and political front-runners. Politicians are the least trusted of all professions, the expenses scandal contributing to historic levels of mistrust in elected representatives. These attitudes, coupled with the trends in political behaviour, are deeply problematic, not least because they challenge the legitimacy of MPs, political parties and governments. Indeed, non-participation in elections has become an area of academic research:

> [I]n the 1950s and the 1960s neglecting turnout seemed reasonable, or at least acceptable, since the vast majority of people regularly voted in general elections. That has changed ... signalling that the turnout decision has become an important aspect of electoral choice in contemporary Britain. (Clarke et al, 2004, p vii)

The crisis in political engagement has been of concern to many a political scientist, some of whom are re-evaluating the purpose of their work. Many of the contributions to the debate have the explicit aim of provoking action. Robert Putnam's *Bowling Alone* (2000), for example, trumpets its aim of stimulating a national debate on how to resurrect civic engagement in America. Colin Hay (2007) challenged his colleagues to take their responsibility towards their subject matter more seriously by working on solutions to political disengagement. Similarly, Professor Gerry Stoker's work is based on the belief that politics matters: 'what happens in wider society matters to us all', he says, 'and that means that politics matters too, because it is through politics that we can influence what happens in that wider world' (Stoker, 2006, p 5).

Of particular concern is that the trend for non-participation in mainstream politics is especially pronounced among certain demographic sections, notably young people. In *Voter Turnout Since 1945: A Global Report*, López Pintor and his colleagues point out that in the UK age is a key factor in explaining involvement in formal politics. The fact that young people are less likely to take part in politics has been taken as indicative of their disillusionment with the political process as a whole; indeed, some have argued that young people who reached the age of 21 just before or just after the turn of the millennium, the so-called 'Millennial Generation', are an 'apolitical generation' (Pirie and Worcester, 1998). Overall, young adults are less likely to be involved in conventional politics, to be knowledgeable about politics, to have attachments to any political party or to view voting as a civic responsibility. The implications of this are far reaching; Forbrig argues that 'in turning their backs on democratic institutions, the young of today are jeopardising the democracy of tomorrow' (Forbrig, 2005, p 7). In the UK, observers have linked young people's disengagement from political institutions and processes to even more immediate problems, such as disengagement from local communities and lack of societal integration; such theories emerged as a particular response to the riots in 2001 in northern British towns (Cantle, 2001; Marsh et al, 2007).

This level of interest has inevitably generated a large body of work attempting to explain the public's reluctance to turn out and vote. Three broad explanations are particularly prominent. The first is that people are generally satisfied with their lives and so, content with their lot, feel no compulsion to vote. This argument rests on the idea that people are more likely to vote if they are unhappy and want to bring about change.

The second argument – and one which holds the most currency at present – is that people are apathetic about politics. They don't believe politics matters or that it has relevance in their lives. Faced with the inability of politicians to effect the things that matter most to individual voters – falling unemployment, low inflation – there is simply not the 'demand' for politics. Again, the fact that there is rising unemployment, and the retrenchment of the welfare state, mean that the connection between the world of politics and individuals' lived experiences of the policies that politicians make and enforce upon publics is real. Milbrath (1965), writing half a century ago about political participation, saw it as a hierarchical activity. He devised a hierarchy of participation, identifying three groups: gladiators (those actively and widely involved); spectators (those having minimal involvement); and apathetics (those abstaining from any activity). However, O'Toole et al (2003) problematise the idea that just because individuals do not take part in mainstream politics they must be apathetic. And this leads to a third reason that is deserving of more attention than it currently receives.

This argument posits that individuals do not vote because they are disillusioned with politics.

This argument follows the logic that it is not that people don't care; rather, they think that they have little influence, that their vote and their voice will count for nothing. These people are not politically apathetic, as has been popularly suggested, but are disillusioned with the 'supply' side – the politicians and policies on offer. This disillusionment does not extend to the political process itself, and this is best evidenced by the demand for the anti-politician, someone who stands for (is seen to stand for) the people and not a political career. The rise in popularity of the Scottish National Party and Respect (albeit briefly) can, in large part, be attributed to the leadership of Alex Salmond and George Galloway, respectively, both of whom have one thing in common with Boris Johnson: they are viewed as anti-politicians. Salmond, Galloway and Johnson appeal to voters because they have carved out identities as passionate, personable and ideologically driven in a wider political culture that largely dismisses politicians as careerists, scripted and self-serving: individuals who'd sell their grannies if it meant winning an election. The anti-politician, in contrast, is not associated with traditional mainstream politics. Instead they are – or at least appear to be – the antithesis of the self-serving, power-hungry, media-savvy and scripted Member of Parliament (MP) (Akhtar, 2012).

A key emphasis of O'Toole's argument is that non-participation is rarely, if ever, seen by researchers as a conscious choice. The suggestion that individuals who do not participate in formal ways are politically apathetic is, O'Toole et al suggest, too simplistic and sweeping (O'Toole et al, 2003). As Marsh et al also argue:

> As researchers, we need to ensure that we are sensitive to how respondents themselves conceive of the political, and this means avoiding making easy assumptions about non-participation. (Marsh et al, 2007, p 24)

Bhavnani's (1991) analysis of the political participation of young people from a psychological perspective argues that young people do have views about political issues, but feel disenfranchised for various reasons. Non-participation in mainstream politics cannot, therefore, automatically be seen as a sign of apathy. Some people abstain from politics not because they are apathetic, but because they are, as in the example of many feminists:

> wary, and/or distrustful of participating in the practices of
> 'formal' politics such as elections, voting, political parties,
> parliament. Engaging in conventional politics without first
> changing its cultural and ideological context has not been
> deemed a rewarding use of energy for many feminists.
> (Corrin, 1999, p 174)

There is a whole body of research that challenges the notion that just because young people are not engaging with mainstream politics they are, de facto, politically apathetic. Henn et al (2002), for example, argue that it is often the case that young people are reluctant to participate in the formal political arena because they believe it is not reflective of the issues and concerns of their lives. They do not engage with the mainstream political system because they feel it does not engage with them. In more recent work, using nation-wide survey data of more than 700 young people, Henn et al (2005) found that many 'support the democratic process, but are sceptical of the way the British political system is organised and led'; furthermore, they are 'turned off by politicians and political parties' (Henn et al, 2005, p 556).

White et al (2000) go further in suggesting that there is an under-accounting for political activities among young people. This is because of the difference between definitions of politics used by the researcher and the young people themselves. So, while an activity may be deemed political by the researcher, the same activity may not be viewed as political by the young person and, as such, may not be mentioned by them – leading the researcher to conclude that the young person was not politically active. In addition, work done by Eden and Roker (2002) suggests that there is a persistent failure among researchers to consider areas of political life where young people are active.

> [T]he claim of widespread alienation and apathy amongst
> young people has been based on a narrow definition of the
> 'political' remit. (Roker et al, 1999, p 185)

In support of this, Marsh et al argue that the literature 'fails to take account of the politics of the personal and thus, the politics of identity'; they argue for a conception of politics that understands it as 'lived experience' (Marsh et al, 2007, p 5). In their view, politics is inseparable from daily life. The forms of engagement that people choose (or do not choose) are embedded in the circumstances and routines of their own lives. As such, they argue, '[if we] treat politics as something outside people's experiences, that is, in a sense, as merely something "done unto"" them, then we negate how people view, experience and live politics' (Marsh et al, 2007, p 24).

Furthermore, research by the Electoral Commission and the Hansard Society shows that people fail to connect politics to their own lives, within their own 'lived experiences': that people often fail to associate the word 'politics' with issues that affect their everyday lives. This is the case 'even among people who seem well-disposed towards politics (those who declare themselves very or fairly interested in politics), many (40%) claim not to have discussed it in the last two or three years' (Electoral Commission and Hansard Society, 2007, p 27). The report addresses the problem of the lack of data and insights into 'the public's political behaviour and attitudes beyond the simple measure of voting in elections' and postulates that 'improving engagement requires a realistic starting-point and an honest appraisal of what motivates people to become involved and, correspondingly, why others choose not to participate' (Electoral Commission and Hansard Society, 2007, p 3). By moving from surveying young people's attitudes towards a limited range of political issues/arenas to conducting in–depth explorations of young people's views and experiences, we begin to develop a much more nuanced understanding of the relationship between young people's conceptions of the political and their engagement with, and interest in, politics.

Young people are 'deeply sceptical' about political parties and elected politicians (Henn et al, 2005, p 571). And while research has indicated that young people are very far from being politically apathetic and are, in fact, often highly articulate about the political issues that affect their lives, as well as about the disconnection between these issues and mainstream politics (O'Toole et al, 2003), Henn et al are cautious to not 'overstate' young people's involvement in alternative political actions, so that while they do argue that 'there is evidence of some support for a different type of politics that is more participative and direct' they also warn that 'it would not be appropriate to explain young people's apparent disengagement with formal politics and the established parties as a consequence of a uniform shift towards a "new politics" value system and orientation' (Henn et al, 2005, p 573).

So far it has been suggested that there is general disillusionment with mainstream politics and this is more pronounced among young people. We turn now to look at minority young people in the British political system in general and thereafter Muslim young people in particular. It is argued that, like their wider British counterparts, they too are disillusioned with the political mainstream, but that they are also disillusioned by community political representation.

Ethnic minority young people

While there is a strong alignment between ethnic minorities and the Labour Party, political engagement among minorities is lower than for the general British public. Concern over the lack of political involvement in ethnic minority communities has led to a number of remedial programmes, including targeted campaigns and resources. In this section we examine issues around minority political participation in the UK.

In multi-ethnic societies, participation within the mainstream political structures is taken as evidence of political integration (Anwar, 1986, p 17) and often seen as a hallmark of support for democratic politics (Layton-Henry, 1992). It can also be construed as a powerful symbol of political belonging. As such, it is both an indicator of and a factor in the incorporation of immigrants into the host society (Garbaye, 2005). While the participation of ethnic minorities within the mainstream political process has been much less common than other forms of political involvement, this does not necessarily imply total disenfranchisement. It is helpful to posit the integration of ethnic minorities in the political system as a continuum (Geddes, 2001, p 134) rather than as a simple integration/alienation dichotomy. Importantly, this continuum of integration is one on which the various minority communities are not positioned in the same place. Until the late 2000s the categories found in the literature on minority political participation were so broad that much of the data on ethnic minorities and political participation was not sensitive to variations between communities and different groups (Layton-Henry, 1990; Purdam et al, 2002). The simple categories of Black, White and Asian used in data collection were ineffective in providing nuanced information and missed the patterns of political behaviour within, as well as between, different communities (Anwar, 1994; Purdam et al, 2002; Richards and Marshall, 2003).

Research by Purdam et al undertaken for the Electoral Commission found that the reasons why some minority communities do not participate in mainstream politics at a national level are not so different from those that apply to the wider population and include: alienation and disenchantment; the belief that participation within the system makes no difference to the outcome; apathy; no interest in politics; impact (that is, the belief that an individual's vote will have no effect); and inconvenience (Purdam et al, 2002). More specifically for minority communities a further explanation for political abstinence lies with the idea of representation: lack of Black and minority ethnic (BME) representation within the political elite is a further barrier to participation (see also Fernandes, Chapter 9 in this volume). Nearly half of those questioned said that better representation of Black people within politics would be the most important factor in encouraging them to vote (Electoral Commission, 2002b). Similarly, two-thirds of Muslim respondents in Anwar's research felt that Muslims lacked a sufficient voice in the political process (Anwar, 2005, p 38). Correspondingly, some have argued that the British Asian community is politically disengaged because the 'equitable, representative decision-making institutions' are not multicultural (Viswanathan, 2002 cited in Electoral Commission, 2005, p 16). This is a view shared by Marsh et al, who argue that

> racialised political discourses, mono-ethnic political and public institutions and ethnic segregation shaped young people's perceptions of political and public institutions. (Marsh et al, 2007, p 208)

Perhaps, too, there are other barriers that restrict the opportunities for ethnic minority candidates; barriers that have less to do with ethnicity and more to do with exclusion based on family background, something that does exist in British politics. Within the Labour Party, for example, it has been argued that some prominent MPs are the descendants of trade union officials and councillors. Indeed, as Kavanagh noted long ago, there is also now 'a Labour establishment based on dynastic and kinship ties' (Kavanagh, 1982, p 104).

The exclusion of minority groups through political non-participation can lead to the dangerous path of societal fragmentation and the breakdown of social cohesion. Indeed, the belief that identity and background influence political participation has led the Electoral Commission to focus on specific groups, organised according to age, gender and ethnic background (Richards and Marshall, 2003). As Karamjit Singh, Electoral Commissioner and Chair of the Commission's research project with the University of Manchester, observed in his preface to the Electoral Commission's report *Voter Engagement among Black and Minority Ethnic Communities*:

> The fact that large numbers of eligible voters are choosing not to exercise their democratic right is increasingly a cause for concern among commentators and politicians of all persuasions. But it would be wrong to seek universal solutions to the problem of voter disengagement. In today's diverse society, it is vitally important that research and

> policy responses in this area are sensitive to the different experiences and perceptions of particular communities. (Electoral Commission, 2002a, p 3)

Thus, although the decline in mainstream political involvement is not exclusive to minority communities, solutions ought to be community specific. To do this, however, it is necessary to have a detailed understanding of the way various community groups view and experience politics. This is clearly the starting point for the 'community-based' responses to the problem of minority non-participation recommended by the Electoral Commission.

Double disillusionment: the particular case of British Pakistani Muslims

The majority of Muslims in the UK have a South Asian, or more specifically Pakistani, heritage. This reflects patterns of migration and settlement after 1945. This chapter focuses on British Pakistani Muslims. While Pakistani Muslim young people, like their counterparts in wider British society, are disillusioned by mainstream politics and the political system, they are also disillusioned with community representatives or biraderi elders. Biraderi or kinship is an important feature of community organisation in Pakistan. It is a mechanism of social protection in a (largely tribal) society with no viable state–society contract to ensure legislative justice or an economic safety net. Individuals and families rely on biraderis in times of need. Political affiliation is along biraderi lines. Indeed, biraderi was the informal network through which many Pakistanis first migrated to Britain in the 1950s and 1960s. Pioneer migrants initially sent word to biraderi members about the employment opportunities in the industrial heartlands of the UK. Once they were in the UK, the biraderi system acted as a buffer for new migrants, as biraderi members helped new arrivals with work, accommodation and settling into life in the UK (Akhtar, 2013).

Initially, most Pakistani migrants abstained from any significant political activity because they believed in the myth of return, thinking they were temporary economic sojourners and would return to Pakistan. However, in time, with legislation restricting migration and the arrival of women and children, Pakistanis densely situated in specific urban constituencies began to see themselves, and were seen by political parties, as an ethnic bloc vote. A relationship of patronage between Pakistani community leaders (often biraderi elders) and aspiring (as well as established) local politicians developed. In return for the promise of the Pakistani ethnic vote, community leaders were promised positions of influence and the prestige of being an intermediary (Akhtar, 2013). One consequence of such a relationship of patronage was the stifling of genuine political dialogue within the community or between Pakistani politicians and the wider political community.

Biraderi networks are hierarchical and patriarchal, and as a consequence young people and women were effectively disenfranchised. The entrenchment of patronage politics in many constituencies with significantly large numbers of Pakistanis has led to a great deal of scepticism among young Pakistanis about the effectiveness of mainstream electoral politics. In her research with young Muslim university students in Bradford, June Edmunds found significant cynicism towards voting and elections (Edmunds, 2010, p 223). In recent years there has been a wider debate within the British Muslim community about whether participating in a man-made political system is permissible in Islam.

To participate or not to participate?

In the run-up to the May 2005 general election, the Muslim Council of Britain (MCB) arranged a number of public gatherings in which it called on Muslims to exercise their democratic right to vote. One such MCB meeting was disrupted by a group of Muslims who claimed it was wrong for Muslims in the UK to endorse a non-Islamic state system. Members of the Saviour sect handed out a leaflet headlined: 'Vote today, become Kufar [unbelievers] tomorrow' (Gillan and Dodd, 2005).

Also known as Al-Ghuraaba, an offspring of the Al-Muhajiroun, which had at the time been disbanded, the crowd of mainly young men forced their way into the meeting. The group also ran an anti-voting campaign website that featured pictures of all Muslims standing as parliamentary candidates with the words 'shame' underneath, followed by the tag:

> They ALL have no excuse unless they repent to Allah and leave their KUFAR. (Gillan and Dodd, 2005)

At the meeting they attacked the MCB for working within the British political system; indeed they went further and accused it of working for the government:

we are here to condemn you for apostasy! ... you are the
mouthpiece of the British government! You are kufar – go
to hellfire! (Cited in Casciani, 2005)

The message in the leaflets they handed out was that participating in
the Western political system is inherently wrong: it is 'major apostasy
and will take you outside the fold of Islam ... It will nullify all your
good deeds ... and guarantees your seat in Hellfire forever!' (Casciani,
2005). However, among the individuals and groups that the author has
worked with in Birmingham very few have taken this view. Indeed,
Naima speaks for many when she argues:

"and in fact this land gives us the opportunity to
democratically protest, this land gives us the opportunity to
democratically stand for election if you want to ... we can
be an MP if we want to make the effort. We can do all those
things, so why should they say no I don't want to take part
in democratic process?" (Naima, Pakistani Muslim, female)

While groups such as the Saviour sect view the state as the nemesis,
Gulbahar, like others I spoke to, does not believe that the British state
is against Muslims:

"I think Britain did quite a lot for the Muslims in Bosnia
and former Yugoslavia and places like that, so I wouldn't
necessarily say that the government is particularly anti-
Muslim, I mean it has policies in Kashmir and things like
that so I wouldn't say it was anti-Muslim, no." (Gulbahar,
Pakistani Muslim, male)

Indeed, Naima points to the freedoms accorded to Muslims in the UK:

"[W]e have our own mosques, our people are freely able
to go to mosques and pray and take part in their festivities
without political interruption from the government."

She goes further in suggesting that if individuals are not satisfied with
the world around them they should utilise the tools of democracy to
bring about change.

"What's that old saying you get the government/politicians
you deserve, so if we're not making that effort to vote in,

vote for people who will represent or take into account our views or good for the benefit of the whole community, then actually we're the ones who are, actually we're the ones who are in the wrong, so for me, you have those opportunities there, don't whinge and moan on the side-line, if you want to create that change, then get involved or shut up … For me, if you want to make or create changes you can do so if you want to, but don't criticise those that do and don't criticise if you don't want to get involved."

There is very clearly support for the democratic process among the majority of British Muslims, even if there is little faith in their representatives within that system.

Biraderi politics across generations

At the same time, there is a clear sense of disillusionment with politicians and community leaders among young Muslims. Much of this stems from the fact that young Pakistanis often feel barred from the mainstream channels of political expression, due to the system of biraderi. Their issue is not with the process of democracy itself but with leadership within the Pakistani community that restricts their access to electoral politics.

"I think a lot of people these days are more aware of double standards/half truths and people aren't giving them the right information, so when people … you have to become political otherwise you become totally isolated (talking about leadership)." (Akrim, Pakistani Muslim, male)

Moreover, not only did many young Muslims feel excluded from mainstream politics through the system of patronage, but they also felt that the biraderi elders, often involved in the formal political sphere, did not understand them or their concerns and therefore could not represent them. The issue of a connection and understanding between political leadership and young people is crucial for effective political representation, but also for young people's faith in the political system. There are Pakistani Muslim politicians in all the three main political parties, but as one of my interviewee stated:

"We see them as part of the system/problem. Even if they are not part of the biraderi system. They aren't the

antithesis/solution the Muslim youth are looking for."
(Mohammed, Pakistani Muslim, male)

Simple demographic representation does not necessarily equate to representation of ideas and values, and Mohammed's concerns are not 'just Muslim concerns'. Instead, he is interested in tuition fees and whether his vote in the 2010 election actually mattered in a system where the country ends up with a government no one voted for:

"Like I voted in [the] last election for Lib Dem. No one in the country voted for [a] coalition. But that's what we got. So what was the point of voting? And Clegg went back on his word about student fees. So we see it as a broken system."

Like many of the young Pakistanis I have spoken to, Mohammed places less emphasis on the background of political leaders than the biraderi system allows:

"I think we would rather vote for a white person we felt represented us, such as Galloway, rather than vote simply 'cause they are Muslim. Muslim identity kind of plays a big part in Pakistani identity, so it is important someone represents that side. And Galloway seems to be doing [the] best job."

The tensions between the younger and older Pakistanis over the issue of biraderi politics expose a level of disconnect between the generations. Many of the younger generation criticise the older generation for the tendency to do as figures in authority (biraderi elders) say without question. At the same time, the identity concerns of young people are dismissed by the older generation, most of whom do not understand issues to do with identity. They see themselves as realistic and pragmatic, while the younger people are seen as essentially naïve. As one older interviewee said: "Young people have either too idealistic or romantic ideals of politics, they think it is really simple" (Ali, Pakistani Muslim, male). He continued: "the identity issue is simply a question of things being misinterpreted". However, Shareefa Fulat, a worker at the confidential Muslim Youth Helpline, which acts as an 'agony aunt' service for the Muslim community, suggests that the most common problems raised by callers concern family, relationships, sexuality, drugs and mental health issues, such as depression. Furthermore, she contends that "What exacerbates these problems is that there are no support services, or support from within the [Muslim] community, for people struggling with resolving their identities.... There are huge cultural and generational differences within the community, which also play a role" (BBC NewsOnline, 2004).

It is important to remember, however, that there is not a simple generational divide. While economic migration from Pakistan and South Asia to the UK is now limited, marriage patterns still mean that third-generation Pakistanis born in the UK marry partners from Pakistan (Charlsey, 2013). This means that there is no clear delineation between the generations and many young Pakistanis who come to England as spouses do not have any more familiarity with the English language than their elders, and they may hold equally strong ties to traditional social systems like biraderi.

Yet, there are also instances where young and old Pakistanis work together to get their voices heard. For example, Unity FM, a local radio station run by Muslims for the Muslim community, has a range of ages working together. Working on a voluntary basis, members run a number of programmes to get individuals involved in politics and the civic sphere more widely. Many of the young people who are a part of the station are in higher education and university is one arena where Muslim young people build up their political acumen. One young university student spoke about working to be a part of the student union:

> "We just need to get our foot in ... we're not going to change the university, we're just there to make sure no one affects us lot to get representation." (Rizwan, Pakistani Muslim, male)

Access to higher education is fundamental in allowing Muslim students admission to a range of networks and resources that will shape future political activism. As Edmunds notes:

> Extensive networking with diverse groups, contrasting with their parents' intensive networking within largely homogeneous groups in their home and host country, provides a richer source of 'social capital', adding to the improved 'human capital' they obtain from higher education. (Edmunds, 2010, p 236)

While many of the older generation of Pakistanis are in politics through mobilisations around biraderi, university activism provides young

Pakistanis with opportunities to build upon their social and human capital and also their political capital. As Rizwan continues with regard to joining the student union:

> "It's not harder, well it is harder in the sense that they're never done it before, so if you never done something before then you don't know what to do when you get into that position … You need to get people to get their foot in, next year you have people who know a little more, and next year and then slowly, slowly until you know what is going on inside."

Getting involved in politics and representation at universities and institutions of higher learning is one avenue through which some young Muslims engage in the public sphere. But there are also other non-mainstream ways in which young Muslims have expressed their political beliefs and ambitions. Unity FM, the Muslim community radio station, has many sister stations across the UK and there are a number of local community organisations with which Muslims have got involved (Akhtar, 2013). Political consumerism, when 'consumer behaviour such as the buying or boycotting of products and services for political and ethical reasons can take on political significance' (Stolle et al, 2005, p 245), is another area of activism popular with young Muslims (Mustapha, 2014). Research by Van Zoonen et al examines the multimedia environment, in particular videos uploaded to YouTube in response to the Dutch anti-Islam video *Fitna*,[1] and shows how video-upload channels have become 'important arenas for political activity and communication' (Van Zoonen et al, 2010, p 250). O'Toole in this Chapter Eight of this edited collection argues that:

> Conceptually, these forms of engagement should be seen not simply as additions to an increasing battery of repertoires of political action, but as underscored by different kinds of political subjectivities that were characterised by a preference for more immediate, personal, direct, hands-on, everyday forms of activism.

Though they feel disenfranchised from electoral politics, in part due to biraderi networks, it is clear that many young British Muslims remain engaged in the wider arena of politics. Drawing on 'different kinds of political subjectivities' they continue to engage in the public sphere. Involvement in alternative forms of activism, including university politics and community radio, highlights a commitment to civic engagement more broadly.

Conclusion

While it is important to expand our conceptualisations of political engagement and to recognise that different groups of individuals engage in alternative and creative ways in the public sphere it is still nevertheless the case that mainstream politics is an important facet of the legitimation of political life. Bhavnani has argued that 'while the processes of parliamentary democracy are too limited to, by themselves, encompass all that is political, they are however, a necessary part of what constitutes politics' (Bhavnani, 1991, p 38). That individuals are disillusioned with and are abstaining from mainstream politics remains problematic because disengagement from the formal arena of politics is problematic for the future of democracy (Stoker, 2006), a view echoed by Paul Webb:

> while interest groups or media actors might be equally (or more) effective in articulating sectional demands and placing issues on the political agenda, the fact remains that it is only the political parties (or individual candidates in candidate-centred systems of politics) that can legitimately perform the key function of aggregating demands into more or less coherent programmatic packages in democratic contexts. While this task is undoubtedly increasingly difficult, parties remain central to it. (Webb, 2007, p 8)

Perhaps Bang (2004, p 4) puts the issue most clearly, arguing that political authorities 'cannot make and implement authoritative decisions for a society unless lay people accept them and recognise themselves as bounded by them'. Indeed, as Whiteley and Seyd (2002) postulate, the decline of high-intensity participation within British political parties means that these organisations will perform their functions less effectively in the future. A further possible consequence of the decline in mainstream politics is that 'the erosion of fragile democratic cultures will lead to the breakthrough and dominance of a far more basic and violent form of identity politics' (Bentley, 2005, p 17). Indeed, Putnam argues that the rise of extreme politics is an inevitable result of this decline:

> if participation in political deliberation declines – if fewer and fewer voices engage in democratic debate – our politics will become more shrill and less balanced. When most people skip the meeting, those who are left tend to be the more extreme, because they care most about the outcome. (Putnam, 2000, p 348)

In addition, as Stoker argues, this rise of the more extreme, populist aspects of politics:

> does not respect the core features of politics – the search for compromise between different interests, the need to understand another's position and the complexities of implementation. It fails to do this because it does not allow for the presence of differences between citizens. (Stoker, 2006, p 139)

It remains the case that engagement in mainstream politics is important: it matters. Disillusionment with electoral and party politics is problematic. Yet, in the UK as well as in other advanced democracies across the globe, it is in decline. Individuals are increasingly abstaining from electoral politics, be it voting, joining political parties or high-intensity activities such as street canvassing. This decline is most pronounced among cohorts of young people many of whom have little faith in politicians, highlighted by, but preceding, the MPs' expenses scandal. And there is a backlash against a political culture that is seen as self-interested and self-serving. Muslim young people, like their mainstream counterparts, are also disillusioned with mainstream politics. However, unlike their non-Muslim counterparts, they are further disillusioned by their community representatives, often biraderi elders who dominate positions of political power. Yet biraderi has often been overlooked in understanding Muslim engagement with politics. Initiatives to counter non-participation among ethnic minorities are wide ranging but also generic. For example, the report *Voter Engagement among Black and Minority Ethnic Communities* (Purdam et al, 2002) recommended various policy responses and possible initiatives for increasing engagement among BME communities. Among these were measures to: make registration and voting easier; encourage political parties and others to review BME representation within UK politics; and ensure that public-awareness campaigns reflect the diversity of BME communities and their consumption of culture and media. However, community-specific understandings of political participation are necessary for more nuanced understandings of political behaviour. The system of biraderi deeply embedded in the political culture of Pakistani communities in the UK is by its nature inherently hierarchical and patriarchal and effectively disenfranchises young people and women. While young people in general are disillusioned with politicians, Pakistani Muslim young people are doubly disillusioned: by politicians in general and also by community leaders and, more specifically, biraderi elders. The system of patronage that developed in the 1970s served the interests of local politicians and community elders. Bloc community votes were offered for the reward of community prestige and local power. This stifled genuine political exchange. As a consequence, those outside of the biraderi system, or those at the bottom of the biraderi hierarchical order, feel isolated from mainstream politics. Some politically inclined young Muslims have sought creative ways of political engagement to bypass the biraderi system and still be involved in civic and political life. George Galloway's surprise electoral win in the Bradford West by-election in 2012 was, in part, built on the disillusionment many Muslims felt with electoral politics in the constituency (Akhtar, 2012). Regardless of Galloway's performance in office, his victory highlighted the potential for mobilisation against the biraderi system (Peace and Akhtar, 2014). Young British Muslims may be doubly disillusioned with electoral politics but they have demonstrated an enthusiasm for engagement and a desire for change.

Note

[1] Produced in 2008 by Gert Wilders, a member of the Dutch Parliament.

References

Akhtar, P. (2012) 'British Muslim Politics: After Bradford', *Political Quarterly*, vol 83, no 4, pp 762–6.

Akhtar, P. (2013) *British Muslim Politics*, Basingstoke: Palgrave.

Anwar, M. (1986) *Race and Politics: Ethnic Minorities and the British Political System*, London: Tavistock.

Anwar, M. (1994) *Race and Elections: the Participation of Ethnic Minorities in Politics*, Coventry: Centre for Research in Ethnic Relation.

Anwar, M. (2005) 'Muslims in Britain: Issues, Policies and Practice', in T. Abbas (ed) *Muslim Britain: Communities Under Pressure*, London: Zed Books.

Bang, H. (2004) 'Everyday Makers and Expert Citizens Building Political not Social Capital', ANU Politics Programme, available at: http://dspace.anu.edu.au/handle/1885/42117 (accessed 6 May 2006).

BBC NewsOnline (2004) 'Disaffection Among British Muslim Youth', available at: http://news.bbc.co.uk/1/hi/uk/3586421.stm (accessed 31 March 2004).

Bentley, T. (2005) *Everyday Democracy: Why we get the Politicians we Deserve*, London: Demos.

Bhavnani, K.-K. (1991) *Talking Politics: a Psychological Framing for Views from Youth in Britain,* Cambridge: Cambridge University Press.

Cantle, T. (2001) *Community Cohesion: A Report of the Independent Review Team,* London: Home Office.

Casciani, D (2005) 'From election launch to PR panic', BBC NewsOnline http://news.bbc.co.uk/go/pr/fr/-/1/hi/uk_politics/vote_2005/frontpage/4461695 (accessed 23 July 2005).

Charsley, K. (2013) *Transnational Pakistani Connections: Marrying 'Back Home',* London: Routledge.

Clarke, H.D., Sanders, D., Stewart, M.C. and Whiteley, P. (2004) *Political Choice in Britain,* Oxford: Oxford University Press.

Corrin, C. (1999) *Feminist Perspectives on Politics,* London: Longman.

Eden, K. and Roker, D. (2002) *'Doing Something': Young People as Social Actors*, Leicester: National Youth Agency.

Electoral Commission (2002a) *Voter Engagement among Black and Minority Ethnic Communities* – available to download at: http://www.electoralcommission.org.uk/__data/assets/electoral_commission_pdf_file/0020/16094/Ethnicfinalreport_11586-6190__E__N__S__W__.pdf.

Electoral Commission (2002b) *Campaign to Increase Electoral Registration Amongst Black and Minority Ethnic Communities*, available at: http://www.electoralcommission.org.uk/media-centre/newsreleasecampaigns.cfm/news/63 (accessed 15 January 2007.

Edmunds, June (2010) '"Elite" young Muslims in Britain: from transnational to global politics', *Contemporary Islam*, vol 4, no 2 pp 215–38.

Electoral Commission (2005) *Social Exclusion and Political Engagement*, available at: http://www.electoralcommission.org.uk/__data/assets/pdf_file/0007/63835/Social-exclusion-and-political-engagement.pdf (accessed 3 November 2014).

Electoral Commission and Hansard Society (2007) *An Audit of Political Engagement 4: Research Report*, available at: http://www. electoralcommission.org.uk/files/dms/Audit-4-Report-Web-2007-03-27_25163-18662__E__N__S__W__.pdf (accessed 19 January 2007).

Forbrig, J. (2005) 'Introduction', in J. Forbrig (ed) *Revisiting Youth Political Participation: Challenges for Research and Democratic Practice in Europe,* Strasbourg: Council of Europe Publishing.

Garbaye, R. (2005) *Getting into Local Power: the Politics of Ethnic Minorities in British and French cities,* Oxford: Blackwell.

Geddes, A. (2001) 'Explaining Ethnic Minority Representation: Contemporary Trends in the Shadow of the Past', in Bennie, L., Denver, D., Harrison, L. and Tonge, J. (eds) *The British Elections and Parties Review 2001,* London: Frank Cass.

Gillan, A and Vikram, Dodd, (2005) 'Islamists step up campaign to stop Muslims voting', *Guardian*, http://www.theguardian.com/politics/2005/apr/22/uk.election20052 (accessed 23 July 2005).

Henn, M., Weinstein, M. and Wring, D. (2002) 'A Generation Apart? Youth and Political Participation in Britain', *British Journal of Politics and International Relations*, vol 4, pp 167–92.

Hay, C. (2007) *Why we Hate Politics*, Cambridge: Polity Press.

Henn, M., Weinstein, M. and Forrest, S. (2005) 'Uninterested youth? Young people's attitudes towards party politics in Britain', *Political studies*, vol 53, no 3, pp 556–78.

Kavanagh, D. (1982) *Politics of the Labour Party*, London: Allen & Unwin.

Layton-Henry, Z. (1990) 'Black Electoral Participation: an Analysis of Recent Trends', in Goulbourne, H. (ed) *Black Politics in Britain*, Aldershot: Avebury.

Layton-Henry, Z. (1992) *Politics of Immigration: Race and Race Relations in Postwar Britain,* Oxford: Blackwell.

Lopez Pintor, R. and Gratschew, M. (2002) *Voter Turnout Since 1945: a Global Report*, available at: http://www.idea.int/publications/voter_turnout_weurope/index.cfm (accessed 12 June 2006).

Marsh, D., O'Toole, T. and Jones, S. (2007) *Young People and Politics in the UK: Apathy or Alienation?* Basingstoke: Palgrave Macmillan.

Milbrath, L.W. (1965) *Political Participation: How and Why do People Get Involved in Politics?,* Chicago: Rand McNally.

Mustafa, A. (2014) *Identity and political participation among young British Muslims*, Palgrave Macmillan (forthcoming).

O'Toole, T., Marsh, D. and Jones, S. (2003) 'Political Literacy Cuts Both Ways: The Politics of non-Participation among Young People', *Political Quarterly,* vol 74, pp 349–60.

Peace, T. and Akhtar, P. (2014) 'Biraderi, Bloc Votes and Bradford: Investigating the Respect Party's Campaign Strategy', *The British Journal of Politics & International Relations,* doi: 10.1111/1467-856X.12057, available at: http://onlinelibrary.wiley.com/doi/10.1111/1467-856X.12057/full

Pirie, M. and Worcester, R.M. (1998) *The Millennial Generation,* London: Adam Smith Institute.

Purdam, K., Fieldhouse, E., Kalra, V. and Russell, V. (2002) *Voter engagement among black and minority ethnic communities,* London: Electoral Commission.

Putnam, R.D. (2000) *Bowling Alone: the Collapse and Revival of American Community,* New York: Simon & Schuster.

Richards, L. and Marshall, B. (2003) *Political Engagement Among Black and Minority Ethnic Communities: What We Know and What We Need To Know,* available at: http://www.electoralcommission.gov.uk/files/dms/BMEresearchseminarpaper_11354-8831__E__N__S__W__.pdf (accessed 2 November 2006).

Roker, D., Player, K. and Coleman, J. (1999) 'Young people's voluntary and campaigning activities as sources of political education', *Oxford Review of Education,* vol 25, nos 1–2, pp 185–98.

Stolle, D., Hooghe, M. and Micheletti, M. (2005) 'Politics in the supermarket: Political consumerism as a form of political participation', *International political science review,* vol 26, no 3, pp 245–69.

Stoker, G. (2006) *Why Politics Matters: Making Democracy Work,* Basingstoke: Palgrave Macmillan.

Webb, P. (2007) *Democracy and Political Parties,* available at: http://www.democracyseries.org.uk/sites/democracyseries.org.uk/files/HANSARD%20DEM%20POLITICAL%20COMPLETE.pdf (accessed 15 December 2007).

White, C., Bruce, C. and Ritchie, J. (2000) 'Young people's politics: Political Interest and Engagement Amongst 14–24 year olds, available at: http://www.jrf.org.uk/bookshop/eBooks/1859353096.pdf (accessed 1 November 2007).

Whiteley, P. and Seyd, P. (2002) *High-intensity Participation: the Dynamics of Party Activism in Britain,* Ann Arbor: The University of Michigan Press.

Van Zoonen, L., Vis, F. and Mihelj, S. (2010) 'Performing citizenship on YouTube: Activism, satire and online debate around the anti-Islam video Fitna', *Critical Discourse Studies*, vol 7, no 4, pp 249–62.

Viswanathan, A. (2002) 'Doing nothing not an option', in *Disengaged and disinterested: deliberations on voter apathy*, New Politics Network (winter).

Part Three: The politics of identity and marginalisation

Political engagement among ethnic minority young people: exploring new grammars of action

Therese O'Toole

Introduction

For some time now, the crisis narratives that have attended young people's political participation have been qualified by a growing body of research demonstrating the significance of forms of political action outside of electoral and party politics (Marsh et al, 2007). There is in the literature a growing recognition of the range of alternative, informal and everyday repertoires of political action in which citizens, and perhaps young citizens especially, are engaging (Zukin et al, 2006; Dalton, 2008). The study of youth participation has also seen greater attention to differences among young people, particularly of gender and educational status and, more irregularly, of ethnicity. The latter focus has received on-going attention in public and government discourses though, where ethnic minority young people have been the objects of particular concern. For instance, in the anxious debates about youth political apathy in the UK in recent years, connected to the low levels of electoral participation among 18- to 24-year-olds in elections since 2001 (Marsh et al, 2007), it is often suggested that ethnic minority young people are even less likely to turn out to vote, as compared to young people in general or older ethnic minority groups (Purdam et al, 2002; Electoral Commission, 2003, 2005), and that ethnic minority young people are less civically engaged (Janmaat, 2008). In the aftermath of disturbances in 2001 and the 2005 London bombings, such narratives have increasingly converged on the issue of religious, and particularly Muslim, youth identities, centring on concerns about political disaffection, failed integration, a lack of social capital consonant with democratic participation, or violent political extremism.

In this chapter I argue that the evidence base underpinning perceptions that participation in democratic life among ethnic minority and Muslim young people is lower than for other groups of young people is rather weak, while those studies that do exist do not necessarily sustain such generalised crisis narratives. Furthermore, public and academic discourses on ethnic minority young people have paid insufficient attention to the ways in which ethnic minority young people *do* politically engage. In this chapter, I address the varied forms of political action among ethnic minority young people within and beyond mainstream electoral politics, drawing on qualitative research with ethnic minority young activists carried out in the UK. In so doing, I suggest that the study of political engagement among ethnic minority young people should be situated alongside the growing literatures on changing patterns of political engagement; the significance of globalisation and globalised information and communication technologies for the modes and scales of political participation; and the political implications of the emergence of 'new ethnicities' and hybrid identities in underpinning more reflexive and less collectivist expressions of social identities. These broader processes have some profound implications for the ways in which ethnic minority and Muslim young people politically engage.

A crisis of participation?

In the UK, dominant discourses on ethnic minority young people have focused on concerns about political disaffection as well as violent political extremism. These have been driven by events such as the disturbances that took place in 2001 in the northern English towns of Bradford, Burnley and Oldham, characterised by confrontations between young people of Pakistani and Bangladeshi heritage and the police (Casciani, 2004), as well as the bombings of 7 July 2005 in London, which involved British Muslims. While the official report on the 2001 disturbances, the Cantle Report (2001), focused largely on ethnicity rather than religion as a key division within the three areas where the disturbances took place, following the 9/11 attacks in the US, these events were read post hoc as a conflict between young Muslims and the police, and increasingly focused on Muslim, as opposed to 'Asian', communities' 'self-segregation' (Phillips, 2006). The motif of 'failed integration' of British Muslims intensified following the London bombings of 2005 (Bagguley and Hussain, 2008) and featured prominently in the ensuing debates on the failures of British multiculturalism and the nature of political disaffection and extremism among young Muslims (see PET Working Groups, 2005).

Given the extent of public and media attention paid to political disengagement among ethnic minority and Muslim young people, it is surprising how few studies there have been that directly explore their political experiences and engagement. In the UK, where ethnicity statistics are routinely collected in a range of domains, there are relatively few survey-based studies of political and electoral participation that disaggregate by both ethnicity and age. Similarly, although anxieties about young Muslims' political disengagement or radicalisation have to some degree overtaken discourses on ethnic minority young people, there are few survey studies that disaggregate patterns of political engagement by age and religion. As such, then, there has been rather little by way of robust analysis of turnouts, voting preferences or forms of political engagement among either ethnic minority or Muslim young people. Moreover, those studies that do exist often suggest a rather different perspective.

For instance, the view that political disengagement is more pronounced among ethnic minority young people is challenged by findings from the recent Ethnic Minority British Election Study (EMBES) of electoral engagement among ethnic minorities in the 2010 general election. This study found that while age is a statistically significant factor determining turnout across all ethnic groups, such that younger people are less likely to vote, the effect of age is actually *weaker* among ethnic minorities than it is for White British (Heath et al, 2011, p 262). Interestingly, Quintelier's (2009) study of patterns of political participation among immigrant youth in Belgium analysed a range of repertoires of political action including voting, party membership, protesting, boycotting and buycotting, and found that migrant youth of non-European backgrounds were actually 'the most politically active group, ahead of both Belgian and European immigrants' (Quintelier, 2009, p 929). Her work also dispels views of young Muslims as politically disaffected, finding high levels of activism among young Muslims, and – contrary to prevailing perceptions – Muslim young women especially. This finding echoes recent events in the UK in relation to some successes of the Respect Party – a coalition of Left and anti-war groupings – which in recent times has achieved spectacular electoral victories in areas of Muslim settlement (Peace, 2013) where the activism of young Muslims, and especially Muslim young women, were notable features of the campaigning.

The perceptions of lower levels of political participation among ethnic minority young people, then, are not well substantiated – indeed within those relatively few surveys of ethnic minority and Muslim young people's political engagement that do exist there are some indications that they are not necessarily less likely to vote than White young people. In this chapter, I argue that our view of political participation should in any case extend beyond electoral turnouts, and look more widely than conventional, or violent extremist, forms of politics to take account of the range of forms of activism in which young people engage and the issues and concerns that animate their political activism. Before discussing these forms of activism, I set out the nature of the qualitative data on which this chapter draws.

Research design

This chapter draws on research from a qualitative project with ethnic minority young activists in Birmingham and Bradford that I conducted from 2004 to 2007 with Richard Gale. As many youth studies researchers have argued (Eden and Roker, 2000), crisis narratives about youth political apathy have tended to displace attention from forms of political participation in which young people *do* engage. The study set out to address this issue by posing the question: in what ways do ethnic minority young people politically engage? To address this question, the study explored modes, targets and repertoires of political action among groups of ethnic minority young participants and activists. The project worked with a range of groups in the two cities, sampled according to a broad conception of political participation that included different levels of engagement in formal, informal, youth, community, neighbourhood, gender and campaign politics, including:

- two groups of Members of the Youth Parliament (MYPs) from the Bradford Keighley Youth Parliament (BKYP) and the Birmingham Young People's Parliament;
- a women's group in Birmingham comprising, significantly, Pakistani, Yemeni and Indian women, established to provide women with a 'space of their own' and to challenge community and local state responses to women's concerns;
- an organisation in Bradford providing a range of educational, social and recreational provision for predominantly Muslim young women in a 'women-only' environment;
- a youth group based in Birmingham, focused on addressing experiences of African Caribbean young men and women, organising to inform 'the public and government agencies on gang culture' and to challenge 'the boundaries of local and governmental action'. Following disturbances in 2005, the group began to work with young Bangladeshis to address common issues facing young people in the city;

- a youth group in Bradford engaged in youth, community, self-help and neighbourhood renewal projects; working primarily with Pakistani young men, the group also sets out to include in its activities young Slovenian men newly migrated to the local area;
- four local youth groups in Birmingham and Bradford focused on increasing educational resources and opportunities, working with Pakistani, Yemeni, Somali and White young people;
- a Bradford-based youth group, working with Pakistani, African Caribbean and White young people to 'encourage positive identities' and 'celebrate young people's achievements';
- a Birmingham-based anti-war 'Muslim Justice Movement' organised and led by young Muslim men.

We carried out 12 focus groups (6 in each city) and 50 individual in-depth interviews, involving a total of 76 respondents (39 in Birmingham and 37 in Bradford). Our respondents were aged 16 to 25, with slightly more men than women in the sample. The self-ascribed ethnicity of respondents included: Pakistani, British Pakistani, Muslim, Kashmiri, Mirpuri, Yemeni, Afro-Caribbean, Black British, Somali, Indian, Black African and Mixed Race. Corresponding to the demographics of each city, a little over half of our sample were Muslim.

The focus groups consisted of a group discussion with between 4 and 12 individuals exploring the groups' activities, membership, experiences and reflections, and their perspectives on political institutions, processes and issues. These were followed by individual in-depth interviews with the focus group members. A key aspect of these interviews was discussion of people's personal political biographies, which explored how and why individuals became politically active, the range of activities in which they participated, their views of their local areas, the issues that concerned them and how they saw their future political interests and participation. Our rationale for including a 'political biographical' perspective was driven by our concern not just to understand the dynamics of a range of groups and their collective experiences but to consider also members' paths into those groups and the range of repertoires of action in which they engaged, including 'everyday' and 'subpolitical' action (Giddens, 1994; Beck, 1997). These interviews were supplemented by interviews with youth workers and local authority and youth services personnel.

The cities of Birmingham and Bradford, where the research was conducted, have significant (young) ethnic minority and Muslim populations, and somewhat different demographic profiles, economic development and histories of political mobilisation. Ethnic minority groups comprised 29.6% of the population in Birmingham and 21.7% in Bradford in 2001, with ethnic minority young people constituting 38% of the 16–24 cohort in Birmingham and 34% in Bradford (Census, 2001). Both cities are former industrial centres that have witnessed major deindustrialisation and were engaged in strategies for regeneration: while Birmingham was reinventing itself as a 'global city' with burgeoning financial, service and cultural sectors, Bradford's local economy had experienced less growth. In both cities there were, and are, marked patterns of geographical concentration of ethnic groups, giving rise to some distinctive patterns of political mobilisation and local community politics. In both cities ethnic minority young people assumed a political visibility as a consequence of disturbances (occurring in 2001 in Bradford and in 2005 in the Lozells area in Birmingham) and concerns about community cohesion, educational attainment, gang culture and political extremism. Nevertheless, the groups with whom we were in contact expressed concerns regarding the mechanisms for addressing the experiences of ethnic minority young people within local democratic structures. These contextual issues certainly had an impact on the issues and policy agendas that pertained in each city, as well as on young people's engagement in their local areas (O'Toole and Gale, 2013).

Changing political participation

I opened by suggesting that crisis narratives on ethnic minority young people tend to focus primarily on electoral non-participation (which is not always well substantiated) and (relatively rare) instances of political extremism – paying too little attention to the range of forms of activism between these poles. I argued that analysis of repertoires of action requires a broader conception of 'the political' – to address engagement that takes place within and outside of mainstream and electoral politics. In this respect, this study links to a broader set of literatures that suggest that declining levels of electoral and political-party participation in established democracies among citizens generally (Hay, 2007) sit alongside increasing levels of engagement in civic, voluntary or other informal modes of political engagement (Dalton, 2008). Seen from this perspective, political participation is not so much declining as changing.

Many locate these changes within broader social and political developments that have been taking place over the last few decades, such as the rise of new social movements since the 1960s, characterised by more informal forms of activism that focus on questions of identity and that are associated with the growth of 'postmaterialist' values and political concerns (Inglehart, 1997; Norris, 2002), engendering a concern with identities and social practices as objectives of action, with social movements providing the spaces for the public articulation of demands and interests in relation to these (Melucci and Avritzer, 2000). Additionally, the end of the Cold War, it is suggested, has had profound implications for political ideologies, diminishing the mass-mobilising role of political parties (Beck, 1997). The growth of the internet since the 1980s is credited with making state boundaries and scales of action more fluid and enabling more creative and personalised repertoires of action (Dahlgren, 2005; Bennett, 2008). This has occurred alongside other effects of globalisation that have resulted in new transnational and global political structures that have diversified the targets of citizens' action. These social and political developments are thought to have transformed citizens' relationships to politics and given rise to new political subjectivities that are more individualised, personalised and reflexive (Giddens, 1994), where citizens increasingly express their engagement in informal, networked forms of political organisation, using hands-on, direct repertoires of action and where questions of identity and culture are increasingly a matter of political concern. This has given rise to new horizons in political participation research exploring more reflexive (Beck, 1997; Giddens, 2002), 'DIY', everyday (Bang, 2005) and life-style forms of activism.

According to Giddens, citizens' political engagement is increasingly founded on a 'life politics' of reflexive engagement with the world, based on a politics of identity and choice (Giddens, 1994, p 91), involving everyday challenges to established rules, practices, norms and decisions – made possible in a context where these are no longer governed by tradition (Giddens, 1994 and 2002). He argues: 'Life politics, and the disputes and struggles connected with it, are about how we should live in a world where everything that used to be natural (or traditional) now has in some sense to be chosen, or decided about' (Giddens, 1994, p 90–1). He suggests that one reason why party politics tied to debates between Left and Right have become unappealing is because they do not address these 'new fields of action'. This resonates with Beck's thesis on the reinvention of politics, in which he argues that the decline in interest in formal politics is not evidence of a lack of political engagement: such conclusions are based on looking for politics 'in the wrong places' (Beck, 1997, p 99). He suggests that new forms of politics are arising (sometimes behind the facades of orthodox institutions), that are concerned not with the aims of political parties, but with citizens' capacity for self-organisation and engagement in everyday, often small-scale, activities that bypass the institutions of the state, which he refers to as 'subpolitics'. Similarly, Bang argues that for contemporary citizens the 'political is increasingly personal and self-reflexive' (Bang, 2005, p 163), manifested in everyday forms of political engagement that eschew formal institutional politics in preference for a politics of direct, self-actualising, 'Do-It-Yourself' (DIY) action. McDonald's (2006) study of the political subjectivities within contemporary global movements suggests that recent years have given rise to new, more personal and interpersonal, networked grammars of political action that are distinct from earlier 'civic-industrial grammars of action' expressed through hierarchical, vertically integrated, highly mediated and collectivist forms of organisation.

New grammars of action

Debates on, as well as the study of, ethnic minority or Muslim young people's politics have generally not been connected to these analyses of shifting trends in citizens' political participation. Our data, however, demonstrates their relevance to the ways in which ethnic minority and Muslim young people express their political engagement. Thus, we found very diverse repertoires of action among our respondents, including but also beyond electoral engagement, and perspectives that give substance to arguments that the political subjectivities of young people are oriented towards more informal, personalised, networked grammars of action, such that, while they did not completely disavow engagement with mainstream politics, neither were they strongly engaged in this arena.

A recurring feature of activists' political engagement was their scepticism towards representative politics and institutions – a common finding in recent studies of young people's political participation (see Marsh et al, 2007). Although most of our respondents were likely to be voters, few cited affiliation to any particular party as a reason for voting: instead, reasons were often local (for example, to block the BNP) or global (such as to register opposition to the war on Iraq). Even respondents who were members of a local youth parliament were ambivalent about its status as a representative institution, and in one focus group there was extensive discussion of whether 'parliament' was an appropriate term for the Birmingham Young People's Parliament. As one MYP argued:

> "You're branding yourself with this, this – and why? [...] [Impassioned] Clearly people are not involved, participating

in that kind of democracy to begin with, why are you giving yourself that label deliberately? [...] It's amazing the number of people you can speak to, both adults and young people, who will say that Westminster no longer actually changes a great deal in terms of policy. And to have that same kind of connotation with a young people's forum [...] And that's, you know, that's actually a much bigger problem, that people are disaffected in that way ..."

Generally, respondents tended to prefer direct involvement in horizontal, informal networks or movements, or ad hoc involvement with particular initiatives, rather than membership of formal political organisations. As an activist from the Saheli women's group in Birmingham,[1] involved in working with local women from different ethnic and religious communities as well as in local community politics and protest activities, explained:

"personally, I would never become like, people have joked like 'Why don't you become a ward Councillor or something?' but [...] that's not where I'm at, you know. I come to it from a more questioning, learning point of view, as opposed to becoming bogged down with the bureaucracy of, like trying to make change, 'cos I don't think that's my way of doing it. I think there's more benefit in doing it in, through my role here at Saheli or, you know in another position where I'm hopefully impacting on the real people, as opposed to getting bogged down with party lines and, like party agendas and stuff, that doesn't interest me."

Where we found engagement in electoral and institutional politics, this tended to be expressed in highly personalised, DIY approaches. For example, one activist had campaigned for the Respect Party in the 2005 general election, leafleting and street canvassing – although he had not joined Respect. As he explained:

"it's not that I have any affiliation with Respect in terms of its ideology, or anything, 'cause I'm still trying to unravel that myself [...] I'm still trying to look for some kind of coherent aim, some agenda [...] And, I'm just flirting with various different groups. [...] I'll never join any of them. They've all asked us, because they would do, but I've never joined any of them."

This stance was also replicated in his relationships with other organisations, which were based on hands-on involvement rather than formal membership or affiliation. Thus activists tended to avoid submerging their identities into formally constituted, vertically integrated political organisations.

Most activists were engaged in, and oriented towards, 'subpolitical' activism (Beck, 1997) in relation to local spaces or specific social issues, and through actions such as voluntary activity (for example, volunteering for charitable organisations, such as Islamic Relief, or as mentors); career choices (for example, working in an Asian women's refuge or as a youth worker); political shopping (for example, buycotting Fair Trade (Micheletti et al, 2004) or boycotting Israeli goods); life-style choices (such as limiting personal consumption or energy use); web-based action (such as blogging or website construction); or discursive political action (to challenge perceptions of Muslim women or Black or Muslim youth in mainstream media and public discourses). Thus our study found plenty of (often intensive) activism that was located outside of mainstream political arenas. As one Muslim volunteer and mentor working with Muslim young men in Bradford commented:

> "I think as a person, as an individual I don't think I can make that change on a bigger scale. [...] whereas with my skills as a youth worker I can make a difference on a smaller scale, where I live [...] I have my own politics in a way."

Conceptually, these forms of engagement should be seen not simply as additions to an increasing battery of repertoires of political action, but as underscored by different kinds of political subjectivities that were characterised by a preference for more immediate, personal, direct, hands-on, everyday forms of activism. These kinds of subjectivities constitute, borrowing from McDonald (2006), 'new grammars of action'. Thus, even where activists were engaged in institutional politics, they did so in ways that suggested reluctance to assimilate to 'civic-industrial' grammars of action.

New technologies, global engagement and DIY activism

For many activists, the possibilities for everyday engagement in direct forms of action were facilitated by access to web-based forms of activism. There is a literature suggesting that globalised forms of communication and networking have made internet-based political action increasingly significant (Norris, 2002; Dahlgren, 2005; Bennett,

2008, and that, facilitated by new technologies, contemporary forms of action are increasingly concerned with global issues. An important aspect of this development is the scope for networking and consciousness raising afforded by globalised communication systems. For McDonald, globalisation (albeit in highly uneven ways) creates a space of flows, facilitated by network logics that engage with personal experiences linking individuals across space (although not uniformly) (McDonald, 2006, p 32), and such changes in apprehensions of space potentially create very different ways of engaging politically. These developments, aligned with the emergence of more direct, personalised grammars of political engagement, have given rise to greater use of communications technologies as a means of DIY political action (Häyhtiö and Rinne, 2007).

This was particularly evident in the practices of Muslim Justice Movement (MJM) activists in Birmingham who were critically engaged with a range of media, not only analysing messages about Islam through consumption of a global range of broadcast and internet media sources, but also as producers of media communications – through blogging and website construction – as a form of direct action that allowed them to circumvent conventional mediated forms of politics. The communication tactics of MJM activists drew on the internet not only as a tool that facilitated de-medialised, direct forms of activism, the group also viewed web-based communication itself as a terrain of political action, particularly in terms of disrupting discursive constructions of Muslims/Islam found within mainstream media (MSM). As the MJM focus group explained in relation to the logic of web-activism and protesting, much of its activism was at the level of discursive politics.

Respondent 1: That's what we see as our only effective means for doing something. But, in order to draw people to come and protest with us, or to take on board the issues that we are trying to portray, and to let people know about, it's, it's difficult because it's hard to defeat the logic behind what Bush and Blair are doing over in the Middle East, and, and the whole war on terror. The whole lot, we have to defeat the logic of the war on terror before we can get the real points across. Because […] they portray it as like a clash of cultures. Bush would say, you know, 'they hate our values, that's why they are doing this', you know, and 'they don't like our way of life' and all that crap.

Several: Yeah, yeah, yeah, yeah.

Respondent 1: But it's, it's not that. They don't like your actions, what you're doing, your government. They, they mix up the issue [...] so when we are protesting Lebanon, you know ...

Respondent 2: Extremism is going on over there! [Laughter]

Respondent 1: [The public] don't wanna, they don't even debate the issue. Talking about Palestine and Israel, you know, the standard conception that you have of Palestine and Israel is that these terrorists are terrorising the Israelis. And that's, that's the common understanding. So, we, I think we have to defeat the logic behind these stories.

The role of information and communication technologies (ICTs) in facilitating more direct forms of action, and in global and international issues, created possibilities among our respondents for direct political engagement on issues such as Palestine, Iraq, Afghanistan, Islamic Relief, tsunami relief, debt, or the terms of international trade and development. Political engagement with global and international issues and campaigns captured the imaginations of many activists, in ways that found little equivalence at the level of national politics, as one Saheli activist elaborated:

Interviewer: What does 'politics' mean to you?

Respondent: What does it mean? [...] middle-aged men in suits, talking endlessly and not really doing anything constructive! It's got quite a negative impact on me. But I think that's due to you know, all of these individuals not really making it accessible [...] on the flip side of that [...] politics does kind of grab me as well. How do we function internationally and how I feel all of that, that's more interesting to me than nationally.

It is important to note here that such engagement was not solely an outcome of diasporic ties, in which young people engaged with the issues and politics of their countries of heritage – as was the case in Eade and Garbin's (2002) study of Bengali young activists in the East End of London. While these were often important, engagement was also underpinned by more globalised orientations, made possible through their use of ICTs, which enabled access to a range of media and information sources; enhanced possibilities for creating and disseminating, rather than only consuming, information and political messages; enhanced their ability to engage in campaigns with little need to invest in organisation building; and facilitated engagement in personalised, horizontal and networked forms of activism, which was a recurring characteristic of the activist preferences of most of our respondents.

DIY ethnicity, reflexive religiosity and political activism

Much of my argument so far concerning the significance of new grammars of action could be applied to young people generally – and in many ways respondents' politics and concerns reflected their identities and positions as young people. Yet, it is important not to decontextualise these, particularly in relation to the significance of salient social differences among young people. Both the concepts of reflexive individualisation and subpolitics have been criticised for their lack of attention to the specific contexts to political activism or social identities. Bakardjieva (2009) is critical of the lack of attention to the significance of *collective* identities in both Beck's and Giddens' accounts of sub/life politics, suggesting that their theory 'downplays and almost cancels the significance of collective identities for citizenship and political life in general' (Bakardjieva, 2009, p 95). In particular, critics (Bernstein, 2005; Adams and Raisborough, 2008; Bakardjieva, 2009) have cited the continuing salience of class, gender, race and ethnicity in shaping personal subjectivities and political mobilisations.

The literatures on contemporary conceptions of ethnic and religious identities frequently argue, nevertheless, that there has been a fracturing of stable group identities, and the emergence of more reflexive, complex, hybrid identities. This theoretical literature has focused a great deal on young people, who are often seen as bearers of 'hybrid identities' and 'new ethnicities' (Hall, 2000; Alexander, 2002; Back, 2002). While there has been a great deal of writing on the impact of complex and intersecting identities in undermining Black identity politics (Mercer, 2000; Modood, 2000; Meer, 2010), and the rise of ethnic and cultural movements in fragmenting anti-racist and Black political movements (Alexander, 2002), there has been relatively little empirical research on the ways in which new ethnicities and complex, hybrid identities might find political expression and little attempt to examine the implications of changing identities among ethnic minority or Muslim young people for their political engagement.

Our research found that ethnic and religious *group* identities were significant in animating political action among our respondents – not least as a consequence of their experiences of being othered through categories of ethnicity, race or religion. Thus, for many activists, experiences of racism, or of encountering pathologising discourses on ethnic minorities or Muslims, were politicising. For example, one MYP in Bradford talked of being politicised by her early school experiences of teachers' highly ethnocentric perspectives on her and other young people of Asian heritage. This translated into anger, challenge and ultimately her emergence as an advocate for young people at school, in the youth parliament and in the field of youth activism generally, as she recounted:

> "[W]hat used to frustrate me was when I used to hear the school teachers saying something like 'oh those Asian lads they are so and so' or 'those Asian girls and their parents came in and said that'. I didn't like that, because I thought well it's not all like that. The only reason it is like that is because you don't listen to [the issues that] these young people have got […] and as a young student I couldn't really step in, you know, I was powerless to do that. […] I think that's where I was really passionate. I thought to myself, one of these days you know I will be able to say these things."

The salience of public debates and policies on ethnic diversity, multiculturalism and cohesion, Black youth, Muslim youth, security or urban conflict were important in defining the contours of the political field in which activists formed their political perspectives and engagement. The period in which we were working was characterised by intense debate on and critique of multiculturalism as a consequence of both the disturbances in 2001 and the London bombings of 2005, following which the community cohesion paradigm emerged as a dominant discourse on the governance of diversity. A particular feature of this discourse was its assertion of ethnic and cultural group differences as a social problem, and its emphasis on the mixing of ethnic groups as a solution. For young activists in our study, some implications of the disturbances involved a heightened sense of their lives as shaped by their association with areas of ethnic minority concentration that were also stigmatised by incidents of urban disorder and perceptions of maladjustment and failed integration – an awareness that manifested itself in a critical stance on outside characterisations of cities like Bradford or neighbourhoods such as Aston, Handsworth or Lozells in Birmingham as sites of urban disorder and high crime, and attendant racialised moral commentaries on Black and minority-ethnic residents in those areas. A further implication of the community cohesion paradigm, particularly in the aftermath of the London bombings, was that it intensified debates on the place of Muslims, and particularly young Muslims, within British society. These factors underpinned policy interventions that placed particular emphasis on inculcating in young Muslims' norms of active citizenship and identification with core British values (pursued under the community cohesion agenda, and later through the government's community engagement-focused, counter-terrorism 'Prevent' strategy). These broader debates and issues shaped the political terrain on which young activists formed their political identities and trajectories, and meant that identity issues were in many ways highly politically charged – sometimes perceived as constraints on or a stimulus to activism. Thus we found many instances of young activists reflecting on their own identities and responding to and seeking to shape wider debates on ethnic groups, Muslims or the governance of diversity.

There is a growing literature on the identities of young Muslims across Europe that points to the decoupling of ethnic and religious identities among many young Muslims, with religious identities emerging as a more focal reference for identity and political engagement (Jacobson, 1997; Eade and Garbin, 2006; Mushaben, 2008; Gale and O'Toole, 2009). Among our respondents, the significance of religious identities in shaping political activism was important in three senses: as objects of governmental action (for example, through community cohesion or counterterrorism policies); as 'highly polarised and stigmatic' identities (Mandaville, 2009, p 493); and as a mode of identity giving form and substance to patterns of political engagement (Brah, 1996; Gale and O'Toole, 2009; Modood, 2009; Meer, 2010).

For many of the young Muslims in our study, the events of 9/11, the war on Iraq or the 2005 London bombings and the ensuing heightened surveillance of young Muslims were politicising experiences. One Saheli member, reflecting on the experience of her younger brother being subject to a stop-and-search by the police under prevention of terrorism measures, linked this with international events in relation to the war in Iraq, such that she perceived local and international events as cohering in a more generalised attack on Muslims and Islam, and she reflected: "So – that's why I got active and used the first demonstration I went in was in College. And then I went in one to London."

Encounters with public and institutional discourses on race and religion frequently gave rise to direct and personal forms of action to contest representations of ethnic minority and Muslim young people. As one Muslim woman explained, her decision to participate in the BKYP, media interviews and public debates had been underpinned by her desire to challenge dominant representations of Muslims and Muslim women following the 2005 London bombings:

> "I think now like as a Muslim woman, as you know, coming from a Black background, it feels more important [...] that we are seen to be out there and be active, because well, probably always thinking about the Muslim community secluding itself from everyone and sort of isolating itself, especially Muslim women being oppressed and, you know, subjected to their fathers and tied to [...] their religion. Whatever the nonsense they have said, [...] and I think that there are lot of assumptions made about people like myself and it was important and thinking back on it, that I did get involved in challenging things and that I did have an opinion and I was, I was assertive, without being too aggressive and I think yeah, Muslims have opinions too."

For many respondents, such a sensibility was underpinned by their awareness of a broader global Muslim community of the umma, animated by global events such as the Iraq War and the publication of cartoons of Muhammad in Denmark and elsewhere in 2005, as one MYP from Birmingham explained:

> "something about Islam is that everyone feels you, you're connected with it, it's called the brotherhood, so if there has been an injustice against Muslims on the other side of the world, Muslims here will care about it, and then [...] obviously, the foreign policy of our country has meant that youths feel just as much as adults or their parents and we do care about that and I think that's something that [...] really affects us [...] the feeling that, it's a war on Islam ..."

Significantly, young Muslims in our study were active in seeking out an understanding of religious identity and of what it means to be a Muslim in diaspora, in ways that concurred with the growing literature on reflexive, DIY religiosity among young Muslims elsewhere. As Harris and Roose (2013, p 14) suggest, 'religiosity is emerging as important to many young Muslims as a much more self-fashioned form of expression and moral guidance'. Based on their research with Muslim young people in Australia, they found that 'the moral reference points provided by a religious tradition could be seen to intersect with the requirement of modern self-making in particular ways. Islam was a spark for personal action and individual responsibility' (Harris and Roose, 2013, p 15; and see Mushaben, 2008). Our research also found that religious identity was cited as a framework for linking ethics and action, which sometimes provided a legitimacy to political activism in the face of parental opposition, as one male member of the MJM explained:

> "My religion has given me more freedom than anyone. I mean things like arranged marriages which is more culture than religion, I mean parents they bring up their kids more culturally, especially Pakistani, Indian and Bangladeshis. It's quite, I don't know, when they read Islamically it's, it's, it gives them more freedom the way I see it, and it's given me more freedom to do things, and more freedom to speak out. It's like when my parents say to me, 'Don't go to a protest, they're gonna arrest you'but Islamically it tells me to, yeah, go to a protest and I see the word of God greater than my dad's any day."

Responses to identity concerns among our respondents tended to be expressed in ways that were highly personalised and focused on DIY action and achieving 'concrete influence on the articulation and delivery of social policy' rather than engaging in deliberation over 'abstract political rights' (Bang, 2009, p 123). This was expressed, for instance, in the practical ways in which the West Bowling Youth Initiative in Bradford worked to counter educational inequalities among Muslim young men. It was manifested in the search for personal ways to resist particular representations of, for instance, Black youth or young Muslims or Asian women, such as in the web-based discursive political action of the MJM that set out to disrupt mainstream representations of Muslims and Islam, or in the aims of the 'Young Disciples' activists in Birmingham to inform 'the public and government agencies on gang culture' and to challenge 'the boundaries of local and governmental action' in relation to representations of areas of Black settlement and Black young people in Birmingham. It can also be seen in the activities of the Saheli women's group in Birmingham in campaigning for a women's gym in Balsall Heath to tackle health inequalities among

South Asian women in Balsall Heath, where challenging funders' and the local authority's perceptions of Asian women formed key aspects of their mobilisation.

While activists demonstrated political commitments that were framed by ethnic or religious identities, these tended to be referenced to general principles of recognition of difference and were expressed in terms of a willingness to extend recognition of differences across groups, but in ways that were non-essentialist, non-reductive and that resisted reducing individuals to their membership of groups. This sentiment was reflected in one Bradford-based MYP's reflections on the politics of representation:

> "[I]t doesn't matter whether a man or woman is in that particular role as long as you are meeting the needs, that is the important thing but you need to be able, to be able to empathise with those people, to understand, to know that you are part of that, and you don't have to be Asian, Black, White, Muslim, Jew to not experience those people's feelings [...]"

Similarly, while concerns with global issues, campaigns or organisations were often underpinned by a political consciousness that was shaped by a concern with Muslim values or identification with a broader Muslim community, these were typically not confined to a concern with Muslim issues or societies. For instance, one MYP in Birmingham was involved in voluntary humanitarian work for Islamic Relief, yet her interests in volunteering extended to a broad range of humanitarian work and sat alongside her membership of Amnesty International and her everyday commitments to ethical shopping, limiting personal consumption and environmentalism. There were numerous instances of activists expressing concerns with global issues such as the international terms of trade, debt, development, humanitarian and emergency relief, or the maldistribution of resources globally. Concerns with global issues were typically not confined to regions to which respondents held diasporic or ummatic attachments, but were frequently underpinned by a broader concern with unequal global social relations – a concern that is captured in this reflection from an MJM activist: "Islam teaches us to stand up against any injustice that is happening around the world. It doesn't matter whether it's happening to a non-Muslim or a Muslim."

Conclusion

In recent years, ethnic minority and Muslim young people have become increasingly visible in a variety of public debates that have rested upon claims concerning these groups' political disaffection and – in the case of Muslims – their tendency to be drawn towards forms of political extremism. As I suggested, however, neither of these claims is particularly well substantiated by empirical data. What information there is on the interaction between age, ethnicity and religion as factors underlying differences across young people in mainstream political participation is patchy at best, and certainly insufficiently robust to support such crisis narratives. Typically, claims about the limited extent of ethnic minority young people's democratic engagement rest upon a narrow definition of 'the political', which is restricted to participation in electoral politics. Through the research presented here, I have argued for a broader understanding of political engagement. I suggested that a reconceptualising of the nature of political participation alerts us to the significance of the varied repertoires and modes of activism among ethnic minority young people – which can be obscured by a conceptual focus on forms of mainstream and electoral participation alone.

Founded on this broader conception of participation, I highlighted the fluidity of activism between scales – and particularly at the level of the global – suggesting that information technologies have facilitated opportunities for DIY activism across different scales. The limited significance of the national in the concerns and activism of ethnic minority young people was not a manifestation of political apathy, but provides some important critical insights into the democratic and participatory limitations of political institutions at this scale, and potentially reveals some of the ways in which these might be enervated. In particular, the experiences of the activists in our study demonstrate grammars of action that are founded in: a preference for hands-on, direct forms of activism; a tendency to mobilise in horizontal, loosely organised groups or networks rather than vertically integrated institutions with highly formalised regulation of membership or activity; engagement with concrete projects rather than abstract debate; personalised (rather than individualised) modes of interaction that do not require activists to submerge their identities into formal organisations; and, above all, a politics founded on the scope for activists to make a difference.

Finally, I highlighted the importance of identities in underpinning political activism in ways that show the significance of ethnic and religious identities as well as the enduring power of group identities, but crucially these were expressed through a politics of personalised action and a commitment to a politics of difference that was not separatist or inimical to concerns with universal rights or broader conceptions of social justice.

Note

[1] Saheli (meaning '(female) friend' in Urdu) was set up in 1998 to 'meet the needs of local women' in Balsall Heath, Birmingham by creating a centre organised by and for women, see: http://www.saheli.co.uk/the-history-of-saheli/.

References

Adams, M. and Raisborough, J. (2008) 'What Can Sociology Say About FairTrade? : Class, Reflexivity and Ethical Consumption', *Sociology*, vol 42, no 6, pp 1165–82.

Alexander, C. (2002) 'Beyond Black: Rethinking the Colour/Culture Divide', *Ethnic and Racial Studies*, vol 25, no 4, pp 552–71.

Back, L. (2002) 'The Fact of Hybridity: Youth, Ethnicity and Racism' in D.T. Goldberg and J. Solomos (eds) *A Companion to Racial and Ethnic Studies*, London: Blackwell, pp 439–54.

Bagguley, P. and Hussain, Y. (2008) *Riotous Citizens: Ethnic Conflict in Multicultural Britain*, Aldershot: Ashgate.

Bakardjieva, M. (2009) 'Subactivism: Lifeworld and Politics in the Age of the Internet', *The Information Society*, vol 25, no 2, pp 91–104.

Bang, H. (2005) 'Among everyday makers and expert citizens' in J. Newman (ed) *Remaking Governance: Peoples, politics and the public sphere,* Bristol: Policy Press.

Bang, H.P. (2009) '"Yes we can": identity politics and project politics for a late-modern world', *Urban Research & Practice*, vol 2, no 2, pp 117–37.

Beck, U. (1997) *The Reinvention of Politics: Rethinking Modernity in the Global Social Order*, Cambridge: Polity Press.

Bennett, W.L. (2008) 'Changing Citizenship in the Digital Age', *Civic Life Online: Learning How Digital Media Can Engage Youth*, W. Lance Bennett (ed), Cambridge, MA: The MIT Press.

Bernstein, M. (2005) 'Identity Politics', *Annual Review of Sociology*, vol 31, pp 47–74.

Brah, A. (1996) *Cartographies of Diaspora: Contesting identities*, Abingdon: Routledge.

Cantle, T. (2001) *Community Cohesion: A Report of the Independent Review Team*, London: Home Office.

Casciani, D. (2004) 'Disaffection among British Muslim Youth', news.bbc.co.uk, 31.3.04: http://news.bbc.co.uk/go/pr/fr/-/1/hi/uk/3586421.stm (accessed 24 May 2004).

Dahlgren, P. (2005) 'The Internet, Public Spheres, and Political Communication: Dispersion and Deliberation', *Political Communication*, vol 2, no 2, pp 147–62.

Dalton, R. (2008) 'Citizenship Norms and the Expansion of Political Participation', *Political Studies*, vol 56, no 1, pp 76–98.

Eade, J. and Garbin, D. (2002) 'Changing Narratives of Violence, Struggle and Resistance: Bangladeshis and the Competition for Resources in the Global City', *Oxford Development Studies*, vol 30, no 2, pp 137–49.

Eade, J. and Garbin, D. (2006) 'Competing Visions of Identity and Space: Bangladeshi Muslims in Britain', *Contemporary South Asia*, vol 15, no 2, pp 181–93.

Eden, K. and Roker, D. (2000) *'You've Gotta Do Something…': A Longitudinal Study of Young People's Involvement in Social Action*, Keele: Youth Research 2000 Conference, University of Keele.

Electoral Commission (2003) *Political Engagement among Black and Minority Ethnic Communities: What We Know, What We Need to Know*, London: Electoral Commission.

Electoral Commission (2005) *Black and Minority Ethnic Survey*, London: Electoral Commission.

Gale, R. and O'Toole, T. (2009) 'Young People and Faith Activism: British Muslim Youth, Glocalisation and the *Umma*', in A. Dinham, R. Furbey and V. Lowndes (eds) *Faith in the Public Realm: Controversies, Policies and Practices*, Bristol: Policy Press, pp 143–62.

Giddens, A. (1994) *Beyond Left and Right*, Cambridge: Polity Press.

Giddens, A. (2002) *Runaway World: How Globalisation Is Reshaping Our Lives*, London: Profile.

Hall, S. (2000) 'Old and New Identities, Old and New Ethnicities' in L. Back and J. Solomos (eds) *Theories of Race and Racism*, London: Routledge, pp 144–53.

Harris, A. and Roose, J. (2013) 'DIY Citizenship amongst young Muslims: experiences of the "ordinary"', *Journal of Youth Studies,* doi: 10.1080/13676261.2013.844782.

Hay, C. (2007) *Why We Hate Politics*, Cambridge: Polity Press.

Häyhtiö, T. and Rinne, J. (2007) 'Hard Rock Hallelujah! Empowering Reflexive Political Action on the Internet', *Journal for Cultural Research*, vol 11, no 4, pp 337–58.

Heath, A.F., Fisher, S., Sanders, D., Sobolewska, M. and Rosenblatt, G. (2011) 'Ethnic Heterogeneity in the Social Bases of Voting at the 2010 General Election', *Journal of Elections, Public Opinion and Parties*, vol 21, no 2, pp 255–77.

Inglehart, R. (1997) *Modernization and Postmodernization: Cultural, Economic and Political Change*, Princeton, NJ: Princeton University Press.

Jacobson, L. (1997) 'Religion and Ethnicity: Dual and Alternative Sources of Identity Among Young British Pakistanis', *Ethnic and Racial Studies*, vol 20, no 2, pp 238–56.

Janmaat, J.G. (2008) 'The Civic Attitudes of Ethnic Minority Youth and the Impact of Citizenship Education', *Journal of Ethnic and Migration Studies*, vol 34, no 1, pp 27–54.

Mandaville, P. (2009) 'Muslim Transnational Identity and State Responses in Europe and the UK After 9/11: Political Community, Ideology and Authority', *Journal of Ethnic and Migration Studies*, vol 35, no 3, pp 491–506.

Marsh, D., O'Toole, T. and Jones, S.(2007) *Young People and Politics in the UK: Apathy or Alienation?* Basingstoke: Palgrave Macmillan.

McDonald, K. (2006) *Global Movements: Action and Culture*, Oxford: Blackwell.

Meer, N. (2010) *Citizenship, Identity and the Politics of Multiculturalism*, Basingstoke: Palgrave Macmillan).

Melucci, A. and Avritzer, L. (2000) 'Complexity, cultural pluralism and democracy: collective action in the public space', *Social Science Information*, vol 39, no 4, pp 507–27.

Mercer, K. (2000) 'Identity and Diversity in Postmodern Politics' in L. Back and J. Solomos (eds), *Theories of Race and Racism*, London: Routledge, pp 503–20.

Micheletti, M., Follesdal, A. and Stolle, D. (2004) *Politics, Products, Markets: Exploring Political Consumerism Past and Present*, New Brunswick: Transaction Publishers.

Modood, T. (2000) 'Anti-essentialism, multiculturalism and the "recognition"' of religious groups', in W. Kymlicka and W. Norman (eds) *Citizenship in Diverse Societies*, Oxford: Oxford University Press, pp 175–98.

Modood, T. (2009) 'Muslims and the Politics of Difference', in *Muslims in Britain: Race, Place and Identities*, Edinburgh: Edinburgh University Press, pp 193–209.

Mushaben, J.M. (2008) 'Gender, HipHop and Pop-Islam: The Urban Identities of Muslim Youth in Germany', *Citizenship Studies*, vol 12, no 5, pp 507–26.

Norris, P. (2002) *Democratic Phoenix: Revinventing Political Activism*, Cambridge: Cambridge University Press.

O'Toole, T. and Gale, R. (2013) *Political Engagement Amongst Ethnic-minority young People: Making A Difference*, Basingstoke: Palgrave Macmillan.

Peace, T. (2013) 'All I'm Asking, Is For a Little Respect: Assessing the Performance of Britain's Most Successful Radical Left Party', *Parliamentary Affairs,* vol 66, no 2, pp 405–24.

PET Working Groups (2005) *Working Together to Prevent Extremism*, London: Home Office.

Phillips, D. (2006) 'Parallel lives? Challenging discourses of British Muslim self-segregation', *Environment and Planning D: Society and Space*, vol 24, pp 25–40.

Purdam, K., Fieldhouse, E., Kalra, V. and Russell, A. (2002) *Voter engagement among black and minority ethnic communities*, London: Electoral Commission.

Quintelier, E. (2009) 'The Political Participation of Immigrant Youth in Belgium', *Journal of Ethnic and Migration Studies*, vol 35, no 6, pp 919–37.

Zukin, C., Keeter, S., Andolina, M., Jenkins, K. and DelliCarpini, M.X. (2006) *A New Engagement? Political Participation, Civic Life and the Changing American Citizen*, New York: Oxford University Press.

NINE

'Injustice anywhere is a threat to justice everywhere'

Francine Fernandes

Established in 1996, Operation Black Vote (OBV) is a national, non-partisan organisation. All the main political parties have recognised the work of OBV in helping to encourage the positive engagement of Black and minority ethnic (BME) communities and in helping to address BME under-representation in political and public bodies. Written by OBV's deputy director Francine Fernandes, the chapter begins by sharing her early motivations for becoming politically active. It then outlines the political backdrop of BME representation in the UK, reveals particular patterns of BME disengagement and outlines the societal and policy consequences that this creates. Despite the bleak picture, this is a narrative that fundamentally believes that the systemic inequalities can be challenged through positive political activity. The chapter closes with examples of OBV's work that demonstrate that many BME individuals want to engage, and do engage when presented with the opportunity, and celebrates those who have moved from being political bystanders to being political activists.

Introduction

I am the deputy director of OBV, a leading national not-for-profit campaign group established to address the BME democratic deficit. This democratic deficit refers to the lack of BME political participation and representation within the political discourse. Through raising political awareness and promoting political education, OBV seeks to persuade BME communities to recognise their power and to inspire them to participate positively, for the benefit of all communities.

Think global, act local

Politics has been a lifelong interest for me, with my political awareness sparked when I was a child. At the time I would not have classed it as politics but, reflecting upon it, I realise that my upbringing was one of the catalysts for my desire to make a difference.

I grew up in Kenya and was fortunate to receive a good education and enjoy a good standard of living. I was lucky to enjoy many privileges and therefore, in a way, did not have an urgent need to fight. However, the overwhelming economic and racial inequities were too strong to ignore.

Beautiful mansions set back from the road with huge, immaculate private gardens were flanked by shanty towns that offered the most basic of accommodation. A simple construction of mud walls and corrugated roofs fashioned into a one- or two-room facility for a family of four was very commonplace. A mansion for a rich family of four would occupy the same amount of land as that occupied by 100 people living in the shanty town.

I suppose the acceptance of and apparent indifference to the stark economic inequities and consequent limiting of life opportunities did not sit right with me. I believe that the fortune or misfortune of where you are born and the subsequent positive or negative effects that this brings is a complete accident of birth. Thus the people who lived in impoverished conditions in those shanty towns did not do anything to warrant their circumstances, nor has someone who happens to be born in a rich country like the UK and therefore enjoys all the accompanying benefits.

The racial inequity was also very visible to me. Although I may have been young – only six or seven – it was clear to me that a race hierarchy existed – a living relic of colonialism. Although Kenya had gained its independence 20 years previously, the legacy of 70 years of colonialism is not easily shaken off. The shackles of empire were very much at work and the racial hierarchy was clear to me in the way that people were treated or often mistreated. Fellow Kenyan US President Obama succinctly captured this notion of a racial hierarchy when he spoke about it during his inauguration speech in 2009.

> If you're white – you're alright.
> If you're brown – stick around.
> If you're black – get to the back.

Just before I became a teenager, I moved to the UK and, with a greater awareness of racism and social injustice, not only did I want to, but I felt it was my obligation to become socially active. I felt that it was incumbent upon me to do this: I had access to an education – and in the UK, I had access to a platform. I felt empowered, and inspired that the harsh inequalities I had seen as a child could be challenged and perhaps I could give a voice to the voiceless and become an agent of change. By getting involved in local initiatives, such as boycotting the Springboks rugby team when it came on a UK tour, I could help support the global anti-apartheid movement (Figure 9.1).

As Dr Martin Luther King so eloquently put it: 'Injustice anywhere is a threat to justice everywhere'.[1]

Figure 9.1: Think global, act local: 1992 – the author as a teenager at an anti-apartheid demonstration

Spot the Black MP

Under-representation of BME communities exists in key areas of political and civic society at local, regional and national levels.

If we look at our national Parliament, the highest democratic body in the country, the lack of representation is starkly evident and it becomes apparent that the road to progress has been painfully slow.

In 1892, Dadabhai Nairoji grasped the political mantle and became the first Asian and first BME member of Parliament when he served as the Liberal Party's MP for Finsbury Central. Nairoji had set a precedent, and within 20 years another two BME MPs were elected, namely Conservative Mancherjee Bhowajee (Bethnal Green North) and Communist Shaprurji Saklatvala (Battersea North).

Despite the initial surge, nearly 100 years later the numbers of BME MPs remained stubbornly low, with none being elected between 1929 and 1982. In 1983 there was only one BME MP, Jonathan Sayeed, who represented Mid Bedfordshire. Four years later, the 1987 general election heralded what seemed like a political breakthrough, with the election of four MPs – known as the 'Gang of Four' – namely, Keith Vaz, Diane Abbott, Paul Boateng and the late Bernie Grant. However, this 'breakthrough' really served only to magnify how little progress had actually been made. In a period of nearly 100 years, eight BME individuals had been elected, as compared to a total of 16,654 White MPs (Figure 9.2).

Figure 9.2: Spot the Black MP, general election 2001 OBV campaign

In the 1990s and 2000s the numbers crept up, and in 2010 a historic high of 27 BME MPs were elected. Although a considerable increase from 30 years ago, the level of BME representation is still woefully low, as illustrated in Table 9.1. To be representative, we should have 84 BME MPs – nearly triple the present number.

At local level the disparities continue, with the numbers of councillors less than a quarter of what they should be to be representative. When we take gender into account the picture of under-representation is further accentuated. To be more reflective of society as a whole, the number of BME women councillors would need increase more than seven-fold – from fewer than 200 of all councillors in England to nearer 1,500. The proportion of BME women councillors increased from 0.6% in 1997 to 0.9% in 2006, meaning that at the current rate of increase it could take more than 130 years to reach proportionate levels of representation.

Even in London, where approximately 60% of Britain's BME communities live, the London Assembly Members remain distinctly undiverse, with only 5 BME members out of a total of 25.

As Table 9.1 demonstrates, there are systemic levels of under-representation of BME communities in our local, regional and national democratic institutions. In the next section I will illustrate the consequences of under-representation and why it is imperative for it to be addressed for the benefit of all communities.

Table 9.1: Political representation: the facts

Area of public life	BME representation		BME women	
	Actual	To be representative	Actual	To be representative
House of Commons (MPs)	27	84	10	42
House of Lords (peers)	46	110	16	55
European Parliament (MEPs)	7	9	1	4/5
Scottish Assembly (MSPs)	1	5	0	2/3
Welsh Assembly (AMs)	2	3	0	1/2
London Assembly (AMs)	5	10	1	5
Local government councillors (the figures below are given as percentages because exact numbers are difficult to establish)				
England	4%	14.7%	1%	7.35%
Wales	0.8%	4.4%	0.2%	2.2%
London	20%	40%	5%	20%
Scotland	1.4%	4%	0.03%	2%

Note: Figures correct as of December 2014.
Source: Author's own research.

Political participation: patterns of disengagement

> Two nations: between whom there is no intercourse and no sympathy; who are as ignorant of each other's habits, thoughts, and feelings, as if they were dwellers in different zones, or inhabitants of different planets... (Disraeli, 1845)

These sentiments, penned nearly 150 years ago by Benjamin Disraeli, the 19th-century British prime minister, ring as true today as when they were written, succinctly describing the state of British democracy.

Despite reams of legislation and countless initiatives to engender greater political participation, the British democratic system still remains essentially a relationship of those who govern and those who are governed. This is evidenced by the United Kingdom's ranking in 21st place in the Economist Intelligence Unit's Democracy Index 2008, a relatively low position, due almost entirely to its political participation score, which is the lowest of all 30 countries categorised as 'full democracies'. In fact, in the Audit of Political Engagement 2013, just 41% of the public said that in the event of an immediate general election they would be certain to vote – a decline of seven percentage points in a year and the lowest level in the history of the Audit. Political engagement is the second facet of the democratic deficit that OBV focuses on.

While our parliamentary democracy can continue to function with low levels of participation, there is a strong link between governmental effectiveness and high levels of political participation. Governance tends to be most effective in countries with high levels of participation and turnout, two areas that have dropped significantly in Britain in recent years, as Table 9.2 indicates.

Table 9.2: International comparisons of political participation rates during four general elections

Country	Highest rate of voter turnout (post-war)	Year – voter turnout level	Year – voter turnout level	Year – voter turnout level	Year voter turnout level
UK	84% (1950)	1997 – 71%	2001 – 59%	2005 – 61%	2010 – 66%
France*	84% (2007)	1995 – 80%	2002 – 80%	2007 – 84%	2012 – 80%
Germany	91% (1972)	1998 – 82%	2002 – 79%	2005 – 78%	2009 – 71%

Note: *France has had 84% voter turnout levels in 1965, 1974, 1988 and 2007.

Source: International Institute for Democracy and Electoral Assistance (IDEA) Voter Turnout, http://www.idea.int/vt/countryview.cfm?CountryCode=FR

As shown in Table 9.2, in the UK the turnout in the 2001 general election was 59%, 12 percentage points lower than in 1997 and 25 points lower than the post-war high of 84% in 1950. Levels rose in 2005 and 2010, but only to 61% and 66%, respectively. When examining the political participation rates of BME communities, among all age groups they are worrying low.

BME electoral participation rates

The political activity levels demonstrated through voting have been in decline among the general population, and BME communities are even less politically active. As Table 9.3 makes plain, voter–registration levels among all BME communities remain significantly lower than for the wider community. The self-reported voter–registration levels for the population as a whole are 95%. For White communities the figure is reported by the Electoral Commission as 86% (White, 2014).

Table 9.3: Voter registration (data based on UK 2010 general election)

Ethnicity	Voter registration levels (self-reported)	Voter registration levels (validated)
White	90%	86%
Pakistani	88%	78%
Bangladeshi	88%	73%
Indian	87%	78%
Black African	71%	59%
Black Caribbean	84%	72%

Source: Fisher et al (2011)

While it is clear that BME voter-registration levels are lower than those of the wider public, what is even more alarming is that there is also confusion among BME communities about whether they indeed are registered to vote and this further widens the gap, in terms of voter-registration levels, between BME communities and the wider community.

As the *Ethnic Minority British Election Study* (Fisher et al, 2011) demonstrates, there is a worrying trend among all communities for people to believe that they are registered to vote when in fact they are not. It can be seen that while 90% of the White population think they are registered to vote, validated registration for this group is 86%, showing that a lack of understanding about voter registration is a serious problem for all communities. This is amplified for BME communities, with 88% of the BME community as a whole believing they are registered (self-reported registered to vote), but validated registrations showing the figure to be around 75%, more than 10 percentage points lower than for the White community. Moreover, there are stark differences within the ethnic groups surveyed, with Africans being the least likely to be registered, at 59%.

The study also revealed that Pakistanis and Bangladeshis were least likely to have filled in their voter registration forms themselves (Fisher et al, 2011). Therefore the impact of new legislation such as Individual Electoral Registration in 2014, replacing Household Registration, could be significantly greater in these communities and could result in the further disenfranchisement of an already politically fragile community, resulting in what some call 'the missing millions'.

The cost of disengagement

This lack of political engagement and absence of representation is not just damaging to a healthy and vibrant democracy where, ideally, all citizens will feel empowered and engaged. Lack of political participation means that politicians are not held to account for policy decisions, and because of the lack of representation and engagement, policies particular to BME communities are often not adequately voiced. The result for BME communities is persistent and far-reaching inequalities affecting social justice and their quality of life in terms of health, education, housing and a myriad other public policy areas. The human and financial costs are extremely high.

Employment

The employment gap between BME communities and the rest of the population currently stands at 15%, and employed Pakistani, Bangladeshi and Black African men demonstrate a 13–21% differential in pay, as compared to White British males of the same age, qualifications and occupation (*The Price of Race Inequality: The Black Manifesto*, 2010). In terms of youth unemployment, the figures are even more dramatic. Office for National Statistics research in 2011 suggested that more than 50% of Black men under 25 were unemployed, as compared with 20% for young people overall (Ball, 2012).

These figures clearly demonstrate that in terms of employment there is a youth penalty; but while you grow out of the youth penalty, you don't grow out of your ethnicity.

Poverty

For a G8 country, it is shocking that four million UK children live in poverty. When we look at those figures broken down by ethnic groups, there is a clear link between ethnicity and poverty (Table 9.4).

Table 9.4: UK children living in poverty, by ethnicity

Ethnicity	Children (%)
White	25
African	56
Pakistani	60
Bangladeshi	72

Source: Commission for Racial Equality (2007)

Criminal justice system

Twenty-seven per cent of the British prison population is BME. BME prisoners have longer sentences than their White counterparts and are more likely to be imprisoned for certain crimes (Ball, Bowcott and Rogers, 2011). The DNA database, ruled unlawful by the European Court of Human Rights, holds information on people arrested but never charged or found guilty of a crime; OBV estimates that Black young men (including mixed race) make up 50% of this database.

Moreover, this criminalisation of BME communities seems to be perpetuated by the media's selection and coverage of stories creating and then reinforcing negative stereotypes. The *REACH Media Monitoring Report* (Cushion et al, 2011) demonstrated that news about Black young men and boys was heavily focused upon crime, with crime stories making up 66.9% of the coverage. For national print, this figure is 73%. This far outweighs the coverage of other, more positive stories; for example, news items about the achievement or positive role of young people in the community (3.8%), or other local activities, school events, club activities or charity work (1.4%). Writing in the *Guardian* in 2008, Eric Allison succinctly captured this negative spiral: 'While negative stories about black teenagers are almost guaranteed headlines, the positive achievements of black youth go largely ignored' (Allison, 2008).

As if these staggering human costs were not enough, the financial costs are highly significant. The REACH Report (2007) identified an annual cost of £808 million annually to tackle educational under-achievement, unemployment and BME over-representation in school exclusions and the criminal justice system.

Operation Black Vote: our future in is in our hands

Highlighted above are a myriad of shocking reasons why it is of paramount importance to dramatically reduce the negative and debilitating effects of racism that blight the progress of BME communities in the UK. This is what OBV aims to achieve.

Below are two examples of the work that OBV has carried out. The first describes how OBV aims to positively address the issue of lack of representation and its consequences, through a long-term programme of mentoring and leadership programmes. The second is an example of reactive politics – a one-off campaign response to proposed changes in legislation.

Informing and inspiring agents of change

Despite the plethora of negative statistics and daunting facts, what always amaze and inspire me are the numbers of BME individuals from across the country who contact us at OBV with a sincere desire to learn how to make a difference to society and become agents of positive change. As highlighted earlier, in every area of political governance, bar the Welsh Assembly, there is a lack of political representation of BME communities. The lack of BME representation within our elected chambers leads many people from within BME communities to believe that, whether by design or default, there is little or no place for BME communities to have an equitable voice. Justice and equality are the driving forces behind achieving representative democracy for BME communities. By involving those from minority backgrounds, different talents and different experiences will be brought to decision-making arenas and can only enhance our collective understanding of the people our governance system seeks to serve.

BME individuals and their communities often feel disempowered, due to both lack of understanding of, and experience in dealing with, local and national, civic/democratic institutions. Many feel, sometimes rightly, that decisions are imposed upon them, with little or no input from themselves. Although some of the inequalities and injustices must be challenged by holding politicians to account through the voting process and ongoing democratic dialogue, we also believe that it is incumbent upon our communities to become agents of positive change, rather than sit on the political side-lines. Our vision is to fully empower BME communities so as to ensure that we are better placed to deal with and challenge those persistent elements of race inequality. When individuals can play a full and positive role in all areas and at all levels of society, everyone benefits.

As deputy director of OBV, I have been involved in managing and overseeing a number of nonpartisan political and civic shadowing schemes, including MP, councillor, magistrate, parole board member, school governor, and safer neighbourhood panel member among others. The aim of this work is to encourage and inspire greater political and civic participation and representation from BME communities by raising awareness and demystifying the processes of key areas of public life.

Managing the schemes is an area of our work that I particularly enjoy. Working in race equality is a very challenging and thankless environment, as the statistics above demonstrate. However, the schemes are consistently over-subscribed, clearly demonstrating that BME individuals are keen to engage when offered a meaningful platform to do so.

National

Our last parliamentary shadowing scheme attracted more than 800 applications for the 25 coveted places. Each shadowing scheme is customised in its formulation and structure, depending upon the area of public life it is focusing upon, but the key elements are always the same:

- addressing a deficit of BME representation in key areas of public life
- nurturing and supporting BME individuals to become political/civic leaders, with the intention that they eventually take up public/civic posts
- participants become Community Ambassadors, informing and inspiring others with the skills and knowledge they have learned by participating in outreach work in their workplace, at local community centres/schools, places of worship and so on
- a diversity of BME communities working together, the benefits of which will be enjoyed by wider society
- positive publicity about BME communities actively participating as role models for civic engagement to encourage and inspire others
- empowering communities to engage effectively with both local and national civic and democratic institutions to address their concerns

- narrowing the gap between BME communities and the policies that often bear little resemblance to the concerns of these communities
- inspiring confidence in BME individuals that civic and public bodies are trying to be more inclusive and representative of all the communities they seek to serve.

The schemes have enjoyed tremendous success and many plaudits for their ability to help transform both the lives of hundreds of individuals and the institutions they work in. They have also helped to empower many thousands and changed the perception of what BME individuals can achieve in the UK, with Prime Minister David Cameron stating that OBV has done incredible work to ensure that BME communities engage positively in civic society (Operation Black Vote, 2011, p 5).

In no small measure we have helped to transform national governance both directly and indirectly: the first two ministers in the Coalition government to come from the BME community are both from the OBV family. Helen Grant MP, who made political history as the first woman of African Caribbean descent to become an MP for the Conservative Party, and Baroness Sayeeda Warsi, the first Muslim woman to attend Cabinet, are both OBV alumni. The Conservative Party has paid tribute to the work of OBV in helping to increase the number of its BME MPs from 2 to a historic 12. The Labour Party too acknowledges OBV's support, particularly with regard to a younger cadre now coming through, such as OBV graduate Clive Lewis, prospective parliamentary candidate (PPC) for Norwich South in the 2015 general election, and graduate Tanmanjeet Dhesi, who is the PPC for Gravesend.

Regional

At regional level, we worked with the National Assembly for Wales in 2007–08, delivering the dynamic Welsh Assembly Shadowing Scheme. Rt Hon Lord Dafydd Elis-Thomas, speaking as Presiding Officer of the National Assembly for Wales at the Graduation of the programme in 2008, said:

> "When I sit in my chair in our new debating chamber, I am ashamed when I look out and see before me a sea of white faces."

The Assembly has been a dynamic force for change in addressing the gender inequality in politics. In 2003 it achieved the first gender-balanced elected political body in the world and through the scheme it has made a substantial impact in illuminating the corridors of power, unlocking political talent and providing a meaningful platform for BME political engagement in Wales. Through the cross-party initiative, all participants of the shadowing scheme have been inspired to become more politically active. At the start of the scheme, none of the eight participants had even considered standing for elected office. After completing the scheme, three of the participants were selected to represent their parties, two as parliamentary candidates and one as an Assembly candidate. While still in its founding year the scheme received national recognition and was awarded the highly acclaimed Channel 4/ Hansard Society 'Democracy Award', which recognises innovative ways to encourage greater public involvement in the democratic process.

Local

At local level, OBV has worked in Bristol and Liverpool and the Councillor Shadowing Scheme has helped to transform the political landscape. When the first shadowing scheme was established in 2006, there was only one BME councillor in Bristol, out of nearly 70 seats. By 2008 the historic increase to four BME councillors, representing all of the three main political parties, could in part be attributed to OBV's work. As suggested by Bristol City Councillor Abdul Malik:

> "I feel the scheme in Bristol has encouraged people to come forward and represent their communities. This scheme has indeed been the reason behind the awareness within council groups that more BME representation is required and that we need to tackle this issue by becoming proactively involved with providing ourselves as extended advocates to enroll more diversity into our political groups."

In Liverpool, the scheme enjoyed equal success. Despite the city's having a BME population for over 400 years, the elected chamber had only one BME councillor out of 90, herself an OBV graduate. Through our work with the Councillor Shadowing Scheme, the levels of BME representation have now tripled to a historic high of three, in which two of the three BME councillors are OBV graduates.

Transforming civic society: Magistrates Shadowing Scheme

The impact of the civic programmes has been equally considerable and I will focus on just one of these, the Magistrates Shadowing Scheme. As highlighted earlier in this chapter, there is a very difficult relationship between BME communities and the criminal justice system, where BME individuals often feel that they are being over-policed, over-sentenced and under-protected.

In order to combat some of this negativity we worked in partnership with the Ministry of Justice (at that time the Lord Chancellor's Department) to develop the Magistrates Shadowing Scheme, as the magistrates courts are the cornerstone of the judicial system, dealing with over 95% of criminal cases.

Looking like the community it serves

"Magistrates are the epitome of justice in the community – they are from the community and for the community. And, it is vitally important that magistrates represent the diverse communities they serve. Confidence in the justice system depends on it."

These sentiments of Rt Hon Jack Straw MP, expressed when he was Lord Chancellor and Secretary of State for Justice, epitomise the aims and objectives of the OBV and Ministry of Justice Magistrates Shadowing Scheme.

The scheme has helped improve Black and other minority ethnic representation within the magistracy and to increase BME awareness of the criminal justice process, with over 100 graduates of the scheme having been appointed as magistrates around the country. The scheme has not only helped to increase the level of representation, but also promoted greater cultural diversity on the benches and, crucially, has given magistrates the opportunity to gain greater insights into the experiences of BME communities.

Significantly, the average age of OBV appointees is dramatically lower than the overall average age of magistrates. The average age of OBV-graduate magistrates is 37, as compared to the overall average age of 57. This is important not only because it highlights another under-represented aspect of public life, but also because the lower age represents an important cost saving, as the OBV graduates will be able to serve for a further 20 years, representing thousands of hours of volunteering.

Having worked for and developed these programmes for over 10 years, it is clear to me that an abundance of talent is available that, when provided with the right guidance, support and networks, can transform individuals, who in turn can transform communities. This to me is what politics is all about.

Stop 'whitewashing' history

> The black Florence Nightingale and the making of the PC myth: One historian explains how Mary Seacole's story never stood up. (*Daily Mail*, 31 December 2012)

Enjoying the Christmas break after a packed year of activities, you can imagine our dismay to see the above headline in the *Daily Mail*.

Leaked drafts of the history curriculum showed that the then Secretary of State for Education, Rt Hon Michael Gove, MP was seeking to change the school curriculum. The government was looking to make the history curriculum more 'traditional' and 'back to basics', determined not to let it be skewed by 'political correctness themes'. The impact of this leaked report was beginning to show its ugly head, as clearly evidenced by the *Daily Mail* article, which wrongly diminished the role of Victorian heroines such as Mary Seacole as a 'PC' (politically correct) myth.

Great social reformers such as Olaudah Equiano and Mary Seacole, among others, were to be consigned to the educational dustbin, depriving millions of children of the chance to learn about them, even as an optional subject chosen by their teachers. We at OBV believed these changes would amount to what can only be described as the systematic removal of positive references to the contributions of Black and Asian people to British history. Not only that, but the proposed history curriculum also belittled the revolutionary movements of the working classes, as well as denigrating the achievements of women in history.

Although this was not a campaign that we had intended to undertake, the 'whitewashing' of history was far too important not to be challenged.

Within days of our return from the Christmas break, the OBV office was a flurry of activity. We wrote an open letter to Michael Gove pointing out the huge contributions that these Great Black Britons had made. Seacole had worked bravely in the Crimean War and her extraordinary efforts were recognised at the time; upon her return home, the decorated war heroine was greeted by 80,000 people.

Equiano, an emancipated slave, played a pivotal role in the abolition of the slave trade and his memoirs served to highlight the injustice and brutality of slavery. The first freed slave to write his autobiography, he wrote in a flowery prose to artfully challenge the degrading effects of slavery. His book petitioned Parliament and even the queen to abolish slavery, and the best-seller inspired thousands to reconsider their views on slavery.

We argued that 'it is not political correctness to keep them in, but it is historically and culturally incorrect to remove them from the rich tapestry of the UK's history, just as it would be for the struggle for women's rights'. Within days, the simple open letter had created a political hot potato for the Education Secretary. Over a period of just three weeks, it received massive levels of support, with over 35,000 signatories, including 72 MPs from all parties, Christine Blower, Head of the National Union of Teachers, Children's Laureate Michael Rosen, award-winning author Zadie Smith and even US civil rights legend the Reverend Jesse Jackson signing up to the petition.

In response to this surge of support, demanding that reference to these two great reformers not be withdrawn from the curriculum, an unexpected, but very welcome U-turn happened. The Secretary of State wrote personally to OBV in response to the campaign:

> We are lucky to be heirs to a very rich mix of exceptional thinkers, bold reformers and courageous political activists. I agree that it is important that our children learn about the difference that these figures have made, and it is right that we do more, not less to make subjects relevant to the lives of our children. (http://www.obv.org.uk/news-blogs/we-ve-won-mary-seacole-olaudah-equiano)

By February 2013, the Secretary of State agreed not only for them not to be omitted from the history curriculum, but in fact that they were now to be included as a mandatory, rather than optional, part of that curriculum.

While it is true that Mary Seacole has gone from being in the guidance notes, to nearly being erased, to finding herself at centre stage, other key aspects of the history curriculum seem to have disappeared, in particular, the teaching of African civilisations before the slave trade. This is critically important. African history lessons that start with European conquest not only deny Black children of knowledge of their complete and true heritage but also, shockingly, distort the view of Africans that is presented to white students. This is an area that we will watch vigilantly, but for the meantime we were pleased that this win represented an opportunity for all our children to learn about a diversity of Great Britons.

This campaign demonstrated that a not-for-profit group can lead a campaign against the government and win. The sheer speed of the campaign is also notable, lasting approximately one month in all, as is the fact that significant levels of media coverage and exposure were won not as the result of a large public relations budget. In fact, there were no financial costs to this campaign and the victory was testament to people power.

Conclusion

BME communities face a number of critical challenges, and persistent race inequalities stubbornly continue. The tendency to treat the symptoms, rather than the causes, in part explains the persistence of these inequalities. In addition, the political barometer oscillates wildly from recognition that long-term empowerment of BME communities is beneficial to a vibrant democracy, to race equality being consigned to the political wilderness. Despite this difficult political environment, and the difficulties inherent with the work that we do, OBV provides an example that activism can work and change is possible.

Our schemes are helping to change the political and civic landscapes, locally, regionally and nationally, equipping and empowering hundreds of individuals to become beacons of hope in their communities and drivers for change throughout society.

OBV's work demonstrates that the condition of racial inequality need not be insurmountable. When we are equipped with a clear vision, a plan of action and a group of activists who passionately believe, change is always possible. As the OBV motto reads:

> Our future is in our hands.

Note
[1] Letter from Birmingham Jail, 16 April 1963.

References

Allison, E. (2008) 'The Silenced Majority', *Guardian*, 25 August, available online at: http://www.theguardian.com/world/2008/aug/25/race.knifecrime.

Ball, J. (2012) 'Data showing how young black men have been hit by unemployment', *Guardian,* 9 March, available online at: http://www.theguardian.com/news/datablog/2012/mar/09/black-unemployed-young-men?intcmp=239.

Ball, J., Bowcott, O. and Rogers, S. (2011) 'Race variation in jail sentences, study suggests', *Guardian,* 25 November, available online at: http://www.theguardian.com/law/2011/nov/25/ethnic-variations-jail-sentences-study.

Commission for Racial Equality (2007) *A lot done, a lot to do: Our vision for an integrated Britain,* Commission for Racial Equality, London, available online at: http://resources.cohesioninstitute.org.uk/Publications/Documents/Document/Default.aspx?recordId=47.

Cushion, S., Moore, K. and Jewell, J. (2011) *Media representations of black young men and boys: Report of the REACH Media Monitoring Project,* Department of Communities and Local Government, available online at: http://www.cardiff.ac.uk/jomec/research/researchgroups/racerepresentationandculturalpolitics/fundedprojects/08reachresearch.html.

Disraeli, B. (1845) *Sybil; or, The Two Nations,* Henry Colburn: London, p 149.

Fisher, S., Heath, A., Rosenblatt, G., Sanders, D. and Sobolewska, M. (2011) *Ethnic Minority British Election Study: Electoral registration and turnout data,* available online at: http://www.runnymedetrust.org/uploads/EMBES%20Turnout%20and%20Registration.pdf

Operation Black Vote (2011) *OBV Special Anniversary Issue: 15 Years of Change,* available online at: http://www.obv.org.uk/sites/default/files/images/newsletter/nletter-issue6.pdf.

REACH (2007) *An independent report to Government on raising the aspirations and attainment of Black boys and young Black men,* Department of Communities and Local Government, available online at: http://dera.ioe.ac.uk/7609/.

The Price of Inequality: The Black Manifesto 2010 (2010) available online at: http://equanomics.org/news/the-black-manifesto.

White, I. (2014) 'Individual Electoral a Registration', Parliamentary Briefing Paper, October 2014, *House of Commons Library* available online at: http://www.parliament.uk/Templates/BriefingPapers/Pages/BPPdfDownload.aspx?bp-id=sn06764.

TEN

Political participation is self-interest ... but not in the way you might think

Stephen Reicher, Yashpal Jogdand and Caoimhe Ryan

Introduction

Our argument in this chapter is very simple. People participate politically when it is in their interest to do so.

This may not be a wise way to start. Already, much of our audience will be alienated and many may be drifting away. On the one hand, the statement seems so bland as to be meaningless. Of course people participate because it is in their interest to do so. Everything people do, they do because it is in their interest. So the statement tells us nothing unless we are in a position to specify what these interests are and how they play out in specific contexts, from voting to joining a political party to participating in a demonstration. This is a position we have some sympathy with.

On the other hand, the statement can be rejected as palpably untrue. As many commentators have pointed out, most people vote in the certain knowledge that their individual vote will have no effect on the outcome and that all the effort involved in going to the polling station and casting their ballot will bring them no individual benefit at all. If the idea of acting in one's individual interest falls at such a low hurdle, how can it be of any use when dealing with more complex political acts? What of those in Timisoara, years ago during the Romanian revolution of 1989, and those in Kiev in 2014, as we write, who are prepared to risk their very lives in political action? Were they – are they – really acting in terms of dry calculations of what they have to gain from their sacrifices? Surely not. This is a position with which we have even more sympathy.

But now we have created another problem for ourselves. How can we agree both that everything is a matter of acting in one's interests and also that acting in one's interests explains little or nothing? Are we not a perfectly lubricated academic weathervane? Well, no. The problem here lies less with us than with the way that the term 'interest' is commonly understood and used in explaining human action in general, and political participation in particular.

In the social sciences, the notion of 'interest' is primarily associated with rational choice theory (Downs, 1957; Homans, 1961; Elster, 1986). This assumes that human beings act to maximise individual utility. Utility is, of course, a very tricky concept. What counts as utility is hard to gauge. But on the whole, it is easiest to measure and define in economic terms. Hence utility frequently means money. Our concern, however, is not primarily to do with the concept of utility (although we will be addressing the issue in due course). It is more with the assumption that it is individual utility that counts.

To make the point slightly differently, when it is claimed that people act in their interests, this is a contraction of the idea that action is governed by *self-interest*. On the whole, it is assumed that this self is the individual self – that which defines me as a unique individual, distinct from other individuals, the 'I' versus the 'you'. Anything we do is oriented to the needs, aspirations and desires of this individual self. If I do anything for others, it is because this ultimately rebounds to my own benefit. Perhaps it makes others more likely to give me something in return, perhaps it enhances my status and reputation in ways that bring gain in the future. But in the end, even acts which appear to undermine personal gain are always about personal gain.

Now, of course, this is a simplification. And of course there are many caveats and qualifications to this stark picture. All sorts of factors, including social factors, impact on the choices we make, including the information we have, how we assess that information, the way we process complex information, our relationship to others and our trust in them and so on. But ultimately, it remains true that the self of 'self-interest' in rational choice theory is an individual self. It is axiomatic that something counts as a benefit only if it accrues (either directly or indirectly) to me personally.

It is this that we wish to challenge in this chapter. Our aim, drawing on recent social psychological theory, is to rethink the 'self' element in the concept of self-interest. More specifically, we make three arguments.

First, the self can be defined on different levels, notably in terms of our group memberships and what makes these groups distinctive ('we' vs 'they') as well as in terms of our individuality and what makes us personally distinctive ('I' vs 'you'). Correspondingly, interest can be defined in terms of benefits accruing to the group as well as to ourselves personally.

Second, precisely because interest and social action can be tied to the group and, to the extent that it does, influence the choices of all group members, so the nature of group identity (and hence, what precisely satisfies the group interest) is contested and provides a focus of argument.

Third, we argue that notions of identity and, hence, of interest are not calculations made by isolated individuals, but rather, that such understandings are mobilised by organisations, leaders and activists.

Having laid out these three arguments in general terms, we then apply them to the specific matter of concern in this book: political participation. We examine how notions of identity and interest are invoked both directly (involving explicit notions of 'who we are' and how we relate to others) and indirectly (involving emotional appeals that imply 'who we are' and how we relate to others) in the context of mobilising people to take part in two very different social movements: the one concerning anti-deportation campaigns in the UK, the other concerning Dalit movements in India.

Before we start, though, we want to stress that the arguments here are not about the rationality or irrationality of our choices – more specifically, the choice to become involved in political action. They are about the grounds of rationality. They rest on the understanding that one cannot have an interest without having a self. To cite Ringmar (1996):

> It is only as *some-one* that we can have an interest in *some-thing*; it is *only once we know who we are that we can know what we want*. Once the problem is seen in this fashion, however, it should be obvious that all the real analytic work is carried out not by the concept of interest but rather by the concept of self. The former concept may perhaps still be given an independent definition, but this can only be done once the latter concept has been defined. (Ringmar, 1996, p 53, emphases in the original)

Similarly, our claim – that people participate politically when it is in their interest to do so –becomes intelligible only once it is seen in the light of a radical rethink of the self in self-interest.

Rethinking self and interest

The self as a system

If we were to ask you, the reader, to tell us who you are, you would no doubt respond by listing some of the things that characterise you as a distinctive individual – that you are tall, fair haired, friendly, a little shy ... and so on. But equally, you would tell us something about the groups that you belong to – that you are a woman, a political scientist, British ... whatever.

The fact is that identity is not singular, but rather, a complex system. It consists of some elements at the personal level that distinguish the 'I' from the 'you' and some at the collective level that distinguish the 'we' from the 'they'. This is the starting point for the 'social identity tradition' that, in recent years, has come to dominate the social psychology of group processes (Tajfel and Turner, 1979; Turner, Hogg, Oakes, Reicher and Wetherell, 1987; for a recent overview, see Reicher, Spears and Haslam, 2010).

The second key point for social identity theorists is that, at different times and in different places, different elements of the self-system will be salient. So, for instance, in the lecture theatre one's academic identity will take precedence, whereas, say, at a demonstration a political identity will take precedence. What is more, when a given identity is salient, my concerns and my actions are framed by the definition of that identity. To continue with the foregoing example, in the lecture theatre I aim to enact academic values of precision, of reason, of analytic even-handedness. That is not what I seek to do at the demonstration. Here, group values of solidarity and commitment take precedence.

Already, this points to the way in which group (or social) identities define interests. They tell us what counts, what is 'utility' and what we should therefore seek to maximise through our choices. But there is another way in which social identity impacts on interest, this time relating less to what constitutes utility than to when something counts as accruing to ourselves. Thus, for group members, what counts is the fate of the group. To the extent that we define ourselves in terms of a social identity, then the fate of other group members serves to define our own fate. An insult to one is an insult to all – just as a benefit to one is a benefit to all. For British Muslims, to the extent that their Muslim identity is important, the humiliation of fellow Muslims in Gaza is experienced as their own humiliation. For British Jews, to the extent that the fate of Israel is bound up with their Jewish identity, missiles targeted at Tel Aviv are experienced as missiles targeted at them. Quite clearly, where social identities are in play, cost and benefit are not limited to their link with the 'I' but are extended to the 'we'. Utility can accrue to or be taken away from ourselves without ever touching us as individuals.

It follows from the above that the way that interest in construed – both what counts as an interest and when something counts as an interest – depends, respectively, on the ways that the content and the boundaries of the group identity are defined. In terms of content, it is only when an outcome is relevant to something valued by the group that it is seen to be 'of interest'. In terms of boundaries, it is only when another is included as part of 'us' that their fate inherently engages our interest (we stress 'inherently' because there may be times when the fate of an outgroup member may engage our interest, but it does not necessarily do so).

Here, we come to a third key step in the social identity approach. Identities are not predefined or static mental structures. Rather, an identity is always a matter of defining the distinctiveness of the self relative to the other (which can be defined either individually as another person or collectively as another group) and so it varies as a function of this other. Social identity theorists (or, to be more accurate, self-categorisation theorists) therefore argue that self-categories are a variable function of the comparative context (Turner, Oakes, Haslam and McGarty, 1994).

Let us illustrate the point in relation to the questions both of boundaries (who we are) and of content (what we are). Let us also use rather different types of evidence in relation to the two. In 1981, in the context of new nationality legislation, the status of the Falkland Islanders was downgraded from full British citizenship to that of British Dependent Territories Citizenship. There was little dissent. However, in the context of an invasion of the islands by Argentina in 1982, the Falkland Islanders were rapidly constituted as prototypically British. On the day after the invasion, 3 April 1982, the *Daily Express* commented: 'The right of the Falkland Islanders, people who are wholly British in origin, sentiment and loyalty, to remain British and to continue to live under British rule must be defended as if it were the Isle of Wight which had been invaded.' So, once the Falkland Islanders become British, their fate becomes our fate, their humiliation becomes critical to our interest to repair the damage. That is, the reconstrual of group boundaries is critical to the choice to go to war. Equally, and unsurprisingly, the war led to the restoration of full citizenship rights to the islanders through the British Nationality (Falkland Islands) Act, 1983.

Turning now from the issues of boundaries to the question of content, and from geopolitical evidence to laboratory findings, there are a wealth of studies that show that, far from being fixed, group stereotypes vary as a function of who the ingroup is compared with: Australians are seen very differently as a function of whether they are compared with Americans or not; Scots see themselves as happy-go-lucky compared to the English, but as hard working compared to the Greeks, and so on (Haslam et al, 1992; Hopkins, Regan and Abell, 1997). The same applies when it comes to what we value. Thus Sonnenberg (2003) showed that, when compared to economists, psychologists see themselves as less concerned with money than when compared to theologians. The utility of monetary reward, it seems, varies alongside variations in the values associated with our social identities.

In sum, then, one cannot determine interest without determining the self and, conversely, by determining the self one can determine what people see as their interest. This makes the question of how identity is determined – that is, which of our various possible identities is salient in any given context and how that identity is defined in terms of both boundaries and content – a matter of public and political (as well as private and psychological) importance. We turn to this matter next.

Contesting social identity

To understand how social identity researchers have approached the question of how identity is determined, it is necessary to address the wider context in which the approach was developed. This can be encapsulated in a phrase. Groups have generally been viewed – both within academic psychology and beyond – as being bad for you (Brown, 1999). They are seen to diminish the individual both cognitively and morally. They diminish society through disorder and violence. In particular, it is assumed that group-level perception is a distortion of reality. Ideally, we should look at people in terms of their distinct individuality. And while – for the sake of simplifying an overly complex reality – we sometimes look at people as group members, this comes at the cost of pernicious phenomena such as stereotyping and prejudice (see Oakes, Haslam and Turner, 1994).

Self-categorisation theory centres on a radical re-analysis of the relationship between social categorisation and social reality. The core argument is that, far from being a distortion, categorical perception reflects the structure of social reality. We see ourselves and others as group members to the extent that the local context is organised in categorical terms – that is, differences between members of the one group are small, as compared to differences between the members of that group and those of another. Indeed the distortion (were there one) would be to view people in terms of individual difference in social settings that are structured in terms of category memberships.

By way of illustration, Oakes and colleagues illustrate the cover of their book on *Stereotyping and Social Reality* (Oakes et al, 1994) with a picture of a riot – London's Poll Tax Riot of March 1990, to be more precise. The significance of the image is that, in a riot, it would make little sense for demonstrators to look at the onrushing police and consider how each officer is distinctively different from the other. The important thing is to consider instead what they have in common, particularly in how they relate to the crowd.

We have already seen a similar argument used to explain how we see the group (category content) as well as when we see people in group terms (category salience). Here again, the ratio of intra- to inter-category differences (the 'meta-contrast ratio' is crucial). That is, the position that exemplifies our own group is that which best distinguishes it from other groups. Who we are is a variable function of who we are compared to. What it means to be a liberal depends on whether the comparison is with conservatives or with liberals. What it means to be Scottish, as noted above, depends upon whether the comparison other is the English or the Greeks.

But all this is only one side of the story – or, rather, of the relationship between categorisation and reality. Consider, for instance, the case of nationhood. It is quite true that we use national categories to the extent that we live in a world of nations: we take it for granted that sport, the economy, politics, even the weather reference the nation because, in the contemporary world, these tend to be organised around national differences (Billig, 1995). However, it is equally true that nations came into being through nationalist movements, which imagined the world in terms of nation-states and were able to mobilise people in order to create state structures. In other words, self-categories do not just reflect the nature of the world as it is. Categories are also actively constructed in order to create the world as it should be. Indeed, if, as we have argued, category definitions create and shape collective action – if, in other words, they constitute the social forces through which the social world can be shaped and reshaped – then anyone who is interested in moulding the social will need to concentrate on the ways that categories are defined. Those who have different notions of how the world should be will also necessarily have different notions of the definition of social categories. Hence, precisely because they are so consequential, self-categories will always be contested.

Sometimes this is a matter of employing different categories. For instance, Margaret Thatcher used her speech to the 1984 Conservative Party conference to mobilise opposition to the miners' strike. She characterised the strike as an attack on the British people by an alien revolutionary clique, the executive of the National Union of Miners (NUM). By contrast, Neil Kinnock, the Labour leader, used his speech to rally support for the miners, if not for the strike itself, by portraying the dispute as an attack upon the livelihoods of ordinary working people by an unrepresentative elite in the Tory cabinet who were completely out of touch with the realities of ordinary lives. In both cases the speaker and the audience were aligned with a majority category (respectively, 'British people' and 'ordinary working people') against an alien and destructive outgroup (respectively, the 'revolutionary' NUM leadership and the Tory cabinet). But while the group structure was the same, the actual groups were very different (see Reicher and Hopkins, 1996 for a full analysis).

Sometimes, though, it is about contesting the definition of the same category. This is often the case with national identity, which is particularly significant in terms of addressing broad electorates that are organised on national grounds. As an example, a while back we examined the use of Scottishness by Scottish politicians (Reicher and Hopkins, 2001). The first thing to note was that members of all the major parties – Conservatives, Labour and Liberal Democrats as well as the pro-independence Scottish National Party (SNP) – were equally vehement in asserting their national identity. It certainly was not *strength* of national identification that distinguished them. The second thing to note was that they all employed equally broad definitions of Scottishness that included those who had moved to Scotland as well as those who were born in Scotland. This was in contrast to some non-parliamentary pressure groups that employed narrow ethnic definitions of who is Scottish. So, it was not the way national boundaries were set that distinguished between parties, all of them seeking to appeal to the same broad electoral audience. Where the differences did lie was in the way that the content of national identity was defined.

For the Conservatives, the Scots were a self-reliant and entrepreneurial people, as exemplified by Andrew Carnegie and others who had built industrial empires in Britain, the United States and elsewhere. For Labour politicians, the Scots were a radical, communal and welfarist people, as exemplified by Robert Burns and his famous 'a man's a man for a' that' (a poem of human solidarity much featured on trades union and socialist banners). For the SNP, the Scots were a fiercely independent people, as exemplified by Robert the Bruce and Bannockburn. In each case, then, the content of national identity is elided with party policy, such that those policies are an expression of (rather than an imposition on) national values and, hence, national interests.

It follows that it is fundamentally misguided to seek a singular definition of national identity or national interest. Even to ask is to suggest that there is a single answer, and this is to privilege one specific definition over others. Instead of viewing identity in terms of a specific message, we need to consider it, first, in terms of the audience for whom the message is designed. Those who appeal to a common (electoral) audience are prone to employ a common (national) identity that encompasses them all. Second, we need to consider the consequences of different identity definitions upon that audience. How does any given definition constitute who this audience is, what their interest is and how the proposals of the source impact that interest? In short, we should ask about what identity does, not what identity is.

So there is a two-way relationship between categories and social reality: on the one hand, social reality frames our categories of self and social understanding. On the other hand, self-categories frame social action and hence constitute social forces with the potential to shape social reality. But these two should not be seen as a duality. Rather, they are different moments of a single historical dynamic. Those who construct new notions of who we are in order to create new forms of social organisation are not exempt from the need to match rhetorical forms and social structures. Indeed if what they propose cannot be brought into being, then their versions of identity are likely to be rejected as, literally, useless. There may be some leeway between making proposals and achieving results, but this cannot last forever. Conversely, given social structures do not in and of themselves guarantee a particular understanding of social categories. They may be interpreted in multiple ways or else condemned as designed to impede our view of more 'fundamental' realities. A world of nations can be rejected as cloaking the transcendental truth of religion, class, race or whatever.

In sum, our understanding of self (and self-interest) is always an interaction of structure and rhetoric. Self and self-interest are always actively invoked, whether we are talking about reproducing old structures or creating new structures. Self and self-interest are never just perceived, they are always mobilised (and, conversely, all those who seek to mobilise others will be concerned with the construction of self and self-interest). And this takes us to the third part of our argument.

From perception to mobilisation

For the last half century or so, the dominant paradigm in psychology, including social psychology, has been cognitive and perceptual. Researchers have addressed how people assimilate, store, retrieve and use information. In social psychology this has led to a focus on how we perceive others, particular members of our own and other groups. In the previous section we focused on the way in which group-level perceptions have generally been considered to be flawed. But even among those who reject this assumption, the notion that our views of other groups are based on perceiving has generally gone unchallenged.

The impression that is given is that human beings come to their understandings of the world through silent contemplation. While this might be a reasonable description of the world of the psychological laboratory – where, ostensibly in the interests of rigorous scientific control, in general people sit on their own, barred from interacting with others, barred from speaking, looking at information presented on a computer screen (see Haslam and McGarty, 2001) – it is not a very good way of conceptualising the wider social world. Here we are rarely alone. Here, there is rarely silence. On every issue that matters we are generally assailed from all sides by different voices describing the world in different terms, invoking different obligations, telling us to do different things.

The dilemma that confronts us is which of these many voices should we trust, heed and follow? Hence, what we think and what we do is less a function of contemplation than of our choice of engagements among those who seek to recruit us. Neither they nor we are passive and, hence, innocent in this process. All make active choices to recruit and to be recruited. We therefore need to shift from a paradigm of perception to a psychology of mobilisation.

Even when social psychologists are dealing with mobilisation, they still manage to ignore mobilisation. Thus there is increasing interest in our discipline in the processes by which people come to be involved in collective action – especially in contentious and violent forms of action (see, for instance, the virtual special issue of the *European Journal of Social Psychology* on theory and research on collective action edited by Becker (2012)). This research looks at factors like calculations of interest, social identification with the group, feelings of efficacy, perceptions of injustice, emotions and others besides.

While these factors are no doubt relevant, the question is how people come to see themselves and the world in ways that impel a collective response. By omission, if not by commission, the implication is that these are individual percepts that come about through an unmediated relationship between the individual and the social world. There is certainly no mention of leadership, of the role of activists, of the ways in which they frame events and appeal to people, nor of when and why they do so. This is a model of collective action without collective activists.

But the importance of a mobilisation perspective is certainly not limited to processes of collective action. It should be part of the bread and butter of social psychology. Take, for instance, the issue of racism and discrimination (which, more than anything else, and especially in the aftermath of the Second World War, has been the issue that has preoccupied social psychologists). We do not come to conclusions about matters like immigration in anything like a state of detachment. Rather, every time we read a newspaper or turn on the television we are confronted by multiple different voices that advocate for and against stricter controls. All of them, in different ways, purport to speak to our interests, about protecting our culture from destruction and saving our jobs, or else about enriching our society and expressing our finer values.

A mobilisation perspective asks entirely new questions about racist views and racist practices (see Reicher, 2007, 2012). On the one hand, why do mobilisers propose such views? On the other hand, why do people accept such views – or rather, given that there are always multiple views on offer, why and when do they accept racist versions over others?

These are clearly enormous questions, each worthy of (at least) another chapter of their own. However, very briefly, our response to the former is that it is by constituting a social category and by being seen to represent its interests that actors gain social power. They become able to act on the world through influencing the actions of others. The one gains the force of a multitude applying their efforts to a common end (see Turner, 2005). What is more, identifying enemies is a very good way of constituting an ingroup constituency and of constituting oneself as defending the ingroup against a threat that one's opponents are either too incompetent to notice, too indolent to meet or even too corrupt to care about (Rabbie and Bekkers, 1978).

Our response to the latter flows from our more general analysis of the categorisation process – more specifically, of the interactive nature of the category–reality relationship. So, there is a rhetorical dimension to the success of racist constructions. They must be vivid, clear and concise, weaving in accepted tropes and symbols of group identity and constructing a narrative in which these meld with the proposals on offer. They must, to use Mick Billig's term, employ appropriate witchcraft (Billig, 1987).

But there is also a practical dimension involved. Racist constructions must make sense of and respond to the lived experiences of their target audience. Thus, for instance, as migrant labourers came to Britain during the 1950s and 1960s, they could be defined either as fellow workers who should be included in a common struggle for increased social provision and adequate wages, or else as racial aliens who should be kept out of the locality and the country. It was the failure to organise and develop inclusive campaigns that led to the gradual domination of the exclusive racist version, which led to Labour as well as Conservatives constituting migrants as a problem and which led to the passing of immigration legislation that then institutionalised the notion of migrants as an 'other' who constitute a problem for 'us' (Reicher, 1986; see also Miles and Phizacklea, 1984).

At this juncture it is worth reiterating that our argument is not meant to be restricted to collective action or, indeed, racism or any other specific phenomenon. It is a general argument about social understanding and action. These are always mobilised. And, while mobilisation tends to be thought of specifically in relation to how people act to change existing social realities, we view mobilisation as equally relevant when it comes to maintaining social reality. Indeed, as much work (and much the same work) is involved in reproducing the status quo as in resisting it.

This point is also important to the extent that social reproduction is often taken for granted in psychology and that only when there is a challenge to existing power relations does it become worthy of notice. Another way of putting this is to say that the discipline suffers from a conformity bias (compare Moscovici, 1976). Various approaches use various arguments to suggest that human beings are inherently prone to accept and do the bidding of authority. This reaches a height in what is possibly the most famous body of research ever conducted in psychology – Stanley Milgram's Yale Obedience studies. Milgram induced participants to inflict what appeared to be lethal levels of electric shock on victims under the bidding of an authoritative, white-coated experimenter. He explained this as due to the fact that people automatically enter into an agentic state whereby they are solely focused on fulfilling their obligations to authority and are all but unaware of the plight of the victim (Milgram, 1974). In popular terms, people cannot help but follow orders, no matter how toxic.

But the problem is that people can and do disobey orders. In different variants of the Milgram paradigm, compliance varies from 0% to 100%.

Even when people do obey they still visibly orient to the victim. Indeed the drama of the studies derives from the fact that people are torn between contradictory demands from the authority and the victim. They have to make an active choice and that choice depends upon their identification, and hence engagement, with the science of the study versus the victim (see Reicher, Haslam and Smith, 2012). What is more, as Milgram himself notes in his unpublished notebooks, the whole set-up of the study was designed to invoke an engagement with science. This is especially clear when participants arrive at the laboratory and are assured that they are taking part in an important and indeed noble enterprise that is to deepen our understanding of human learning. Obedience doesn't just happen, it is the outcome of detailed work by Milgram and his experimenter.

The point, then, is that, whatever the topic, and whether it is a matter of creating consent or discontent, we always will find a dimension of mobilisation (even if those who wish to avoid accountability will try to hide it, claiming that action stems from human nature). On this basis, we have all the strands of our argument in place. We can now draw them together in order to explain what we mean by 'self-interest' and hence explain what we mean when we propose that people participate politically when it is in their interest to do so.

Our position has been to interrogate the notion of 'self-interest' by subjecting the notion of self to critical enquiry, in terms of both content and process. The first step was to problematise the notion of self, showing that, far from being singular or unitary, we have a complex system. Any notion of self-interest therefore depends on asking 'what self?' on determining who is included in that self (because social identities based on group memberships include fellow category members), and on determining what is valued and hence what counts as a good for that self.

The second step was to show that the choice, boundaries and normative content of self-categories is rarely if ever self-evident. While the structure of context may lend more or less plausibility to different category constructions, it does not determine the various dimensions in the definition of self. Rather, in any given context, the nature of self, and consequently of self-interest, is always open to argument – and indeed is characteristically a focus of contestation.

The third step was to argue that understandings of self and self-interest are not argued over innocently. They are proposed precisely in order to engage the audience with the speaker and in order to recruit people in favour of the speaker's proposals. If we want to understand how people construe their interests and, hence, decide whether and how to participate in political activities, we have to look at this in the context of active attempts at mobilisation.

Only if we take all three steps into account does it make sense to argue that people participate politically out of self-interest. Moreover, to make this claim is not, in and of itself, to settle anything about political participation, precisely because we can presuppose neither what the self is nor what is in the actor's self-interest. Instead, it is to point to where the focus of our analytic work needs to lie. That is, we need to examine the ways in which people are mobilised through the active construction of the self of self-interest.

In the second part of this chapter, we provide two brief examples to illustrate our analysis. While we have stressed that the construction of self-categories occurs along many dimensions – including the structuring of social practices, the organisation of physical space, the creation of forms of embodied coordination and more besides (see Haslam, Reicher and Platow, 2011) – our focus here will be on the rhetorical. In the first case we look at the various ways in which notions of self-interest are used in mobilising people to oppose forms of racist exclusion. In the second case, we look at a case where, ostensibly, the focus of mobilising rhetoric is focused on appeals to emotion and where notions of self and of interest might appear to be irrelevant. But, as a more robust test of our approach, we show that the use of emotion and the forms of action it is used to support are indexed upon a particular construction of where the self stands in social relations, and hence what paths are available to advance self-interest.

Mobilising participation through construing interest

Challenging deportation

As we have already noted, work on racism and discrimination lies at the very heart of social psychology. The great majority of the work is concerned with the discriminatory ideas, feelings and actions of dominant group members. There is little focus on those who are on the receiving end. There is still less work on dissent from and resistance to racist practices. And yet, even in the grimmest of circumstances, there is always resistance (Haslam and Reicher, 2012).

What little study there has been of resistance has generally looked at individual acts of heroism – for instance those who put themselves and their families at immense risk in order to rescue individuals from the Nazis (for example, Moore, 2010). Yet there were also instances where communities acted collectively to protect Jews and others from deportation. The defiance of the people of Le Chambon in France is a case in point (Hallie, 1979). The rescue of Danish Jews is another (Werner, 2002). But perhaps the most impressive tale of rescue relates to what happened in Bulgaria. Alone among the countries under Axis control during the Second World War, none of the Jews of old Bulgaria was deported to the death camps. Twice the Nazis tried. Twice they were thwarted by mass mobilisation, first in 1941/42, again in 1943.

Todorov (2001) provides a history of these mobilisations and he reproduces the key texts used to enjoin people to join in. Three broad arguments can be discerned (see Reicher et al, 2006). The first is a matter of group inclusion. Jews are rarely referred to as such, but as a national minority. Where they are referred to it is to stress how Bulgarian they are in culture and sensibility. Deportation is thereby transformed from on attack on *them* to an attack on *us*. The second is a matter of group content. Bulgarians are defined as born in a struggle against (Turkish) tyranny, and as instinctively standing with the weak against the powerful. Deportation thereby becomes an attack not only on *us*, but upon *our deepest values*. The third is a matter of group reputation. To allow people to be deported would be to bar Bulgaria, post-war, from acceptance among the civilised nations (this argument was particularly prevalent in 1943, when it began to be clear that the Axis forces were losing the struggle). Deportation thereby becomes an attack not only on *us* and upon our *deepest values*, but also upon our *standing in the world*.

All three arguments therefore turn on the construction of selfhood. All three serve to constitute the deportations as an attack on key dimensions of the self – its constituents, its values and its standing – and hence upon self-interest. All three therefore render opposition to the deportations as action in the national self-interest.

It could be argued that we are dealing here with an exceptional situation that cannot be extrapolated to the (thankfully) less extreme circumstances of contemporary life. Accordingly, we have recently been examining acts of mobilisation in the context of campaigns against the deportation of migrants (typically, people of African or Asian origin) from the UK.

As in Bulgaria, these anti-deportation campaigns deploy arguments about category inclusion, category content and category reputation. In contrast to the Bulgarian case, however, the nature of the ingroup category varies from case to case. Sometimes it is indeed national, but often it is a matter of locality, of ethnicity or of social class. Much of the variability has to do with the nature of the audience that is being addressed. Thus, when seeking to mobilise Black and Asian communities, the category of 'race' would be used. For instance, to quote from a leaflet distributed by the Anwar Ditta Defence Committee: 'A victory for Anwar Ditta will be a victory for all black people.' Or again, to quote from the campaign literature of the Viraj Mendis Defence Campaign, a campaign heavily based on mobilising trades unionists and radical groups: 'are they serious enough to make an open stand with black people, or will they let racism block the path to a determined struggle against a Tory government?' What is notable here is the way in which participation is constituted as a challenge to see if people authentically support category norms (racial solidarity) and are prepared to act for the category interest (by challenging the Conservative government).

Another major difference between the UK and Bulgarian cases concerns the nature of the perpetrator. In the Bulgarian case no one contests that those behind the expulsion of Jews, the Nazi regime, are an oppressive outgroup. In the British case, however, this cannot be taken as a given and much work goes into representing the source of deportations – the government and the relevant ministry (the Home Office) – as being alien, as violating ingroup values and as acting against ingroup interests.

This was particularly apparent in a campaign to defend Florence Mhango and her daughter Precious, who were living in Glasgow. In a context where certain powers are devolved to the Scottish Parliament, but control over immigration remains with the Home Office in Westminster, deportation moves could be described as originating from a source that is alien not only in class and political terms, but in national terms (for similar arguments used to mobilise opposition to the Gulf War, see Elcheroth and Reicher, 2014). Indeed, in the context of the growing clamour for Scottish independence at the time of the campaign, orchestrated by the SNP, the opposition between Scotland and the British government served as a frame in which to interpret the Mhango case. To cite one example: 'SNP leader James Dornan said: We in Glasgow pride ourselves in recognising we are all Jock Tamson's bairns [a colloquialism meaning we are all of one family] and recognise the need for Scotland to attract talented young people. So can someone please tell me why the UK government is so determined to deport Florence and Precious Mhango who are well integrated into the local community' (Nicoll, 2010, p 22).

So, in contemporary Britain, as in wartime Bulgaria, the arguments used to mobilise ethnic/racial solidarity all ultimately turn on issues of selfhood and self-interest. Depending on the context, more or less work may have to go into establishing particular aspects of the category argument (for example, in what ways the victims are 'us' and in what ways the perpetrators are 'them'). But this represents the way rhetorical resources need to adapt to the particular terrain in order to achieve a common end. That is, to the extent that attacks on particular individuals can be construed as an attack by 'them' on 'us' (our people, our values, our standing in the world), then these become attacks on our self-interest and people can be mobilised to participate in anti-deportation campaigns.

Contesting untouchability

Even accepting the validity of the foregoing analysis, the cases we have considered remain heavily circumscribed. To start with, those being enjoined to act are not themselves directly affected by the issue of concern: non-Jewish Bulgarians or British citizens were and are under no personal threat of deportation. They were and are acting in solidarity with those who do face such threats. Perhaps this puts the self in play in a way that doesn't apply where one's own safety or very survival is in question. In such situations, participation may be expected to be based on more visceral concerns. Next, and relatedly, it can be argued that our stress on construction and representation ignores the critical role of emotions in political action, especially collective action. In many cases feelings may play a greater role in determining participation than thoughts. Last, although we make a virtue of the breadth of study sites in the previous section (from mid-20th-century Bulgaria to 21st-century Britain), we still remain limited to the Western heartlands of social science. Things may be very different in other parts of the world.

Accordingly, we now turn to the self-mobilisation of Dalits (previously 'untouchables') in India. More specifically, we turn to the words of Dr B.R. Ambedkar, the most important of Dalit leaders who twice, in 1927 and 1936, led major mobilisations against the iniquities of the caste system.

Certainly, emotion plays a major part in Ambedkar's rhetoric. The rejection of humiliation is at the core of Ambedkar's call to action. For humiliation is at the core of the Dalit experience: a group reduced to the status of 'walking carrion' (as V.S. Naipaul put it), who are treated with disgust and contempt by those around them (Guru, 2009a). However, from the start, Ambedkar's use of emotion invokes rather than supersedes issues of selfhood. Humiliation implies acts that lessen the self and is only conceivable to the extent that one has a valued sense of selfhood that is capable of being diminished (Guru, 2009b, see also Margalit, 1998).

This was something that could by no means be taken for granted. Therefore, by the very act of speaking in terms of humiliation, Ambedkar sought to provide Dalits with a way of seeing themselves as subjects of rights and of interests and worthy of respect. He set up the grounds from which people could mobilise to defend these rights, advance their interests and achieve respect. Indeed, once such grounds were established, Dalits were obliged to act in order to be true to their selves. The challenge is clear in one of Ambedkar's most significant speeches in the 1927 campaign: 'In the view of Touchables, animal's dung and urine is more pious than the human touch of the Untouchable. Is such a life worth living? Is this living just for the sake of existence worth living?' (this, and all the following Ambedkar quotes, are taken from Jadhav, 2013).

But that is not the end of the matter. There are important differences in the ways that Ambedkar sought to mobilise people in 1927 and 1936. In the earlier period his aim was to raise a non-violent campaign for Hindu reform. But he lost faith in the capacity of Hinduism to change itself, believing that Gandhi and the other Congress leaders would always put the National Question before the Social Question. By 1936 Ambedkar concluded that the only way that the condition of Dalits could be improved was to leave the Hindu fold and join another religion that would accord them human rights (the Conversion Movement).

These differences are evident in the way that Ambedkar spoke about humiliation. Compare the extract we have just cited concerning the touch of Untouchables with the following extract from 1936: 'Thousands of Untouchables tolerate insult, tyranny, and oppression at the hands of Hindus without a sigh of complaint, because they have no capacity to bear the expenses of the courts. The tolerance of insults and tyranny without grudge and complaint has killed the sense of retort and revolt. Confidence, vigour, and ambition have completely vanished from you.'

At first sight, the two passages might seem very similar: Dalits are diminished, and they must do something about it or else they will lose any value or agency. Yet, crucially, in the earlier passage Untouchables are humiliated by Touchables – a group within Hinduism – whereas in the later passage they are humiliated by Hindus, full stop. This difference is not a matter of chance. It runs systematically through the speeches of 1927, as compared to those of 1936. And it is accompanied by further differences (see Jogdand, 2014).

In 1927, Ambedkar represents the humiliation of Untouchables as something that is at odds with the true nature of Hinduism and that harms all Hindus, not just Dalits. He enjoins Touchables to stand besides Untouchables in a mobilisation for reform: 'It is not that Untouchability has caused loss only to the Untouchables; it has caused loss to the Touchables as well, and has done immense damage to the nation ... this movement for removal of Untouchability, is in a true sense a movement for nation building and fraternity.'

In 1936, Ambedkar represents the humiliation of Untouchables as something that reflects the unchanging and unchangeable essence of Hinduism and that benefits Hindus. He enjoins Dalits to leave Hindus and Hinduism behind: 'We practise Casteism; we observe untouchability, because we are asked to do it by the Hindu religion in which we live ... poison cannot be made into nectar [*Amrit*]. To talk of annihilating caste is like talking of changing poison into nectar.'

Ambedkar's rhetoric of humiliation therefore maps out a rich representation of self in social relations that specifies who is being afflicted (Hindus in 1927, Dalits in 1936), who is afflicting them (Touchables in 1927, Hindus in 1936), who should act against affliction (all Hindus in 1927, Dalits in 1936) and how they should act (Hindu reform in 1927; conversion in 1936). We can see how the use of humiliation provides a powerful and efficient way of framing how events impinge on us and what we can do about it – what, in other words, it is necessary to act in the interests of the self. More generally, we would suggest, emotional appeals gain their effect precisely through the way that different emotions encode the significance of events for the self. So, in India as in Europe, whether emotion is involved or not, whether one is concerned with people acting in solidarity with others or for themselves, mobilisation equally involves the construction and contestation of self and self-interest.

Conclusion

It is possible to make our conclusion as short as our chapter has been long. Social science is replete with debates asking if people act in terms of self-interest or not. This is equally true when it comes to explanations of political participation. Our argument is essentially that this is a false debate. The question shouldn't be about *whether*, it should be about *what it means* to act in terms of self-interest.

Our contention is that the claim means nothing unless we specify the nature of 'self' and hence what constitutes interest. The problem is that this issue tends to be ignored and instead the nature of self is taken for granted – an individual self for which monetary gain is the ultimate metric of value.

By doing this we take the spotlight away from the way in which self and self-interest are constituted, we transform public acts of mobilisation into private acts of cognition, we lose sight of where the real work is done – in rendering particular outcomes and particular acts as an expression of self-interest. The losses are not just to be counted in terms of analytic purchase. As long as we neglect the explicit and (perhaps more importantly) the implicit ways by which different voices engage and mobilise us through rhetorics of selfhood, we diminish our ability to make clear choices between those voices. Equally, we limit our ability to hold speakers to account for what is said and done.

With this in mind, we can finish with a slight reformulation of our opening sentence. People participate politically out of self-interest, so democracy depends on it being a self of their own choosing.

References

Becker, J.C. (2012) 'Virtual special issue on theory and research on collective action', *European Journal of Social Psychology*, vol 42, pp 19–23.

Billig, M. (1987) *Arguing and Thinking*, Cambridge: Cambridge University Press.

Billig, M. (1995) *Banal Nationalism*, London: Sage.

Brown, R. (1999) *Group Processes*, Oxford: Blackwell.

Downs, A. (1957) *An Economic Theory of Democracy*, New York: Harper and Brothers.

Elcheroth, G. and Reicher, S.D. (2014) '"Not our war, not our country": Contents and contexts of Scottish political rhetoric and popular understandings during the invasion of Iraq', *British Journal of Social Psychology*, vol 53, pp 112–33.

Elster, J. (1986) *Rational Choice*, Oxford: Blackwell.

Guru, G. (2009a) Archeology of Untouchability', *Economic and Political Weekly*, vol 44, no 37, pp 49–56.

Guru, G. (2009b) *Humiliation; Claims and Context*, New Delhi: Oxford India.

Hallie, P. (1979) *Lest Innocent Blood be Shed*, New York: Harper & Row.

Haslam, S.A. and McGarty, C. (2001) 'A hundred years of certitude? Social psychology, the experimental method and the management of scientific uncertainty', *British Journal of Social Psychology*, vol 40, pp 1–21.

Haslam, S.A. and Reicher, S.D. (2012) 'When prisoners take over the prison: A social psychology of resistance', *Personality and Social Psychology Review*, vol 16, pp 154–79.

Haslam, A., Reicher, S.D. and Platow, M. (2011) *The New Psychology of Leadership*, London: Psychology Press.

Haslam, S.A., Turner, J.C., Oakes, P.J., McGarty, C. and Hayes, B.K. (1992) 'Context dependent variation in social stereotyping 1: The effects of intergroup relations as mediated by social change and frame reference', *European Journal of Social Psychology*, vol 22, pp 3–20.

Homans, G. (1961) *Social Behaviour: Its Elementary Forms*, London: Routledge and Kegan Paul.

Hopkins, N., Regan, M. and Abell, J. (1997) 'On the context dependence of national stereotypes: Some Scottish data', *British Journal of Social Psychology*, vol 36, pp 553–63.

Jadhav, N. (2013) *Ambedkar Speaks* (vols 1–3), Kindle edition, New Delhi: Konark.

Jogdand, Y.A. (2014) *Humiliation: Examining its Experience & Action Consequences*. Paper presented to the School of Psychology & Neuroscience, University of St Andrews, UK, 13 February.

Margalit, A. (1998) *The Decent Society*, Cambridge, MA: Harvard University Press.

Miles, R. and Phizacklea, A. (1984) *White Man's Country*, London: Pluto.

Milgram, S. (1974) *Obedience to authority*, New York: Harper & Row.

Moore, B. (2010) *Survivors: Jewish Self-Help and Rescue in Nazi-Occupied Western Europe*, Oxford: Oxford University Press.

Moscovici, S. (1976) *Social Influence and Social Change*, London: Academic Press.

Nicoll, V. (2010) 'Council unanimously backs family bid to stay in Glasgow', *The Evening Times (Glasgow)*, 10 September, p 22.

Oakes, P.J., Haslam, S.A. and Turner, J.C. (1994) *Stereotyping and social reality*, Oxford: Blackwell.

Rabbie, J.M. and Bekkers, F. (1978) 'Threatened leadership and intergroup competition', *European Journal of Social Psychology*, vol 8, pp 9–20.

Reicher, S.D. (1986) 'Contact, action and racialization: some British evidence', in R. Brown and M. Hewstone (eds) *Contact, Conflict and Intergroup Encounters*, Oxford: Blackwell, pp 152–68.

Reicher, S.D. (2007) 'Rethinking the paradigm of prejudice', *South African Journal of Psychology*, vol 37, pp 820–34.

Reicher, S.D. (2012) 'From perception to mobilization: the shifting paradigm of prejudice', in J. Dixon and M. Levine (eds) *Beyond Prejudice*, Oxford: Wiley-Blackwell, pp 27–47.

Reicher, S.D. and Hopkins, N. (1996) 'Constructing categories and mobilising masses: an Analysis of Thatcher's and Kinnock's speeches on the British miner's strike 1984–5', *European Journal of Social Psychology*, vol 26, pp 353–71.

Reicher, S.D. and Hopkins, N. (2001) *Self and Nation*, London: Sage.

Reicher, S.D., Haslam, S.A. and Smith, J. (2012) 'Working toward the experimenter: reconceptualizing obedience within the Milgram paradigm as identification-based followership', *Perspectives on Psychological Science*, vol 7, pp 315–24.

Reicher, S.D., Spears, R. and Haslam, S.A. (2010) *The social identity approach in social psychology*. In M.S. Wetherell and C.T. Mohanty (eds), *Sage identities handbook*, London: Sage, pp 45–62.

Reicher, S.D., Cassidy, C., Wolpert, I. Hopkins, N. and Levine, M. (2006) 'Saving Bulgaria's Jews: An analysis of social identity and the mobilisation of social solidarity', *European Journal of Social Psychology*, vol 36, pp 49–72.

Ringmar, E. (1996) *Identity, Interest and Action*, Cambridge: Cambridge University Press.

Sonnenberg, S. (2003) 'Money and "self": Towards a social psychology of money and its usage', Unpublished PhD thesis, University of St Andrews.

Tajfel, H. and Turner, J.C. (1979) 'An integrative theory of intergroup conflict', in W.G. Austin and S. Worchel (eds), *The social psychology of intergroup relations*, Monterey, CA: Brooks/Cole, pp 33–47.

Todorov, T. (2001) *The Fragility of Goodness*, London: Weidenfeld & Nicolson.

Turner, J.C. (2005) 'Explaining the nature of power: A three-process theory', *European Journal of Social Psychology*, vol 35, pp 1–22.

Turner, J.C., Hogg, M.A., Oakes, P.J., Reicher, S.D. and Wetherell, M.S. (1987) *Rediscovering the social group: A self-categorization theory*, Oxford: Blackwell.

Turner, J.C., Oakes, P.J., Haslam, S.A. and McGarty, C.A. (1994) 'Self and collective: Cognition and social context', *Personality and Social Psychology Bulletin*, vol 20, pp 454–63.

Werner, E.E. (2002) *A Conspiracy of Decency*, Boulder, CO: Westview Press.

ELEVEN

Conclusion: politics as open-ended process

Nathan Manning

In this final chapter I attempt to draw together some of the insights revealed in the diverse multi-disciplinary and front-line contributions to this collection. One theme that seems to be shared by our authors is that politics is a dynamic, changing field. Politics in its fullness reflects many parts of social life, including: changing socio-cultural norms, generational change, the impact of new technologies, how we feel about the world around us and our relationship with various elites, the complex implications of global capitalism, patterns of migration and the multifarious ways in which social identity is embroiled in political (dis)engagement. Viewing politics in this way is important, as it is part of crediting citizens with the agency to create new and revive older understandings and practices of politics amid changing social conditions. It also helps to draw our attention to the importance of politics as a process, rather than focusing exclusively on the outcomes of political engagement or forms of political behaviour – the way we understand and go about politics is important.

The first section of the book provided three contrasting examples of the changing landscape of contemporary politics. In Chapter Two Michele Micheletti called upon us to interrogate the democratic qualities of different forms of participation. She used the terms 'participation 1.0' and 'participation 2.0' to refer to the ways in which citizenship expectations have opened up in recent years. These ideal types reflect a shift away from the 'pre-packaged political home' of 'participation 1.0', with its large and typically hierarchical institutions marshalling political participation, towards 'participation 2.0', which is less oriented to electoral politics and the nation-state, involves greater questioning of authority and emphasises do-it-yourself approaches and self-expression. Micheletti then poses some awkward and under-researched questions about the forms of participation that accompany different citizenship expectations. Rather than assuming that all participation is good participation, Micheletti invites us to consider the downside of participation and the implications of a possible value divide between citizens. Might different citizenship expectations work to exclude certain citizens, forms of participation and political questions/ideas? Given that there is some evidence that older citizens are more likely to adhere to the dutiful citizenship of 'participation 1.0' and that younger people are more likely to be the engaged citizens of 'participation 2.0' (see Dalton, 2009; Martin, 2012), we may already be witnessing some of the implications of such a value divide for electoral politics (for example, see Berry, 2014). Not surprisingly, the conceptual frameworks provided by Micheletti are very useful in thinking through some of the forms of participation discussed in other chapters.

In Chapter Three, Andre Banks provided the first of three accounts of politics from the front line. Following Micheletti's conceptualisation of participation, the work of All Out is firmly within 'participation 2.0'. The organisation has a genuinely global orientation, is 'digitally native', it politicises aspects of identity, particularly gender and sexuality, and seeks to mobilise networks of lesbian, gay, bisexual, trans people and their straight allies to take action at a range of targets that include international organisations, corporations and governments. Interestingly, Andre's path as an activist and campaigner has included working within institutions associated with 'participation 1.0', namely a labour union, but for a variety of reasons his work is now more characterised by 'participation 2.0' and forms of transnational solidarity citizenship. Like many other civil society organisations, All Out is part of a complex tapestry that helps citizens provide checks on various forms of power.

Chapter Four, the final chapter in this section, continued a focus on new communications technology and forms of 'participation 2.0' with Marie Gillespie, Nesrine Abdel Sattar and Mina Lami's contribution exploring social media and political participation. They discussed a fascinating case study that took place during the rise and fall of the Arab Spring, wherein the BBC Arabic Service attempted to further global engagement in political debates by incorporating social media within news and current affairs programming. Great hopes are often held out for the ability of social media to promote democratic deliberation and participation. In contrast, the research of Gillespie et al revealed a more mixed, complex picture. For example, the continuity of traditional journalistic practices like gatekeeping meant that journalists retained ultimate control over topics for discussion and the selection of users' contributions. Social media also seemed to be regarded with low esteem; only younger and less-experienced staff were systematically working on social media. The use of social media in this case study also did not result in a diversity of participants, as contributors were predominantly young men. The authors' analysis also revealed little dialogue or sustained interaction among social media contributors. Nonetheless, the authors claim that the BBC Arabic Service saw a significant increase in audiences during the Arab Spring, as citizens were provided an open space to debate topics excluded in other media. Moreover, while the numbers may have been relatively small and dominated by younger citizens, such forms of 'produsage' do provide a space to develop deliberative skills and competencies along with digital literacies, which are increasingly important for contemporary political engagement.

The second section of the book developed a more explicit focus on political disengagement. My chapter (Chapter Five) argued that developing an understanding of the feelings and emotions involved in citizens' relationship with electoral politics can shed light on growing political disengagement. Politics is emotional – be it mainstream electoral politics or the contentious politics of social movements – and a sustained analysis of the role that feelings and emotions play in our political lives is well overdue. Being attuned to the emotional dimensions of electoral (dis)engagement can help to challenge the common assumption that disengaged citizens are necessarily individualised and apathetic, by highlighting the critical work of citizens and the failures of political elites to meaningfully connect. This was vividly portrayed by the white working-class interviewees who typically viewed politicians as wealthy elites uninterested in the concerns and struggles of 'ordinary people'.

The feelings of disconnection and frustration expressed by these citizens are part of explaining why many of them rarely voted and felt they had little influence over the shape of contemporary politics. Locating citizens like these within the participation 1.0/2.0 framework is problematic on two counts. Firstly, they only have minimal forms of 'participation 1.0' because they are profoundly disillusioned with electoral politics and many of its associated institutions – political parties, trades unions and so on – no longer socialise and marshal the mass political participation of citizens like them. Secondly, the white working-class sample does not reflect the social profile of citizens more involved with 'participation 2.0' repertoires, who tend to be younger, better educated and to earn higher incomes (see for example Norris, 1999; Pattie et al, 2004; Dalton, 2009). It might also be suggested that the kinds of political repertoires associated with 'participation 2.0' align more closely with middle-class values and life-styles.

Gillespie et al's Chapter Four also pointed to the importance of class for the kind of deliberative skills and digital literacies required by the citizen journalism they discuss. Their research showed that 'comments with grammatical problems are also often removed, privileging the voices of the intellectual and eloquent elite and denying representation to less literate sections of the public.' As Micheletti suggests, further research should be undertaken to explore the social correlates of participation 1.0 and 2.0, and social class should be of particular interest.

Tim Street's chapter (Chapter Six) on UK Uncut contributed to the broader context of political disengagement and dissatisfaction addressed in this section. UK Uncut has had remarkable success in politicising and publicising an issue that would ordinarily seem very boring – corporate tax avoidance. It seized on the actions of various high street companies to argue that there is an alternative to austerity and dramatic cuts in public spending and to highlight the inequalities of the government's programme – we're not all in it together. UK Uncut's efforts have worked to rejuvenate political engagement through direct action, for example, flashmob protests occupying the shop fronts of banks, cafes, pharmaceutical retailers and telecommunication companies. Combining online and offline activity, it created a number of tools and spaces for organising simple, creative, fun, exciting and effective actions. It also collaborated with other organisations to help build an inclusive movement. There is a lot here that other groups, and indeed politicians and political parties, could learn from.

There are numerous ways in which UK Uncut can be considered a success – not least, helping to get tax avoidance onto the political agenda, as featured in the Chancellor's 2014 Autumn Statement (Garside and Treanor, 2014; Mostrous, 2014). In conjunction with other civil society groups, academics and public intellectuals, UK Uncut began by 'questioning, criticizing, and publicizing' (Dryzek, 2000, p 131) the problem of corporate tax dodging. If it hasn't yet changed the terms of neoliberal discourse, it is exerting a good deal of pressure, contributing to a vibrant civil society and strengthening democracy in the process. Its efforts call for an augmented politics, one that would reveal that 'necessities' like austerity and public spending cuts are political choices, not economic inevitabilities.

Parveen Akhtar's Chapter Seven was the first of three to address the political (dis)engagement of ethnic minority citizens. Akhtar's chapter saw our focus shift back to electoral politics and disengagement, with a specific focus on the disillusionment of young British Pakistani Muslims. As was further developed in Therese O'Toole's chapter (Chapter Eight), Akhtar outlined how young people in general show a relative lack of engagement with electoral politics, as compared to older citizens. Within this broader context of many young people turning away from electoral politics, Akhtar's research shows how young British Pakistani Muslims face a further cultural barrier to electoral participation in the form of a hierarchical and patriarchal biraderi system. This system of patronage has served the interests of local politicians and community elders, but worked to disenfranchise young people and women, and in turn has suppressed political participation. Akhtar reminds us that while recognising broader understandings of politics and political repertoires is important, electoral politics remains very powerful and important for our democracy. Somewhat like Micheletti, Akhtar is calling for young British Muslims to be involved with both 'participation 1.0' and '2.0'. And, as she suggests, there are some signs that indicate that the hold of biraderi politics is lessening. For example, George Galloway's by-election victory, which in part was achieved by mobilising an alternative to the patronage system (Peace and Akhtar, 2014), and in the numerous creative ways in which young Muslims are engaging with extra-parliamentary participation that by-passes the biraderi system.

Therese O'Toole's Chapter Eight provided an excellent complement to Akhtar's focus on young British Muslim citizens and electoral politics, as her work investigated the extra-parliamentary participation of ethnic minority young citizens. Firstly, O'Toole contested the crisis narratives of political disengagement among ethnic minority and Muslim young people, showing that the evidence base for such claims is rather weak. She calls for a broader notion of politics that reflects engagement both within and outside mainstream and electoral politics. While the young people of O'Toole's study did have some engagement with electoral politics they were much more oriented to the kind of political engagement that Micheletti characterised as 'participation 2.0' – hands-on, direct and everyday forms of activism often located within horizontal or informal networks.

Again we see the importance of new communications technology, particularly for young people's political engagement. Such information and communication technologies (ICTs) facilitated more direct forms of engagement in a range of foreign countries and international issues. As O'Toole points out, this engagement was not simply a product of the young people's diasporic ties. Important though these often were, new ICTs facilitated and enhanced their global orientations. O'Toole's work also revealed the particular ways in which ethnic, religious and group identities were important in the politicisation and political engagements of these ethnic minority young people.

Francine Fernandes addressed ethnic minority political participation in Chapter Nine, through a discussion of her work with Operation Black Vote (OBV). Here, Fernandes set out some of the challenges OBV faces in pursuing the full political and civic participation of Black and minority ethnic (BME) citizens. She outlined the under-representation of BME citizens at all levels of government – the picture is even more unequal when gender is taken into account. Linking this to a wider set of systemic inequalities, Fernandes also argued that BME citizens were less engaged in electoral politics and other areas of civic life.

In response to these inequalities, OBV has waged numerous campaigns and run various highly successful programmes designed to redress the imbalance. Two key examples are the political shadowing schemes that have run at national, regional and local levels and the magistrates shadowing scheme. These programmes have done much to increase BME representation in key political and state institutions. Moreover, that such programmes are routinely over-subscribed and many participants have gone on to have a continued (and sometimes high profile) presence in these institutions is further testament to the fact that BME citizens want to be meaningfully engaged in civic and political life.

While OBV tends to focus its attention on electoral politics and key state institutions, it is significant that its tactics as an organisation also draw upon new communications technologies and, occasionally, online activism. The successful online petition campaign described by Fernandes indicates that organisations with a track record in 'participation 1.0' campaigns can employ 'participation 2.0' campaigns to great effect.

Finally, in Chapter Ten Stephen Reicher, Yashpal Jogdand and Caoimhe Ryan set out a social-psychological approach to the role of self-interest in political engagement. This chapter provided a sustained critique of simplistic rational-choice approaches to political engagement. Typically, when we think about people acting according to their self-interests very little regard is paid to the nature of the self – the self is often assumed to be someone who aims to maximise monetary gains. In contrast, Reicher et al place the focus on the self and argue that having interests and wants requires being a self and knowing one's social identity. The self in self-interest is the concept that does all the heavy lifting and should not be taken for granted. Reicher et al show the numerous ways in which selves are mobilised in the process of shaping interests and political action. As such, the focus of analysis should be on how people are mobilised through the construction of selves and social identities. This chapter conceptually worked through the centrality of social identity for political participation, a view that implicitly and explicitly featured in the other chapters in this book – identity matters for politics. Part of the power of the Occupy movement was its rhetorical skill in drawing together very disparate social groups – 'we are the 99%'. Of course, as is suggested when describing the work of their organisations, Banks, Street and Fernandes all use identity in their efforts to mobilise people for political action. This is perhaps particularly pronounced in the work of All Out and OBV, organisations that combat discrimination against particular social identities and behaviours. However, all three groups (and many more besides) invite identity 'work' – 'I'm the kind of person who speaks out about injustice', or a specific set of issues. When much of this political mobilisation takes place online through social networks, political engagement is further personalised and often forms part of citizens' reflexive identity formation. But, as was suggested in various chapters, the contemporary identities implicated in politics are complex and hybrid intersectional constructs, which may be more fluid and malleable than in the past. Identities (and aspects of our identities) are embroiled and mobilised through politics in ways that problematise earlier notions of identity politics and call upon us to further explore the relationships between politics and identities that are frequently multiple and hybrid.

This focus on identity, its multiple, relational and contested character and the ways in which it is mobilised for political action helps to highlight the dynamic, protean nature of politics. Contemporary political practices and understandings reflect much more than the institutions and conventions of party politics and representative government. As such, numerous contributors to this volume have, to varying degrees, implicitly and explicitly called for a plurality of methodological approaches to be used in helping us to track and interpret changing political practices and understandings. Research methods, and their implementation, must be flexible enough to capture this vibrant field. Rolling out the same surveys year after year not only misses a great deal of political action, it also fails to credit citizens with the agency to change the *nature* and *practice* of politics.

At a time when established forms of democracy in many countries around the world seem to be in a state of crisis, we desperately need to encourage the kinds of 'public-spirited' conversations that promote 'a cultural kind of power, the power to open up public contexts for citizens to question, challenge, debate; the power to become a different kind of person, to create new meanings and ask new questions; to inspire' (Eliasoph, 1998, p 14).

References

Berry, C. (2014) 'Young People and the Ageing Electorate: Breaking the Unwritten Rule of Representative Democracy', *Parliamentary Affairs*, vol 67, no 3, pp 708–25.

Dalton, R.J. (2009) *The Good Citizen: How a Younger Generation is Reshaping American Politics* (rev edn), Washington: CQ Press.

Dryzek, J.S. (2000) *Deliberative Democracy and Beyond: Liberals, critics and contestations*, New York: Oxford University Press.

Eliasoph, N. (1998) *Avoiding Politics: How Americans produce apathy in everyday life*, Cambridge: Cambridge University Press.

Garside, J. and Treanor, J. (2014) 'Autumn statement 2014: Osborne to introduce "Google tax"', *Guardian,* Available online at: http://www.theguardian.com/business/2014/dec/03/autumn-statement-2014-osborne-to-introduce-google-tax (accessed 18 December 2014).

Martin, A. (2012) 'Political Participation among the Young in Australia: Testing Dalton's Good Citizen Thesis', *Australian Journal of Political Science*, vol 47, no 2, pp 211–26.

Mostrous, A. (2014) 'Tax havens will end in 2018 says OECD', *The Times,* available online at: http://www.thetimes.co.uk/tto/money/tax/article4253248.ece (accessed 18 December 2014).

Norris, P. (1999) *Critical Citizens: Global Support for Democratic Governance*, Oxford: Oxford University Press.

Pattie, C., Seyd, S. and Whiteley, P. (2004) *Citizenship in Britain*, Cambridge: Cambridge University Press.

Peace, T. and Akhtar, P. (2014) 'Biraderi, Bloc Votes and Bradford: Investigating the Respect Party's Campaign Strategy', *The British Journal of Politics & International Relations*. doi:10.1111/1467-856X.12057.

Index

Page references for notes are followed by n